LA GRANGE PUBLIC LIBRA

3 1320 00437 3549

WITHDRAWN

WITHDRAWN

A FINE ROMANCE

Center Point
Large Print

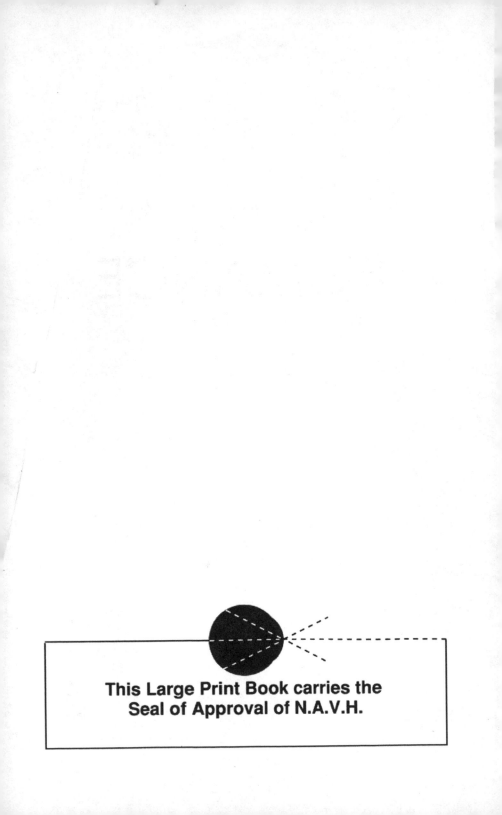

**This Large Print Book carries the
Seal of Approval of N.A.V.H.**

LA GRANGE PUBLIC LIBRARY

10 W. COSSITT AVE.
LA GRANGE, IL 60525
708.215.3200

A FINE ROMANCE

Candice Bergen

CENTER POINT LARGE PRINT
THORNDIKE, MAINE

LA GRANGE PUBLIC LIBR...
10 W. COSSITT AVE.
...

This Center Point Large Print edition is published in the
year 2015 by arrangement with Simon & Schuster.

Copyright © 2015 by Candice Bergen.

All rights reserved.

The text of this Large Print edition is unabridged.
In other aspects, this book may vary
from the original edition.
Printed in the United States of America
on permanent paper.
Set in 16-point Times New Roman type.

ISBN: 978-1-62899-544-2

Library of Congress Cataloging-in-Publication Data

Bergen, Candice, 1946–
A fine romance / Candace Bergen. — Center Point Large Print edition.
pages cm
Summary: "Candice Bergen shares the big events in her life: her
marriage to a famous French director, the birth of her daughter, Murphy
Brown, widowhood, falling in love again, and watching her daughter
blossom"—Provided by publisher.
ISBN 978-1-62899-544-2 (library binding : alk. paper)
1. Bergen, Candice, 1946– 2. Actors—United States—Biography.
I. Title.
PN2287.B434A3 2015b
791.4502´8092—dc23
[B]
2015003350

LT
791.45
BER

For my Bunny

❦ Contents ❧

1

The Arrival

❦{ 1 }❧

It was midway through October 1985, as I waddled in a huge plaid tent dress through the ground floor of Bergdorf's. I'd put on almost fifty pounds since becoming pregnant. A woman kept peering at me, looking away, looking back. Finally she approached. "You know, you have Candice Bergen's face."

"But not her body," I said.

Old friends saw me lurching along the street and burst out laughing. I scowled back. Would this baby be born in a hospital or at SeaWorld?

The due date was the second half of October. I'd been hoping she'd arrive on Halloween, which was the day after my husband Louis Malle's birthday. As the date grew closer, then passed, I went in for a checkup. Whoever was in there, she was hyperactive, that much was sure. She somersaulted and flipped around. Then she landed wrong. Her feet were tangled in the umbilical cord and she was upside down and feet first. There was a high risk of her cutting off the supply of oxygen and nutrients. A risk of brain damage.

My obstetrician, the ironically named Dr. Cherry, was an affable, easygoing guy, but he grew concerned after the recent sonogram. "We need to think about scheduling a Cesarean," he told me. Meanwhile, I was to go home and stay in bed with my feet up. No activity. That would be interesting, as Louis and I lived in a two-story loft and were having people for dinner that night.

That was the beginning of the real bonding. Until that point, I'd kept a bit of distance, thinking of the baby as a kind of invader in my comfortable routines. I'd dragged my feet about preparing her room. No longer. It was ready, wallpapered in tiny pink rosebuds. I'd bought a white rocker and a white crib with pink ticking on the mattress and bumpers and found a pink Kit-Cat clock whose eyes and tail moved rhythmically back and forth.

Now the Alien was in jeopardy. I could not lose her.

Louis and I had been invited to a state dinner at the White House in honor of Prince Charles and Princess Diana. It was the big wingding of the fall, and the royal couple was causing quite the stir. It was possible we could make it if the baby was prompt. The dinner was November 6. I figured we could take the train with the newborn and a baby nurse and stay in DC for a night. I would look like a blimp, but we could attend.

As the date inched closer and there was no sign of a baby, I called Nancy Reagan, who has been a family friend all my life, and apologized for the delayed response. "Mrs. Reagan, she's not moving," I told her. She couldn't have been sweeter. "Well, they'd love you to be there, Candy. Let us know when you can. Of course we understand."

What I didn't understand was where this baby was. What was keeping her?

At almost two and a half weeks past the due date, Dr. Cherry told me he'd decided to extract the baby by cesarean in three days; he was afraid she might have "exhausted prepartal nutrients." Apparently my amniotic fluid was drying up. She was running out of snacks.

The Kit-Cat clock was ticking. I was not in the market for abdominal surgery. I wanted to have this baby naturally. More or less. I did the few primitive things that were suggested to induce labor. Three of my closest girlfriends took me out to dinner and I ate the spiciest things on the menu, hoping to bring on contractions. Sweat streamed down my tiny head and pooled under my newly enlarged breasts. Nothing. I heaved my 180 pounds sixteen floors up to my apartment to see if that would get her moving. Zilch. Louis was giving me a wide berth; I was getting testy.

Louis and I went to Mount Sinai Hospital the next day, November 8, 1985. The surgery was scheduled for 3:00 p.m. We were shown to a pre-op room and I undressed and got into a gown. They gave me oxytocin as a last gasp to start contractions. No dice. The baby was dug in. Dr. Cherry came in with the anesthesiologist and introduced him. He had clammy hands and a mustache that screamed "Shave me!" This was not a guy who seemed cool under pressure. He recognized me and appeared nervous. This was the guy who was going to give me the dreaded epidural? Women had been warning me about this shot, which is given in the base of the spine and is generally successful at blocking pain, except when it results in paralysis. The anesthesiologist told me to curl into the fetal position, which I did, but I was babbling incessantly, compulsively. I am not a good patient. The anesthesiologist also seemed stressed. He mentioned a movie I was in. I was freezing and shivering and the needle looked like a harpoon. Finally, he managed to give me the epidural, and I was wheeled down the battleship gray hall into the operating room. Louis walked beside me in his gown.

The nurses erected a discreet sheet to screen any activity below the waist. Louis sat by my head. They started to swab me but I could feel it, and then I really panicked. The upside of the epidural was, I wasn't paralyzed. The downside was, I wasn't numb. Hey, guys, I'm not numb! I CAN FEEL EVERYTHING! This was a definite crick in the procedure. "Give her a shot of Valium and administer another spinal," someone said. I resumed the fetal position. The anesthesiologist came at me with another harpoon. I wondered, Is this really the best guy you got here?!? Things got blurry; then I got a third epidural. Enough medication for a rhino, which in a sense I had become. I was groggy beyond belief, but I could still feel a prickling in my legs. I might have heard the word *paresthesia*. Was I going to feel it when the surgeon cut through my abdomen? Because I would not be okay with that. I was stoned and ranting and raging.

"Do you feel this?" Dr. Cherry asked as he jabbed a pin in my leg. And then . . . murmuring, movement, a team at work. Louis watched it as the director he was. The curtain set up. People beyond it performing together.

And suddenly a cry. A really loud cry. That would be my daughter crying. Bellowing. All nine pounds two ounces of her had been pried out of my ample abdomen, where she'd made a home— carpet, armchair, reading lamp, sound system— she was *not* happy about moving out. Now the trouble begins, I thought. Schools. Mean girls. Boyfriends. SATs. Now it hits the fan.

Mademoiselle Chloe Malle. I heard Louis singing softly to her in French: "*À la claire fontaine . . .*" She'd been wrapped like a burrito and he held her gently in his arms, crooning. She relaxed and quieted, scrutinizing him. I was sobbing. So much emotion. So many drugs.

She was placed in my arms now, cautiously, since I was so medicated that I was completely gaga. As if I would let anything happen. Again, the tears streamed down my cheeks. My baby girl. My baby girl. Who knew love was this huge? All-enveloping. All-encompassing. My baby girl.

My God, I can't believe I almost didn't do this. It was clearly the beginning of my life.

In the recovery room upstairs, Chloe was brought back to me, steamed and cleaned, fierce and irresistible.

Ali MacGraw and Anne Sterling, two of my closest friends, had been waiting in the hospital lobby. They came up to meet Chloe and give me a pat on the head. I was having trouble speaking clearly, what with my dozens of epidurals, plus I was still weeping. But I was aglow.

Chloe is here. Chloe is here. I was happier than I ever thought possible. *Chloe is here.*

2

Louis at Last

❧ 2 ❧

On September 27, 1980, I married Louis Malle. I'd waited a long time for that moment. It was Louis's second marriage, my first; both of us thought it was a miracle.

Certainly we'd had an inauspicious beginning. We'd met four years earlier at Diane von Furstenberg's home, Cloudwalk Farm, in Connecticut, where we were seated next to each other. I was a houseguest of Mike and Annabel Nichols, who lived nearby. The guests introduced themselves. "I'm Louis Malle," Louis said. "You *are?*" Mike gasped. I was very struck by how socially ill at ease this man was, almost furtive. This was the great director I'd heard so much about? Sparks decidedly did not fly. A few months later, I sat next to Louis again at a dinner in California. I was wearing a designer caftan that kept falling off me. I spent the entire meal trying to straighten it as it kept slipping. The situation was so awkward that we barely spoke.

Undeterred, my great friend, photographer Mary Ellen Mark, kept declaring that Louis Malle was the perfect man for me. She had known him for years. "You're going to marry him. It's absolutely certain." And then, out of the blue, he called from an editing room in Toronto and asked if we could have lunch. Louis and I finally settled into a red leather banquette in the Russian Tea Room for lunch in early March of 1980.

We were still in that banquette four hours later. Two weeks after that, on March 17, we went on our first date, to see *Manon Lescaut* at the Metropolitan Opera House. That night I wrote in my journal: "Uh-oh." It was understood. We knew what we had. And we considered that our anniversary. Louis wrote me two weeks later from Le Coual, his house in the southwest of France.

April 1, 1980
Since we spoke this morning, I have this vision of you standing, still, like hypnotized, waiting for the lightnings, listening to the thunder, and I remember the strange, obsessive sound of rain on your roof. A very dramatic vision, with New-York in front of you as a huge theater, New-York where dreams become monologues, as if everything had to be shouted to cover those millions of heartbeats . . .

My walk took me down to a little canyon, trees still holding the night mist, traces of fog, absolute stillness, the sun just about to appear, birds in a routine frenzy—It was like thousands of years away, before agriculture (and theater) were invented. It is not peace, though, more like a truce, nature neither friendly nor hostile, millions of invisible beings trying to survive this new day, a pre-Virgilian world that hardly notices my interruption. And I see me over there, holding you in the middle of the storm, and I see you here, walking by me, in silence.

This love, you know, our love, is of the essence. Beyond time and space, it has become transcendence and knowledge, and complete abandon. These few days together, they've become eternity. Maybe it is what religious people call contemplation.

Sometimes, I fall into the old traps, pain, even anger or rage. What am I doing here, thousands of miles away, I must see you, and hold you, and kiss you. I throw my hand towards you, like a wrecked sailor in the middle of the ocean. Then I see your smile, the wonderful quietness of your smile, and it helps me to quiet down. Candie, you've brought me wisdom, or the beginning of wisdom, which I never knew before, always restless, always searching. Finding you, I have started to find myself. It's a long way, maybe, but it's here already. And I wonder and wonder how unique, how totally new it is. When I called you that first morning, to say thank you, that's what I meant, because I knew, right away. Everything got suddenly clearer and simpler. And the mandala I brought you is the perfect symbol. You look at it, and you'll feel what I feel.

It gives me such tremendous happiness to write you all this, as clumsily as it comes. It's as if I was writing myself a love letter, for the first time. Sharing, and belonging, I know what it means, now.

L.

Let's be April fools for the rest of our lives. The world can't play tricks on us anymore. The fools are the wise.

That letter swept me off my feet.

Our courtship was entirely backward. We began with the honeymoon in May. We went to Florence, the first time for both of us, and it was a fantastic trip. We stayed above the city at the exclusive Villa le Rondini, the stone balconies overlooking olive groves and Brunelleschi's magisterial Duomo topping the cathedral of Florence below. We just devoured the city. Louis was especially knowledgeable about Renaissance art. His entire family were culture vultures, leaving no cloister stone unturned. We gasped over the sprawling Paolo Uccello triptychs in the Uffizi. We ate in great restaurants at communal tables. Louis was very good at navigating; he'd make a plan, we'd hop in the car, and we'd scoot. It was all a thrilling adventure.

Back home, I was about to start *Rich and Famous* in LA with Jacqueline Bisset, a witty, bitchy script about two lifelong friends and competitors. I was looking forward to digging into it, but an actors' strike held up production. So Louis and I rented a house near the beach in Bridgehampton on Long Island and decided to spend the summer there with his two children from previous relationships, Cuote, nine, and Justine, six. They were wonderful kids. I'd taken to Justine immediately. Her mother, Alexandra Stewart, is a Canadian actress, but lived most of her life in Paris. She was and is uniquely beautiful, vibrant, and funny. Cuote, born in Mexico, named after an Aztec emperor, with a German mother, Gila von Weitershausen, and a French father, was a pancultural windfall. He was more reserved than Justine, but over the summer, after circling each other like cats, the three of us became friends. While Louis worked with Andre Gregory and Wally Shawn on their screenplay, *My Dinner with Andre*, preparing to shoot that winter, Cuote and Justine and I picked strawberries from the field across from the house and swam and played at the beach.

It was an idyllic summer. At the end of it, Louis and I were sitting outside after the children had gone to bed. He turned to me and said suddenly, "If I asked you very politely, would you marry me?" I was overjoyed.

Neither of us was inclined to overmarry. Louis's first, early marriage had been brief, only three years. I'd been on my own for fifteen years, since the age of nineteen. I didn't know how I felt about surrendering my independence, although I'd jokingly tossed off a line in some magazine article about how I'd push my mother down the ramp of the Guggenheim for the chance to find a terrific man. Marlo Thomas promptly sent me a telegram: "You don't fool me. You'd push your mother down the Guggenheim ramp for no good reason."

So: marry Louis, then; marriage didn't necessarily mean losing myself. But then Louis began to equivocate: "Maybe we should just not get married but say we are. Or get married and say we're not." Then we talked about getting married in India. As I would learn, Louis famously had a hard time making decisions. I finally put my foot down. "Let's do it or not do it." We decided to do it.

We planned to get married at Le Coual—the Raven's Cry—at the end of September. We only had about a month to plan. I didn't have a dress. We took the train from Le Coual to Paris. Louis called a costume designer he knew, and she took me shopping to a vintage store, where I bought a Victorian-style ivory silk and lace dress off the rack. It was a beautiful country wedding. Both his kids came from Paris. My mother and brother flew in from LA. Director Terry Malick was there because he happened to be staying at Le Coual. Basha Ferri, a close friend from Paris; Mary Ellen Mark, who had predicted our marriage; and Louis's brother Vincent were our witnesses. By day's end, our guests had scattered and we were left to begin our lives.

The man I married was, in every sense, a dynamo. Louis had almost boundless stamina and energy, and infinite curiosity about everything, especially American sports and politics. He was compulsively creative and productive; if he wasn't shooting a feature, he was shooting a documentary or directing a play. He made a film about American immigrants called *The Pursuit of Happiness* in part to educate himself about that stretch of our history. He had a real gift for getting to the truth of the situation. He was perfectly bilingual in French and English but with the most seductive accent. He could make the word *hemorrhoids* sound lyrical. He used English words like *flabbergasted* but he swore in French.

Louis would routinely do two or three things at a time: walking briskly down the hall, puffing on his pipe while talking on his new portable phone, grabbing a snack, watching the news, doing yoga. He would walk at an angle, tilted forward at the waist, leaning into whatever he was heading for. He was never idle.

He could be incredibly charming and courtly.

He would kiss women's hands on meeting them. I thought Mom would faint when he kissed hers. "Oh, Candy, can't you marry him?" she asked me later. And now I had.

I flew back to LA when the actors' strike ended after three months to finish shooting *Rich and Famous*.

By design, I worked very little. After waiting so long to marry, I wanted to enjoy my new life with Louis. Then a wonderful opportunity arose.

Fifteen years earlier, when I was shooting *The Sand Pebbles* with Steve McQueen and Richard Attenborough in Taiwan and Hong Kong, Dickie told me that he was planning to do a film about the life of Gandhi; he wanted me to play photojournalist Margaret Bourke-White. I loved the idea and I was a huge admirer of Bourke-White's work. It seemed unlikely that Dickie would get funding for a biography of the small brown man who had led his country to independence, and in fact it took him almost twenty years to get a screenplay written, but Attenborough had finally scraped up some money and hired John Briley to write the final script.

I flew to India to do my cameo as Bourke-White. It was all English actors and I was terrified. You don't fool around with those guys; they're incredibly skilled, all business. I felt inept, self-conscious, stiff, and untrained amid such fast company. In fact, I was all of that in *any* company. I rued the time I'd wasted not studying acting. Yes, my life had turned into a miracle, but I suppose I wanted my work to match that. I wanted to feel pride in what I did.

The first week was difficult. I felt lost and lonely. One of my first shots was an exterior tracking shot, with the camera pushed slowly along metal tracks. My job was to walk with Ben Kingsley, kitted out as the Mahatma after three hours of makeup every day, along with round spectacles, sandals, white dhoti, and shawl. I was supposed to be interviewing him, walking backward on the dolly track, photographing him. The problem was that I was wearing high cork wedges and operating a bulky Graflex camera, trying to do my lines while tripping on the camera tracks. We had to do endless takes.

Shooting in India was not uncomplicated. The movie was overscheduled and underfinanced. After six months in India, the British crew had the desperate stare of hostages. They all struggled to keep a stiff upper lip, but I noticed that more often than not, it was tending to droop. Dickie would be shooting all day and fundraising at night. He was at the end of his rope in terms of stamina and strength. It didn't help that people were getting sick on the set, diseases that no one had heard of, chills, fevers, lasting for weeks and weeks. I wasn't immune. Bombay, whose people told you over and over and over that the temperature goes from "hot, hotter, hottest," was set on "hottest." The port city was in the midst of a heat wave of historic proportions. Temperatures above 110 degrees, high humidity. The heat draped itself over you as you came outside, covering you, closing in on you, stopping you midsentence for lack of air. Between takes you sat, trancelike, moving only your eyes.

Despite the terrific tension and tempers on the set, the sense of conviction and commitment to the film was quite extraordinary. And watching Ben as Gandhi walk through a crowd of Indians making a silent path for him was strangely moving.

As we moved through the city in tiny, airtight taxis, beggars clawed and croaked at the windows. "Sistah . . ." Big black eyes as they cawed for money. Small brown hands, asking, asking, until the wide eyes blinked and they darted and disappeared in a flash of color, like ravaged, exotic fish in some sad and savage underwater world, leaving you cowering in your capsule, guilty and grateful. I was sitting in the lobby of the luxurious Dorchester Hotel when someone told me that Martin Sheen had decided, after seeing conditions here, to donate his salary to Indian charities.

Everybody was staying at a hotel outside Bombay (now Mumbai) where the production team had gotten a special rate. Downstairs the bar was filled with drip-dried, short-sleeved Russians in off the latest Aeroflot from Moscow. Someone was playing "Ritorno a Sorrento" and "Chattanooga Choo Choo" on a sitar. Since I didn't know anyone in the cast and didn't want to have room service alone, I took up my friend Mary Ellen Mark's suggestion that I move into the Taj Mahal in the center of Bombay across from Victoria's Gate. Mary Ellen introduced me to Jahangir Gazdar, a lovely, intelligent, gentle man who took me around to meet people and get to know the city.

One Sunday Jahangir took me to Chaupati Beach, to a wonderful fisherman's festival that was a great circus of colors and sights and sounds and smiles and laughter. Hundreds of weathered, splintered, leaking boats were swagged in fluttering pennants, flags of every color, as they bobbed along the thronged beach. Groups of thirty or forty women, all in saris of vibrant colors— citrus yellow, saffron, aqua blue—danced in circles. There was something tough and strong in these small, wiry women, gnarled by life. They offered no barriers, no walls to break through. Their spontaneity was a gift for us Westerners for whom being in the present is so threatening. Their great and enviable freedom made me feel more open, more accessible, giving me no time to defend my position. With their eyes and hearts and colors and flowers and music, they somehow celebrated their lives, consecrated their wretched conditions. There was something indomitable about them, while at the same time so hopeless.

As dusk dimmed it all, the lights came on along the beach, the sky pale and misty. Monkeys did vaudeville acts with their owners. There were tightrope walkers, acrobats, storytellers, faith healers, hoops of fire, incense, jasmine, and always music: drums, flutes, cymbals weaving magic in the night.

Louis met me in India after about a week, an event the *Bombay Standard* chronicled in a headline on its front page: "Louis Malle Is Back in Town." He had been kicked out of India after shooting his nine-hour documentary *Phantom India* in 1968. He'd wanted to show the real country, not the tourist experience wrapped around the luxurious Taj Mahal. Operating the camera himself, he explored how people lived: the caste system, religious expression, politics, dance and other arts. He spent five months shooting, and the result had been shown as a TV miniseries in Europe. Indians in the UK created a stir because they felt Louis had focused too much on poverty and political turmoil and not enough on the country's efforts to modernize. They kicked the BBC out of the country for broadcasting the film. Even though the movie was never released in India, the country banned Louis. Apparently the ban had lapsed; this was his first time back.

After I wrapped up most of my work on the movie, Louis wanted to show me his India. Mary Ellen met us in Bombay. She was the first photographer to gain access to a notorious area there called Falkland Road, an entire primitive metropolis of brothels that had once been stables. The area was legendary for not wanting any intruders; the prostitutes—the so-called Cage Girls of Bombay—would scream, spit, or throw garbage and bottles at any photographer who approached. But Mary Ellen kept returning, bringing gifts for the prostitutes—wigs, bras, nightgowns, Band-Aids, aspirin, whatever they requested. Finally she befriended them and they allowed her access. This time, she took us with her.

It truly was a hellhole: bleak, grinding, excruciating poverty. Here there was no joy. Here there was no hope. Here people lived their lives as quickly as possible and hoped for a better one next time. Surely it could be no worse. The women lived and worked in old horse stalls; Mary Ellen had climbed up to the top of the stables to photograph them from above. She took us to meet the madam of that particular block, who jumped up to greet Mary Ellen. The two women hugged. There were children working there, girls of nine or ten sold by their parents. They earned $45 a month for life in the cages, surrounded by rats and disease. We became dazed and dumb, and we left Falkland Road impotent and enraged.

We wound up back at the Taj Mahal Hotel and we each had a stiff drink. This country was a total bombardment of the senses. It blasted you with sights and sounds and smells and tastes and feelings. It jangled your every nerve, wrung you out, dazzled and disgusted you.

In Rajasthan, Mary Ellen told us to find her dear friend Jungu, a taxi driver, who invited us to visit his little house. His wife served us each a cup of water. Louis and I exchanged glances. Drinking the water is at the top of the list of "don'ts" in India, but we managed a few sips. We waited to die. We didn't. We moved on to Udaipur to spend a night at the famous Lake Palace Hotel, an eighteenth-century marble fantasy floating in the middle of a sacred lake. It was the perfect Western reinterpretation of India, sterile, dusty, jewellike, and lifeless. In Rajasthan, all the old palaces had been made into hotels. Our room at the Umaid Bhawan Palace in Jodhpur, a gorgeous 1930s Art Deco palace repurposed as a hotel, was the size of a stadium. But it was clear that this trip wasn't going to be a tour of the palaces of Rajasthan. With Louis you didn't see the tourist's version of anything.

From Bombay we flew down to Pune so I could do a few more days of work on *Gandhi*. The receptionist at the hotel asked me what movie we were doing.

"It's a movie about the life of Mahatma Gandhi," I told him. He stared at me.

"Is there any singing or dancing in that movie?" he asked. When I said no, he looked disappointed. "Do you not think it would be better with singing and dancing?"

After filming, Louis and I visited the ashram of the Bhagwan Shree Rajneesh. Disciples floated about in saffron- or maroon-colored robes. People swarmed by on their way to lectures, meditation sessions, yoga classes. It was a beehive. There were rumors that Rajneesh presided over collegial shtupping; he advocated tantric sex as a path of enlightenment and was said to be sleeping with a number of his female adherents. Disciples were encouraged to "stimulate their lower chakras." The Bhagwan would later move to Oregon, where his quest for enlightenment appeared to be sated by a vast collection of Rolls-Royces.

March 17 was the anniversary of our first date. We spent this sacred day in this weird and creepy place, staying in the Peshwa Suite with room service and a fine long talk about us. Our marriage. My new passport. Our new life.

The place was full of "Poonies," as the ashram residents were called, all in saffron or maroon. They zoomed around town like maniacs on motorcycles, wild-eyed behind goggles, their hair,

33

beards, and beads flowing behind them. They soared, floated, and chanted. Louis and I found something threatening about their bliss and stayed away.

We have our own ashram, Lou Lou and I told ourselves. A little one on Central Park South, where we have these feelings of love and belonging and purpose and freedom that these Poonies keep searching for.

Pune was hard on us both. So unpleasant and pointless a place. Yet I had a job to do. A job I was steadily not doing well. I continued to feel like the awkward, embarrassing novice I was. While I was on the set, Louis had nothing to do, nowhere to go. He wasn't used to being "the husband." We both became unhappy, tense. We escaped tight-lipped, in a rush, to Madras.

In Madras, I was a tourist, which was more tiring, less involving, more guilt-provoking than having a job in a strange new place. I felt haunted by Martin Sheen. As I walked by the beggars, the lepers, the old women staring, I wondered, what choices should I make? I knew it was a racket, they knew it was a racket, but the second you gave money, they looked pained, brutalized, wounded. Five rupees? That's it? Forget it. And the head wobbled disapprovingly, accusingly. They wanted ten. A month's salary for the average Indian. If you bought something, they wanted you to buy two.

The aggression of the street people was

bludgeoning. And they were all so good at it, so charming, canny, direct, funny. Five-year-olds practically climbed into the car, heads shooting through the windows: "Send me stamps, give me a pen, money." Six-year-olds giving the orders, sending back the tip. Beggars, priests, old men and women, all of them shrieking, cooing, cajoling, and no matter what you gave, it was never enough, ever.

We went south to Madurai, where we visited the Living Temple. The temple sprawled across twelve acres, with an Olympic-sized pool where people would wash their clothes, bathe, and perform pujas and other rituals. The elephants were shiva'ed and vishnu'ed and puja'ed to, washed by hand and taken for walks on the temple grounds, and fed rice balls for lunch at the executive office. There were camels and green parrots, goats, crows, and clumps and clusters of bats. It was a feast for the senses. Women wore bells around their ankles and in their ears; the gentle sound of their ringing was everywhere. They braided their glossy waist-length hair with fragrant jasmine and wore garlands of marigolds. Saris of tangerine, lime, fuchsia, and canary yellow glowed like flowers. Gold sparkled at their ears, wrists, and throats as they knelt to make gifts of slabs of ghee to statues of Shiva, Ganesha, Vishnu, or Hanuman.

We returned to the temple at night to find it lit

up with thousands of candles and lanterns. As was the custom, we took our sandals off—in itself an act of courage—and walked barefoot. Everyone was spitting everywhere. We rounded a corner and almost bumped into an elephant shuffling softly through the colonnades, her forehead and ears painted in paisley patterns and white stencils of religious motifs, an enormous marigold necklace around her gray wrinkled neck. She shuffled slowly away, her face and forehead glowing softly in the low lamplight, gracefully, silently, swaying down a side passage.

The south of India is much more intense than the north, an overwhelming sensory experience. Women walked by wearing anklets and bracelets made of row upon row of tuberose. The heady fragrance lingered after them. The pungent scents of jasmine, cardamom, coriander, clove, cumin, and cinnamon mixed routinely with the smell of shit. You'd drive along and see a row of bare asses as people took their morning dumps in the gutter. I began to understand why the locals never ate with their left hands. I think I can say India raised my consciousness of shit, my own and others'. Never had I seen so much shit by so many. So I too had found enlightenment in India.

In Madras, Louis and I stayed at a little hotel on the sea. It was so hot that even the ocean was almost too warm to swim in. We'd have chai in the morning, a spicy hot milky tea, which was delicious, but you'd pour with sweat after. We ate spicy mughal pancakes for breakfast, spicy curry for dinner. We were always sweating and stoned on the spices, moving through the day with a gentle buzz. One night, we had dinner in a tiny, dark place that was so broiling hot it was as if we were inside an oven. We sat at a counter. A man wearing a torn undershirt was cooking in front of an open fire while customers blew their noses directly onto the ground. I was wearing Calvin Klein sandals. I kept my feet up.

We traveled like maniacs, driving and driving. We saw people brush their teeth, pee, shit, spit, blow their noses with their fingers, take morning chai, wash their cattle, shit, thresh the wheat, bathe, bless themselves, perform pujas, fetch their water, do their wash. India's culture and religions were a celebration of life in every form. Life, love, men, women, gods, demons, animals, nature—in every way they were tied and rooted, a vital part of the whole.

India's gods are found everywhere, their likenesses bathed in milk and ghee, garnished with jasmine, lotus flowers, roses, hibiscus, fed with coconuts, smeared with ash and brilliant red powder. They are living, breathing altars, draped in saris, slid down and climbed upon by kids, puja'ed to in every form: bobbing, circling, tapping, prostrating.

And the West, the West with its immaculate

conception, neutered putti, celibate saints and priests and nuns, and guilt and fear of the almighty God. The silent stone cathedrals that seem places of death more than life, more feared than celebrated. A discouragement of living, a severing of ties, an encouragement of ego. The West with its sterilized, starved, soothed senses. Underarm deodorants, air fresheners. Replacing a natural smell with an artificial one. Removing us, step by step, further from reality.

We felt ourselves disappear, freed. But then we felt naked, shut out—of their skin, their culture, their religion. We snapped, became tired and testy, saw each other stripped of virtue, the glow gone, the magic foiled. We were surprised each one found the other so closed, ungenerous, lost, and angry. It sobered and frightened us both. We wondered if the country would win. Should we leave?

Of course, we stayed. We talked, moved closer, almost immediately. Alert to not letting the other feel ignored, misunderstood, lonely. Finding our sense of humor, we decided not to take India and ourselves too seriously.

Next Louis took me to see the famous temple complex at Khajuraho, one of the seven wonders of India. Hundreds of incredibly detailed erotic carvings from the tenth and eleventh centuries grappled and embraced and intertwined on plinths along the soaring sandstone. The Kama Sutra was said to have originated in the same place. Then it was on to the Rat Temple, where barefoot visitors fed sacred rats as big as poodles. You could barely walk for the rats. I made a quick retreat to the car.

Louis then took me to see the Taj Mahal. The Taj was pale and looming and wondrous, but without the vibrancy of Khajuraho.

We traveled through India for about a month. I'd traveled often on my own to remote and primitive outposts, but Louis was truly hardcore. He never stopped—not even in the middle of the country when we were hiking in 100-degree heat. He'd be crippled with cramps from traveler's diarrhea, but he'd keep going. This was purely French. Louis was an explorer, an adventurer with a bottomless curiosity about Indian art and culture and people. Luxury, physical comfort, were unimportant to him. What mattered was the experience.

We left Delhi for Paris, and then took the train to Le Coual. This was a spring unlike any other: delicate, exquisite, fine, and sure. Lush trees of wild lilacs burst everywhere, thousands of tiny daisies sprinkled across the new grass. Pear and cherry blossoms. Tulips, iris, and clusters of lily of the valley and violets. Fresh, sweet smells.

Spring was splendid in Le Coual. Louis was transformed—radiant and loving, the lines of anger gone from his face. I fell head over heels in love with him all over again. When he was sure and serene in himself, he was utterly irresistible.

Back in LA at last, my mother gave us a lovely wedding reception in the living room of my parents' Holmby Hills home. She was delighted to finally have the chance. She invited a wide circle of friends: Jules and Doris Stein, Billy and Audrey Wilder, Irving and Mary Lazar, Lloyd and Dorothy Bridges, Ricardo and Georgiana Montalban, Vincente and Lee Minnelli, Jennifer Jones, Robert and Rosemarie Stack, Albert Finney, Cary Grant and Barbara Harris, Jimmy and Gloria Stewart, Mervyn and Kitty LeRoy, Greer Garson, George Cukor, who was directing me in *Rich and Famous* at the time, and Jacqueline Bisset, my costar. The women were all beautifully dressed in Chanel and Halston. The men wore dark suits. I wore a vintage gold caftan borrowed from Mom and the heirloom sapphire necklace Louis had found for me in Virginia. Mom served our traditional family meal, which was a Swedish smorgasbord with meatballs and lingonberries, gravlax, and hot, spiced glögg. There were violinists and much laughter. People talked about their hip replacements and drank, some too much. They were all merry. Mom had always been a great hostess.

Touring India was a bold way to begin a marriage. At long last, I'd found my traveling companion.

3

Louis sold his apartment in the West Fifties and moved in with me. I had bought my first apartment in 1976; I was thirty. It was in a landmarked building on Central Park South called the Gainsborough Studios and had a sweeping view of the length of the park. Built in 1908 as artists' studios, it was the first apartment building to go up on Central Park South. It featured twenty-foot ceilings and mullioned windows featuring the northern exposure favored by artists. Each apartment or studio differed in small detail from the next. To me, and to many of my friends, it was the best apartment in the city. Louis had married well.

A gallery ran around the second floor, accessed by a staircase that gave onto a small loft bedroom with a wide window overlooking the living room below and the park beyond. On Thanksgiving Day, you could sit up in bed and watch the parade come down Central Park West. There was a large skylight, as the studio was on the top floor, and the apartment was flooded with light. I had furnished it with two huge sofas covered in white duck and two enormous overstuffed armchairs. In the far corner was a large wingbacked chair with an ottoman under a standing Tiffany poinsettia lamp.

The lamp was the most expensive piece of art I had ever bought and I suffered sharp buyer's remorse. This was pure stupidity on my part. First, it is simply ravishing to look at. Unlike most Tiffany lamps, this one could be viewed from the second floor so you could appreciate the intense colors and pattern of the top of the shade from above. It was the focus of the apartment, and we enjoyed it every evening. Second, it's the best investment I ever made.

There were also trophies from my travels scattered on tabletops: a four-pound chunk of jade that my Hong Kong friend, Shing Lung, had brought from the Jade Market in Burma, a dried opium poppy scored during harvest that perched in a tiny pot, bowls of noodles with chopsticks—realistic plastic display models used in Japan. And my favorite, not for the faint of heart, my bottle of Chinese rat wine, a gift from director Milos Forman, which had fetal rats floating in the amber-colored liquid and was believed to cure anything from headaches to mortality.

In the late 1970s and 1980s, Columbus Circle, which is at the top of Central Park South, was a very different place. When I walked out the door of my building and turned left, it was hookers and dealers. That was it. One was immediately swarmed by wiry guys asking softly, "Sniff? Snort? Blow?" Farther down on the Circle was a hideous 1940s-era convention center, and dilapidated brownstones and rundown buildings. The dazzling Time Warner Center with its collection of restaurants and the gigantic Whole Foods, plus the massive renovation of Columbus Circle itself, was years away. As a neighborhood it was wanting, but it was convenient. You could walk to the theater district, to any museum, and uptown and downtown were equidistant. And it was on Central Park, although the park was not at its subsequent perfect state. That would come years later once it had been taken over by the privately funded Central Park Conservancy. When I moved in, the park's fields and meadows were dust bowls and the benches were broken. Hypodermic needles were strewn in corners of the playground. The park was in a state of total neglect, but it was still the park, and we used it often.

Just before I met Louis, the apartment at the back of the building that was contiguous with mine became available. It was small, with normal, low ceilings, a fireplace, and a single dark bedroom. I bought it, broke through the wall at the end of the hall, and renovated the space. The front apartment was white and filled with light, so I painted the back apartment a pale peach. I had a long L-shaped sofa made, and an armchair with an ottoman. I tore out the wall of the tiny Pullman kitchen and left it open, with a counter, a small fridge, and a small stove. I tiled the kitchen and the fireplace surround in emerald green and built in a desk and media cabinet that went the length of the wall. I faux-painted the mantel to look like honey-colored pine, which matched the desk and bookshelves. Renny Saltzman, who helped me with all of it, had custom carpeting made in sage green with peach Xs.

The back of the apartment had a completely different feeling from the front. It was intimate, warm, and cozy. There were pine bookshelves on two walls. There was Native American pottery from Chaco Canyon and centuries-old baskets and rugs. It was a great place to burrow in for the winter; it was where we really lived. In fact, Louis took over the desk and worked from there, and I worked from my desk in the bedroom upstairs. Hours would go by when we didn't see or hear each other. For two people who had spent a lot of time alone, it was ideal. It gave us room.

Being with Louis upgraded me culturally. Whenever he was on holiday, we would relentlessly visit museums, cloisters, cathedrals; he was a cultural commando. Carnegie Hall was three blocks away, and Lincoln Center was five. Louis especially adored opera: hence our first date at the opening of Puccini's *Manon Lescaut* with Plácido Domingo at the Metropolitan Opera. On our second date, he rented a car and we drove to Philadelphia to see the Barnes Collection—one of the world's greatest private collections of impressionists and post-impressionists.

And of course Louis loved to go to the movies. We'd go to a multiscreen movie theater and he'd watch one movie for fifteen minutes, then hop across the hall to watch the next for twenty, right on down the line, as if the theater were a gigantic smorgasbord.

Louis was innately elegant. Most of the time. He wore custom-made Cerruti suits, bespoke monogrammed shirts. On him, the monograms were never a mark of an arriviste trying too hard; they belonged. And the collars on some of the older shirts were slightly frayed, which he liked. He never looked overly color-coordinated, just tasteful. Sometimes he would add a Fair Isle sweater vest under his sports jackets if it was cold. His shoes were also well worn but handmade, sometimes by Lobb. His dress shoes always had a buffed shine. In them he would launch into his brisk walk, tilting forward, feet slapping the pavement, pipe clenched in his teeth. When we went to the infrequent awards show, Louis would root around in my bag for powder and pat it haphazardly on his face to dull the sheen. His studs were old Cartier, and he had a pair of exquisite cuff links that were iridescent beetles set in gold. They had been a gift from his first wife and they were unlike anything I had ever seen.

He didn't always look so dashing or put together. Working at home or at Le Coual, he wore sweatpants that were so old they had shrunk to midcalf. His sweatshirts were also short and frayed and barely came to the waist, and he was very attached to them all. In cold weather in New York City, he liked to wear my mouse cap, which was a navy knit watch cap with large felt ears, eyes, and nose, and a tail that hung down the back. He would wear this everywhere, and he looked ridiculous, because he would also wear it with suits and an overcoat. He wore it to the theater, to ball games, to pick up food to go, and he looked like a refugee. It was one of the moments I loved him most.

Louis had a really fine mind, a tremendous intellect, and a very sly, dry sense of humor. Once when I flew to Texas to visit him on the set of *Alamo Bay*, he gave me a tour of town: "And there's the little market, just for basics: milk, bread, and guns." A crow in a tree above us cawed and I whipped around. "Did you think it was a fan?" he said.

We would give dinners often in our apartment. We'd serve chicken curry, or our Brazilian housekeeper Roseangela would bring her mother and they'd make feijoada, the national dish with pigs' feet—really graphic but delicious. We made lethal caipirinhas.

We were very happy to entertain. We were fortunate that our separate groups of friends overlapped so much. We'd serve buffet dinners for twenty or twenty-five people at a time. Playwright John Guare and his wife, Adele Chatfield-Taylor, who headed the American Institute in Rome, were frequent guests. So were Richard Avedon and writers Alice and Michael Arlen. Whoever was in town—Bernardo Bertolucci with his wife, Claire Townsend, or Marcello Mastroianni would drop by. Charles Michener, editor of *Newsweek*, with his wife, photographer Diana. Mary Ellen Mark and Martin Bell, actor-playwright Wally Shawn and author Debbie Eisenberg, actor-director Andre Gregory and his wife, Chiquita.

The evenings were low-key, easy, relaxed. If it was New Year's Eve, we'd have late dinners, maybe tamale pie, then turn the lights off at midnight so guests could lift their Champagne glasses while watching the fireworks display set off in Central Park. Afterward we'd watch the whacky Midnight Marathon through the park, with runners dressed as rabbits, pumpkins, reindeer. Later Louis and I would do the dishes, discussing the party like an old couple married for decades. It was bliss.

If we were in LA, Louis would take me to his Bikram yoga class in a windowless room off of Wilshire Boulevard and Doheny. I had no idea what I was getting myself into the first time. When I walked into the studio, the heat was staggering and I had trouble getting my breath.

The room was always heated to a hundred degrees to facilitate stretching. Bikram Choudhury would usually teach the class himself. (Bikram had a collection of vintage cars, one of which was an old white Rolls-Royce with YOGINI on the license plate.) He was a tiny guy, five-feet-three tops, balding with long hair pulled into a pony-tail. He conducted class sitting on a pillow in the lotus position. Behind him sat a favorite female student in a leotard, massaging his shoulders. I took my place with Louis and forty other people, all doing yoga for an hour and a half in the oppressive heat. Halfway through the class, sweat was dripping off all of us, soaking the carpet, which smelled rancid. Quincy Jones was there sometimes, along with Lakers star Kareem Abdul-Jabbar and Raquel Welch. Kareem couldn't stretch fully because the ceiling was so low. It was the stress buster of all time.

Those early years were magic. Next to me in bed was a man who was brilliant by any measure, whom I could never engage with on his level, yet he never seemed to notice the disparity.

Louis could be wonderfully protective of me. His movie *Atlantic City* was nominated for numerous Academy Awards; Louis for director, John Guare for screenplay, and Susan Sarandon for leading actress. Louis had had a relationship with Susan. Fearing tension arising from all of us clubbily seated together at the ceremony, Louis decided we would be in France for the Oscars that year.

Louis had his vulnerable moments too. Especially if he was involved with a film, he'd be plagued with anxiety, turn into a little black ball of despair. He'd have a sleepless night: "You know," he told me, "the Aztecs used to wake up terrified each morning because they were afraid the sun wouldn't rise again."

Once he had a nightmare that I'd left him. I woke in the middle of the night to find him pacing and drinking tea.

"Do you love me?" he asked. "Sometimes I'm afraid you'll leave me for someone else because you'll find out I'm silly."

"You *are* silly," I told him. "And there's no one else. Ever."

Louis's face relaxed. "Well, yes, that's what I feel. Who could be better? We are a perfect fit— but I never take you for granted."

All too soon, Louis would be off to France for whatever movie project he was working on. We really tried to confine these trips to no more than two weeks apart. To be apart for three weeks was too long, too difficult. We would call each other, although the cost was prohibitive. Fortunately, Louis was a wonderful letter writer, *le roi des lettres*, as Alexandra, Justine's mother, said.

Whenever Louis was in New York, I was in

charge. I'd book the reservations and pay for the restaurants. We both felt keeping finances separate was neater. I'd always felt it was important to pay my own way, step up to the plate. I'd often pick up dinner checks for groups of people. Louis was the heir to the Béghin sugar fortune, generated during the Napoleonic Wars; the name Béghin-Say still appears on sugar packets today. He always felt it was not possible to have an equal relationship if you were unequal financially; separate accounts were the only way to steer a straight course.

Ours was not a traditional marriage, yet I was always thrilled when we got to Europe, because in Paris, Louis was in charge, taking me to his favorite restaurants: L'Ambroisie, Chez Georges, Quai Voltaire, La Closerie des Lilas, and his favorite café, Flore.

Outside of it, the dynamic shifted even more, and I had to figure out how to find my place. When I left Paris to go out to the country with Louis, that space was Le Coual, Louis's preserve.

An imposing pale stone château in the southwest of France, it was medieval and mysterious. Built piecemeal over the years in the fifteenth and sixteenth centuries, it was somber in tone, made from the honey-colored stone of the Causses, or limestone cliffs of the region. The architectural vernacular of Le Lot, the region in France where we were, was rugged and very particular to the area. Le Coual's roofs were triangulated and tiled into points. Windows were small and front doors were double and massive. Rising three stories, its turret and roof crowned with terra-cotta-colored tiles, the house had an integrity, a force—and a history. Louis had bought it with his first wife in the late 1960s. The property was in ruins and together they restored it. The marriage ended soon after and then Alexandra moved in with their daughter, Justine.

Le Coual had been painstakingly done to look as though it had never been touched and perfectly reflected Louis's passion for travel, his love for exploring other cultures. The walls were hung with nineteenth-century Indian and European paintings as well as Tibetan thangkas. The floors spread with kilim carpets. Rough-hewn oak beams cradled rooms crowded with deep leather couches. There were towering bookcases over-flowing with dusty volumes, creaky armoires that nipped at the ceiling, nineteenth-century fauteuils covered in antique paisleys, eighteenth-century tapestries, terra-cotta busts.

In the entry hall there was a hearth seven feet high and the floor was laid with large, rounded stones. The fireplace in the entry was designed to give warmth to the stairwell and stave off the damp chill of the winters. The thickness of the walls kept the house fairly cool, even in the baking heat of August. We closed the shutters, windows, and curtains and hunkered down, reading or cooking until the evening when the heat would drop.

The master bedroom was very Italianate, painted a flat salmon and hung with rich ocher velvet-fringed curtains. The carpet was a frayed, fine oriental, the bed antique brass, and the turn-of-the-century settee was an olive tufted velvet. The walls were three feet thick and the ceiling was supported by heavy carved beams. It was beautiful, highly refined, but as a California girl, I sometimes found it oppressive. One night in particular, a raw, cold winter night, as I lay awake in bed it felt like the beams were pressing down on me and squeezing out my breath.

The heart of the kitchen was a huge stone fireplace and a life-size oil of Hecate, goddess of witchcraft and magic, and her dogs. The *cave à vin*, or wine cellar, was one floor down and liberally stocked with wonderful vintages, rats, and rat traps. I'd brace myself whenever I had to run down there for a bottle; the three-foot-thick walls locked in a persistent chill and the low cove ceiling left just enough room to barely stand.

I was always wrestling with that house. I tried to find ways to make Louis's home *our* home. I'd buy wonderful antique posters, including one of a man riding a bicycle as lightning crackled behind his head; it reminded me of Louis on his ever-present bike. I slid wonderful crockery and nineteenth-century kerosene lamps, other antiquing finds, onto tabletops and prayed they'd find favor.

I tried to change things in the garden, because I found it rather enclosed and forbidding. The pool was surrounded by fifteen-foot-high hedges. I found it claustrophobic. Tentatively, I took down one wall of hedges, which opened the pool area to a lovely view of the fields beyond. Louis wasn't pleased. "This is not Bel Air," he informed me. It took me years to take down the remaining three hedges. Finally the pool was open and you could see the massive fifteenth-century stone tower of the house on one side and fields on the other. I was much happier, but Louis was not. He felt that Le Coual had a specific spirit; I should take care not to violate it.

In the cool of the evenings we'd cook dinner and eat outside under the trees and make herb tea from the garden. We were always home for dinners because, for one thing, it was lovely and for another, there was really nowhere to go. Afterward, we'd go upstairs and watch old movies. We had hundreds of movies in Le Coual. It was a library of classics with a few contemporary hits thrown in. We would watch until early morning, then turn in. Days would pass like this in the summer, which could be cold through June. Sometimes we had fires going in the kitchen till July. Mornings were gray and often stayed that way all day; then, in July, it lifted and there was intensive bike riding, swimming races, badminton, and hiking the network of paths that crisscrossed the region.

Le Coual was nestled deep in the country, in *la France profonde*. Life went on as it had a hundred or more years ago. There was an unusually beautiful medieval village fifteen minutes away, Saint-Cirq-Lapopie, which was designated "one of the most beautiful villages in France." It was built on the face of a sheer cliff high above the river and we would sit in the tiny square and have dinner outside the little inn of Saint-Cirq. Lamb was the specialty of the Lot region, but I would always order eggs with truffles since I was not a meat person.

Truffles were the other specialty of the area, and sometimes, on his passport forms, under "occupation," Louis would put *trufficulteur*. We would go hunting with a truffle-sniffing pig or a dog named Rita; there was always a risk that the pigs would eat the truffles they unearthed. You could tell where the truffles would be by the patterns ten feet out from the trunks of the oaks where the roots circled. The pig would lower its pink snout ecstatically and begin to dig; it would take two men to pull it off. The truffles were lumpy, moldering things that looked like cancerous tumors on the tree roots and smelled like a basement. The French called them "black gold," and when the men spaded them up Louis would be buoyant. He'd take them home and soak them to make his specialty, *oeufs aux truffes*. He'd carefully put whole eggs into a bowl, add the fist of truffle, and cover it with a dish towel so that the truffle perfume permeated the eggshells. Then he'd crack the eggs into another bowl, stir in some of the fragrant liquid, slice the truffle very finely into the mixture and cook it slowly, slowly over a makeshift double boiler. We'd have that on toast. With a salad it was all you wanted.

Louis debuted the dish on our wedding day. Somehow a few pieces of hash had gotten thrown into the egg-and-truffle mixture. We had to strain it and pick out the tiny pieces so that no one would eat it accidentally. The dish was so popular that Louis made it every New Year's Eve. Occasionally we brought some home to friends. George Cukor wrote me a thank-you note about how he "oohed and aahed" over them: "I only hope that I don't get too accustomed to them—and then what's going to happen to me? . . . I have scrambled eggs for breakfast every morning, but now I'll eat them with truffles—that's real class."

Each year, there were fewer and fewer truffles on our hunts, which usually happened in February. Louis took it as a foreboding sign. "They're moving to Spain," he would mutter as we came home empty-handed.

We would get crates of white peaches, peel and

puree them, add Champagne, and serve bellinis in the summer. Or we'd make *pêches au vin*: we would peel and slice yellow peaches and put them into a big jug of red wine, a new Beaujolais with cinnamon sticks and a little sugar.

The country roads were lined with hand-laid stone walls covered with blackberry vines. At the end of July and August, the blackberries would ripen and we'd all fan out with baskets to pick them. Everyone's mouth was covered with purple; the berries were sweet and delicious.

Sage, thyme, oregano, and rosemary grew in fragrant beds right outside the kitchen. I'd pick bunches and stuff them into teapots to make Provençal tea, adding lemon and sweetening it with honey from the bee man down the road. The rosemary made everyone pee like crazy. We got our fresh chèvre from the goat man who lived down another country road. We'd mix it with a little olive oil, garlic, chives, and salt and spread it on crusty bread; it was perfect with the zucchini soup that we made from the vines in the *potager*. We also made zucchini bread, stuffed zucchini, sautéed zucchini, and ratatouille. We barely made a dent in the zucchini crop.

Our country neighbors were incredibly sophisticated. They knew how to make everything from scratch. Bakers would pull bread out of sixteenth-century ovens with ten-foot wooden spatulas. You could hear it expanding and crackling as you put it in your basket. Eating it was an interactive experience.

The couple across the road from us were pig farmers. They would invite us for Champagne and serve it with delicate wafers called *langues de chat*, cat's tongues. The pigs were lolling and grunting in the muddy pen right across from the house, but there was always a refinement to things. Armande Gonçalvez, our Portuguese house-keeper, would have us over to her little house on the property for dinner and announce: "*Je vais fatiguer la salade*"—"I'm going to tire"—wilt—"the salad a bit." We found that level of sophistication everywhere.

I was always on my most grown-up behavior in France. I'd spent a year at finishing school in Switzerland when I was fourteen and made a film in French at twenty, so I was comfortable in the language. My accent was good but my grammar was shaky. At Le Coual we would watch the news in French. I would skim *Paris Match* and study my "guide to easy French" textbook. *Je me débrouillais.* I made do. The French have a highly developed sense of wit, but little sense of humor. I don't know how that explains their worship of Jerry Lewis. I was never very successful telling jokes in French. Justine and I took one of our farm dogs to the vet. There was man in the waiting room holding a chicken on his lap. The vet said our dog needed to be on antibiotics.

"But with antibiotics, he wouldn't be able to have alcohol, right?" I asked.

The doctor looked at me and offered a withering rejoinder. "Alcohol is not a good idea for dogs in any case."

Justine was horrified.

Once I made a chili for a couple, both wonderful chefs who collected their own escargots and made their own sorbet and foie gras.

"I'll just leave a little Alka-Seltzer by each glass," I told Louis, anticipating heartburn for these sophisticated palates.

"No, you can't do that!" Louis said, quickly gathering up the packets.

Each town had a marketplace on a different day. The one near us was Villefranche, a medieval sunken square paved with cobblestones. Guarding it on one corner was a fourteenth-century cathedral, very simple and powerful looking, unrelieved by stained glass to lighten its stern façade. There was an arcade of shops around the square and a very large crucifix that loomed some twenty feet over all. To Catholics and non-Catholics alike, it was very forbidding. No traffic was allowed, so there was no contemporary noise, save for the odd honk of a far-off Vespa. The square smelled of cheese, coffee, vegetables spoiling on the ground, the perfume of almonds and coconuts from the macaroons on offer from the bakeries ringing the square. The crowds were so densely packed you could hardly move past the carts.

Louis and I would split up and go around the market on our own—it was too crowded to stay together—and load up our straw bags with salads, vegetables, cheeses, country hams, generous servings from the man with the huge paella pan. This was not the glamorous, tourist-filled south of France by any means; it was very authentic, perhaps too authentic. People still had medieval diseases, like elephantiasis. Some of the women sported beards. Customers strode by carrying live chickens upside down with their feet tied, as if swinging feathered tote bags.

The market radiated along tiny side streets. One cobblestoned street took you past livestock and crates and crates of baby chicks and grown chickens and doves and ducks and geese.

Another side street had tiny stores selling goose livers. We'd see older farm women in the stalls force-feeding their geese, pouring corn and grain down their throats to induce liver disease for foie gras. They'd keep the enormously diseased livers, veined with yellow fat, in great jars before passing them through a sieve to become the visually appealing, fine-grained foie gras with the truffle in the center. This was too much information for someone who tended to be vegetarian.

The market's side streets held carcasses as far

as the eye could see, snouts and hooves on proud display. I found it barbaric and disgusting. Louis lived in terror of what I would say because I loved animals so much that I hadn't eaten beef, veal, pork, or lamb since I was in my twenties. Once in Paris we'd gone to a four-fork restaurant, an enormously elegant place. The waiter recommended *poulet de bresse en vessie.*

"What's a *vessie*?" I'd asked Louis.

"It's like a kind of a bag," he'd replied. Oh, that would be chicken in parchment. Twenty minutes later, the waiter came bearing this huge veined balloon, fully inflated, on a platter.

"Oh my god—what *is* that!" I'd shrieked.

"It's a *vessie*," the waiter told me.

"That's not a bag!"

"I know. It's a pig bladder," he'd said. I blanched.

Derived from a medieval recipe, the pig bladder held chicken with finely sliced truffles inserted under the skin, which was bathed with Madeira and Armagnac. The chicken was tender to the point of exquisiteness. It was the great delicacy of the restaurant, and here I'd been behaving like this rube. It had been humiliating for Louis, who feared similar outbursts at the open-air market.

After we'd gathered our purchases, Louis and I would peruse the antique stores, galleries, pastry shops, and coffee bars ringing the square. We'd meet under the crucifix, and then find a table at

Café des Arcades overlooking the market square, where we'd sit at eye level with Jesus's feet as we sipped our coffee or cappuccino or hot chocolate, looking down over the merry melee of the market. Then we'd schlep our stuff home and start preparing lunch.

We loved to take big driving tours around the very stark, very beautiful countryside surrounding Le Coual. We drove past endless fields of sunflowers to Nîmes in the south of France to see the magnificent stone amphitheater where the Roman garrisons had made their outpost. We'd drive to Arles, Avignon, the mountains. Because Le Coual was fairly close to the Spanish border, we drove to Barcelona. I'm a total Gaudí freak. We explored Parc Güell, Sagrada Familia, saw the new Picasso Museum designed by Richard Meier. The city was designed for walking everywhere. We'd have fantastic seafood at the port in Barceloneta. We couldn't speak Catalan, so we'd point—food, please!

One night we enjoyed an amazing meal at Pinotxo, a highly recommended restaurant. The owner knew Louis's work, so he invited us to meet him at La Boqueria, the huge, covered, bustling marketplace off Las Ramblas the next morning. There the chef bought breakfast fixings—plucking squid from the acres of fish on ice, salty Spanish cheeses from the mongers crowding the center of the market, a bottle of great wine—and then took them to a stand of maybe six barstools at ten o'clock in the morning and told the guy to fry up the fish, cut the cheese, and prepare this incredible meal. We were plastered by the time we staggered out—the most perfect way to start the day.

Another time we drove to Lourdes through gorgeous and completely unspoiled terrain. I'd always had a macabre interest in Lourdes, but the reality of the place was just very depressing. Louis sent his mother a postcard: "*Maman*, I took Candice to Lourdes, and now I limp."

I worked very little during the early years of our marriage; I simply wanted to spend as much time as possible with Louis. I finished my first memoir, *Knock Wood*, after years of halting effort. Much to my astonishment, it found favor with readers. I recorded my surprise in my journal:

I cannot get over it. Have trouble enjoying it. Instead of real joy, pride, I am deeply *relieved*. To have survived the process intact. I have pulled it off. After all that time, all that anguish, all the neurosis and work—I have done it.

The book about which I'd worried so—about my father, mother, friends—this book did honor to them all, but above all, to my father. He had more publicity on my book tour than he had had in the last thirty years of his life. "I have resurrected him," I wrote in my journal. "He is rediscovered." From an admiring daughter who never quite got her father's approval.

The first four years with Louis were the best in the sense that it was very much about the two of us. Okay, sometimes it was about the four of us.

One day I overheard Louis telling Armande in French that Gila, Cuote's mother, and Alexandra, Justine's mother, were coming to stay at Le Coual for Easter. My head ratcheted around and I said, *"What?"* I had a fit. This took Louis by surprise. It would be very unusual for a Frenchwoman to raise her voice.

I couldn't wrap my head around this plan. Once you have a child with someone, of course, they're in your life forever—but usually not in your house. I remember calling my friend Carol in London in tears, saying, "They're coming to stay!"

"Candy, that is absolutely unacceptable. Do not do it," she told me.

The room on the third floor was called Gila's Room. The room on the second floor was called Alexandra's room. Armande suggested we rename the bedrooms: *le chambre du deuxième*—"the room on the second floor"—for Alexandra, and *le chambre du troisième*—"the room on the third floor"—for Gila. *Et voilà.*

In the end, Alexandra came to stay but Gila did not.

Because Alexandra lived outside Paris, I'd had time to establish a relationship with her over many visits. The first time she visited us at Le Coual, we all went to a local pig race. The piglets had numbers sprayed on their sides and were encouraged to trot around a circle in a field. I was surprised the field didn't combust, since I was seething, wondering, "Why is she here?"

Alexandra was a force of nature; when she wasn't weeding in the herb garden, she was in the large family kitchen cooking, which she did brilliantly. She was a natural, instinctive chef, which had a certain appeal for me because I am a natural eater. She was a whirling dervish, running out into the garden to pull herbs, killing a chicken for dinner with a quick wrench of the neck. Her eyes glittered with joy as she told me about how she'd bought a baby goat to cook in the open fireplace in the kitchen. "With cumin—on a spit." My eyes were starting to roll back in my head. That was more than I could ever process. For me, cooking was toasting Parmesan Triscuits in the toaster oven. When I first met Louis, I'd told him, "You know, I don't cook." Later he said, "But you *can't* cook! I thought you were kidding!" His brother Vincent was a gourmet cook who would take four days to make an exquisite bouillon. I would look dumbfounded and say,

"It comes in a can—look at the time you save."

As it turned out, Alexandra was great—dynamic, smart, funny, and generous. She had always loved Le Coual and felt like the chatelaine. It was she who'd made a riding ring next to the barn, renovated the stables, and kept horses. It was thanks to her that we'd had Nanette, the donkey that pulled our wedding cart. She and her *homme*, Olivier, were frequent guests at Le Coual.

The French have very different attitudes about the easy commingling of wives, mistresses, and assorted offspring—they're much more casual and dispassionate about it. They think Americans are primitive and puritanical.

Embarrassed by Alexandra's expertise, I did try to make something of myself in the kitchen, but cooking at Le Coual was not for the faint of heart, which I very much was. The stove was fairly primitive. You had to plunge a long iron stick into the gas to light the fire. I was always afraid my head was going to blow up. Whenever possible, I'd try to get Armande to light the stove for me. The oven was so hot that you needed special potholders that wouldn't burn up on the heavy metal shelf you'd lift out from the cavernous interior. I'd buy special gloves for barbecuing in America, silver, quilted, and heat-resistant.

Once I was carrying a pot of boiling hot pasta from the stove to drain in the sink. There was water on the floor and I slipped. I saw the accident coming and couldn't do anything. The boiling water poured down my thigh. In an instant, it was all hands on deck. Louis had to drive me fifty minutes away to the nearest hospital. I could hardly breathe for the pain. Eventually the length of my thigh was covered by a blister three inches high, which later became infected and turned septic. I considered cooking a high-risk sport.

In truth, I was often unhappy at Le Coual because it was so isolated. Faxes didn't exist then, and it cost a fortune to use the phone. This was President Mitterrand's era, so the television got three channels, one of them dedicated to traditional folkloric dances, usually Bulgarian and in black and white. VHS was just starting, but it was in a very primitive state. Louis and I would play dominoes at the felt-covered game table in the salon. He'd play chess with Cuote and Justine.

To help fight the inevitable cabin fever, I'd have costume dinners. Whenever Louis had a movie project, which was almost always, he would spend his days in the barn, which he turned into a primitive editing facility. I'd commandeer the assistant editors and their girlfriends or wives and make couscous or curry, or stuff a leg of lamb with rosemary so that Louis could paint it with mustard and roast it in the fireplace. The rule was that no one dined without a costume. Everyone was up for it; after all, it was almost always freezing until July, and other entertainment was thin on the ground. I'd dig out trunks filled with clothes from the 1920s, '30s, and '40s that I'd found in the attic. One editor's wife came as the Hunchback of Notre Dame, resourcefully stuffing pillows down her back. Justine wore a crown I made for her that I cut out of cardboard and covered with gold foil and glitter. Cuote wielded the sword I'd cobbled from cardboard and silver foil. We'd celebrate as the fire crackled in the hearth behind us.

Then we'd trundle the guests out to the barn, where Cuote and Justine would put on plays that Justine had written. The two donkeys lived in the stable beneath the barn, which we'd just refloored with a riser that made a perfect stage. Cuote and Justine would perform for the guests, ducking behind an old screen for costume changes. I remember one performance where Justine's entire face and upper body were shrouded in translucent white chiffon, the fabric streaming ghostlike behind her as she wheeled tight circles on her bicycle around Cuote, who recited a poem she'd given him to read. It was all so very . . . French.

Le Coual was beautiful in the winter. It seldom snowed but the weather was raw and very cold. It brought out the mystery of the house, which seemed even more imposing in the winter light.

I brought egg dye kits from home so we could decorate eggs for Easter. One Easter dawned so cold that there was frost and a light dusting of snow. I rushed outside to hang the eggs from the trees so the children wouldn't have to clamber over the frozen ground to find them.

Justine and I would make princess dolls together and undertake various art projects. We stenciled the walls of her bedroom. We made papier-mâché masks.

How could Louis and I have kids of our own? We worked in separate places. We were so much a couple. It was hard enough to make space for our relationship, let alone for a child. Louis was a great father, but he still had to be away from his kids for long periods of time. The logistics seemed insoluble. We spent a lot of time going over our schedules, our respective calendars spread across our knees. Who's where? When did Louis start shooting? When would I finish? We were trying to get some shape out of our lives.

Louis had a huge family; he was the fifth of seven children. He had three brothers and was especially close to the older ones; Vincent, the baby of the family, was much younger and often worked with Louis as a producer. Louis had based his 1971 coming-of-age movie, *Murmur of the Heart*, on his own family—except that unlike the protagonist, Laurent, he hadn't slept with his mother. After the first screening in Paris, Louis's mother got up, hugged him, and said, "Ah, Louis. It brings back such memories!" His family were almost the only people he was close to. Now he had fathered two different children by two different mothers. Where would a child of our own fit into this complicated equation?

Equally important, where would a child fit into the lives we'd chosen? Louis was an internationally acclaimed director with more than twenty films under his belt by the time we married, including *Murmur of the Heart* (for which he'd received an Oscar nomination for Best Screenplay); *Lacombe, Lucien* (nominated for Best Foreign Language Film); *Pretty Baby*; and *Atlantic City* (nominated for Best Director). I'd done an almost equal number of movies by that time, but I considered Louis an artist whereas I dealt strictly in commerce.

Sometimes before he was about to shoot a film, Louis would have a tiny implosion. Before starting one movie, cloistered at the back of the apartment, after furiously pacing back and forth, he burst into tears. Later, he sent me a postcard from location:

What a director does is total self-provocation for me. It's insane for me to do it. You are required to be everything I'm not, everything I hate. I hate to yell at people, for actors to make me their father, pull at me. I understand

69

them; it's frightening. And I am an actor myself sometimes, when I have to I can yell and walk off—give orders if I have to. Sometimes you do. But directing saved me from being passive.

It's the same for many directors. I'm close friends with several; I've seen at what point in the process they leave their bodies as the terror takes over. Mike Nichols's eyes would go yellow. Before they're about to shoot, they lash out at people, almost like cornered animals. No matter how much they've planned the movie they want to shoot, they're tortured with questions. Will the final film end up being remotely close to that vision? The anxiety is overpowering.

If it was a screenplay Louis had worked on himself, he was even more possessive; it was so much more personal. Once he started preparations—piling into a van to scout locations with his crew, shooting—every instinct kicked in, every skill, and he'd function perfectly. He knew every detail of every shot, exactly what he was doing. With the next shoot, he had to climb the mountain all over again. That's one reason he liked documentaries so much. First, because he was so driven by his curiosity; documentaries were a way to explore something that fascinated and interested him. But second, documentaries didn't carry the same fear or anxiety. He'd do his own camera work, so that was fun for him too.

Louis always said the most important things for directors were shoes: "You have to be on your feet eighteen hours a day. Every moment someone is coming to you for a decision in every department." Wardrobe, lighting, financing, sound. Louis thought sound was the most important sense in a movie. He'd listen to a take on his headphones with his eyes closed, chewing gum frantically, listening for the aural style of the film. He could tell if the take worked because of how it sounded. Obviously, camera work was important, but he trusted his sound man, Jean-Claude Laureux, implicitly.

Louis's filmmaking never showed; he was very subtle. While he always dreamed of making a film that was a commercial success, he never wanted to compromise his principles as a filmmaker to do it. (He did that on *Crackers* and the critics attacked him.) He knew that his films weren't accessible for most Americans.

My Dinner with Andre was a script by playwright-actor Wally Shawn that was a conversation between two old friends over dinner. They never got up from the table. Their focus was on themselves and their very different approaches to their art and their lives. The arrival of the waiter was the equivalent of a car chase.

Our first summer together, we were in

Bridgehampton with his kids. Wally Shawn and Andre Gregory rehearsed in the living room, poring over the massive number of lines, while Louis planned his shots. Most directors dread scenes of actors around a table eating. It makes for endless shots of Talking Heads, which are best avoided. There is no movement; it is a nightmare for continuity and they all struggle with ways to keep the scene alive.

Could they shoot the movie in real time? They tried that at the Ginger Man on the Upper West Side. Wally and Andre performed the conversation as written, but Louis discarded that way of shooting because he needed more choices of camera angles than that allowed.

They eventually shot *My Dinner with Andre* in Richmond, Virginia, in the middle of winter. The weather was very cold. Andre was rapturously describing life unembellished, dismissing electric blankets, and defending the experience of cold. Wally's position was the opposite; he took a strong stand for comfort, especially electric blankets, which Andre had hidden under the table on his lap during the entire shoot.

My Dinner with Andre was a surprise hit.

At times, being an artist could feel overwhelming. Once he turned to me, exhausted, discouraged, overworked, overweight. "Working in America has made me into a shadow," he sighed. "A fat shadow." My journal recorded a time of tension when I went to Texas to watch him shoot:

Arrived sick, tense. Lou-Lou working. It is distant. Painful. We are both lonely. I unreasonably resent his absence, preoccupation. Don't see his need. His love. Instead feel shut out, lonely. He knows. Has trouble showing his pain. He understands.

He has heard the rumor from New York that I was having an affair with another actor; in fact, it was a lunch in a group of eight people. Swallowed it. Buried the hurt, fear, anger. The rage that we are treated like any other couple. The terror that we might become any other couple. He would kill himself if that happened. He can't stand it happening.

Work separates us. Divides us. It is no good.

The next night he is restless. Tossing. Sweating. Then goes downstairs and sobs. "I'm not as strong as you think I am. I can't stand when we're not close." We cry together. Hold each other. It is better.

The nature of the beast is that artists are selfish. Their art takes first priority, and while Louis made the two of us his first priority for a while, he was driven as an artist. That was his engine. He saw his life in terms of how much time it took to prepare, shoot, and edit a film. He'd always be asking himself, "How many more films do I have time to make?" He was perennially on a shooting schedule. He always wanted to be doing something; if he didn't have a feature, he'd make a documentary, he'd do an opera, direct a John Guare play. He was always engaged, always on a shooting schedule.

Between the pressures of shooting and the stress of all his travel, it was often too much for Louis. We would have an altercation. "I feel like you are the light and I bring you down," he told me. He was prone to great depressions. When we were first together, they were almost nonexistent, but he'd had them since his early twenties and they could emerge at any time, clobbering him. Rather than impose them on me, Louis would take himself off to a spa in France, where he'd fast, exercise, bicycle—whatever it took to purge himself of the darkness.

With so many battles for Louis to fight, the decision whether to have children, it seemed, fell to me.

⁂ 4 ⁂

In those early days, all we wanted was to spend time with each other. Harold Pinter asked Louis to direct his script of his play *Betrayal.* "I'm very flattered," Louis told him, "but I can't do that now. I just want to be with Candice and love Candice."

Soon after Louis and I began seeing each other, we stayed at a friend's flat in London. One day he left me a huge postcard from Disneyland featuring Jiminy Cricket peering delightedly into the window of a candy store. On the back he wrote:

You're just about to enter the 2nd third of your life, which you will devote entirely to the pleasure principle. You know, it takes that amount of time to get rid of the stiffness, the fears, the hang-ups of adolescence. At 20, you were very old (probably, what do I know??) and it takes time to become young again, to find the child in you. . . . I love you so much, it is like the sun in my eyes, walking in a forest, I am naked because I don't have to hide anything anymore. The world is my nest, my theater, my greenhouse. I feel like a bird. See you to-night.

Whenever we did need to be apart because of work obligations, the blessing in disguise was my discovery of Louis, a legendary letter writer.

From Mr. to Mrs. Louis Bergen:

My darling, I love you more and more, I miss you more and more, and it's fun, fabulous fun to be with you. I am looking forward to all these years ahead of us, we have so much to do together, so much to find about ourselves and the world. I look at everything now with new eyes. I feel differently and you're always with me, flame, heart, body, mind, touch, so tender, so frail, so powerful, your smile in the morning, your innocence and your wisdom.

I am crazy, I am happy, thank you you you you you.

L.B.

A postcard mailed from the Sheraton Carlton in Washington, DC: "Life with you is a feast, Candie, a melody, a delicate happening."

And this, from July 7, 1981: "You is only *you*. There is nobody else you. Love is you, life is you, fun is you, I dance my body and mind with you, I am you. So there! The world is tough without you, you know."

In late 1982 I flew out to Dubrovnik, Yugoslavia,

to vamp it up in a fright wig as the evil Morgan Le Fay in a TV miniseries, *Arthur the King*. It wasn't brilliant filmmaking, but working with Malcolm McDowell, Liam Neeson, and Rupert Everett—who turned out to be a brilliant pianist —was great fun. This was my first major separation from Louis, three weeks apart. The separation was almost worth it because Louis, who'd gone to Paris to visit Justine, wrote me an almost constant stream of love letters.

Nov 12 1982

My darling, I was just speaking to you, your first call from Dubrovnik. Each time I hear your voice, it does go from my ear to my heart and then radiates through my entire body. When your voice says my darling I feel together again, I feel myself again.

I miss you so much, but you're so much with me you know, it's not the real thing but sometimes I smell you, touch you, your body is close, your wonderful smile, your love for me, I feel all that, almost, in front of me. Telepathy, my love, telepathy!

I see you reading at this minute, reading *Salammbô* [a novel by Flaubert] in your little room on the sea.

I love you,

L

Nov 23 1982

My darling, my love, my life, it is tough, isn't it? We so much need each other, we've made our lives so much part of each other, it feels like I have been cut from half of myself. Going to bed, waking up in the middle of the night, having a slight pause in the madness of the shoot, every time the same pain, the same anguish. "Where is she? I miss her, I need her." And I see you in your little room over there, and I know you feel exactly the same.

My love, there may be a good side to it. It's a test, and it's also the proof that we can't live without each other. We knew how much we belonged to each other, but this separation—how tough it is—proves us for good that life without each other is hell. When you were shooting *Rich and Famous* and I was in Richmond, it was not quite as hard—we were in the same country, it was a much shorter time, communications were a lot easier. When I call you in Dubrovnik, it's like the end of the world—

Still, it saves my life to talk to you as often as possible, to hear your voice. And our love should be stronger than our frustration and despair. Soon we will be reunited, and it will be great, great, great. I am working as well as I can, but I have only one thing in mind, when you will come back, our first hug, how good it will be, oh God! I know it's even tougher for you, my love, because of the place, because of the waiting. I think of you, I am with you *all the time.* Our love will come out of this triumphantly.

Your monkey.

Louis signed a number of his letters "Your monkey" or "Hanuman," after the Indian monkey god. Louis always identified with Hanuman because he was so small and agile. A day later, he sent me a single piece of stationery, with "I love you my darling" written over and over across thirty-six lines.

Whenever he was in one of his melancholy spells, Louis wanted my help to chase away his demons.

You are full of grace, a saint, and I am a clumsy priest. . . . I keep thinking that we are going to get old together, pure joy replacing what was pure anguish. . . . Those mornings when I looked ahead, alone, angry, and scared, sad.

Louis and John Guare had worked together very successfully on *Atlantic City*; John had been nominated for an Oscar for Best Screenplay (he lost to *Chariots of Fire*) and Louis for Best

Director (he lost to Warren Beatty for *Reds*). Louis had planned to direct *Moon over Miami*, a political movie about Colombian drug smuggling written by John. The movie was to star John Belushi, but sadly, Belushi died on March 5, 1982, of a drug overdose and the movie never went forward. John Guare produced the stage play of *Moon over Miami* several years later.

I should be devastated by the collapse of *Moon* but I make it with a distance which stuns me, but it comes from you, you being the center of my life, you helping me so much and being the only, yes the only.

Thank you, my love. You've taught me to live, to love, to share—you've made me *almost* great (a little more to do yet!). . . . Remember last night we talked about being one. Well it's happening one + one = 2 = 1 When it happens completely, we'll be invincible.

3

The Cutest
Cactus

⁂ 5 ⁂

A girlfriend with three grown children was adamant: "Don't have a child. You're liberated. Louis is your child. You're each other's children."

Deep down it wasn't what I wanted to hear. For one thing, Louis *wasn't* my child. He was my husband, my friend, my lover. For another, I'd wanted her to urge me on. Tell me not to miss it.

Others did. And were emphatic about it. "It's now or never!" "I don't want you to leave it till it's too late because you're going to want to have a second one." "It's the best thing you'll ever do." "It gives you a sense of purpose." "I don't want you to miss this." "What a difference a baby makes." A friend of mine who ended up adopting said, "Wait until you can't. Your ambivalence will disappear."

It was 1985. I was thirty-nine and pondering getting pregnant at a time when so many women were resisting the idea because of the feminism and careerism of the time. That I would even ponder getting pregnant at that age was pure chutzpah. It was such a struggle to commit to having a child and sacrificing what I thought I might be sacrificing—a career, a life unencumbered. My mother was twenty-three when she had me. I don't think she was ready.

She had a miscarriage when I was four. I found her in a maid's room at the back of the house, resting on the bed. I remember thinking then that having babies can be fatal, obviously high-risk for women. I knew Mom had been frustrated because she'd wanted to have a career as a singer, but she felt thwarted by my father and me. She'd been performing at the St. Regis in New York City and had a chance to go on a six-week tour to New Orleans. Dad refused to let her go, saying, "What, you'd leave the baby?" even though the "baby" was ten or eleven. She didn't go. He didn't want her to have a career. Mine was well established; would having a baby mean giving it all up?

Besides, I didn't go all weak over babies. Or coo over sets of tiny clothes. I'd go to friends' baby showers and feel at a remove. Babies all looked pretty much the same to me. And they all sounded the same. Loud. I found children strangely sinister creatures. Tiny noise machines whose only purpose was to disrupt. I really had no clue how to care for a child. Not even the basics: how to pick them up, comfort them, feed them. Not for me. I wondered if I could love a baby as much as a dog, worried that perhaps I couldn't love a baby more. I was pleased when I visited a friend's newborn and he was quite cute, in fact—grunting, grimacing, not unlike a puppy, actually. Though not quite as cute.

At age thirty-three, I'd gotten the name of an

analyst. I had questions. Why was I single? Why hadn't I found anyone? Should I compromise? How would I know? The doctor was short, color-less—completely unprepossessing. He some-times wore sharkskin suits that changed from teal to ochre in the light.

He may have been small, but his brain was huge. I started seeing him three times a week when I was in New York. I would have to steel myself every time I entered his office because I knew he would hold my feet to the fire. Why did I keep blocking any enjoyment at whatever I'd managed to accomplish? Was he getting too close to the truth? After each session, my ears were ringing like a burglar alarm going off and I'd feel so light-headed that I'd have to squat against the wall while waiting for the elevator.

I sometimes wonder why it was I got to everything rather late in life— everything that truly mattered. A husband. A child. What was holding me back? Were there *so* many demons in my way? God knows I'd met almost every eligible man—and many more not so—but I never came close to marriage.

When I met Louis, it felt like the end of the quest. Finally I'd found the man I was meant to be with. Louis made me more solid, less likely to be swept away in a breeze. Louis gave me a landing, a perch; meeting him gave a depth and substance to my happiness.

85

After we were married, I went to the analyst with the wedding album photos that Mary Ellen Mark had taken. He went through them thoughtfully; then he looked up and said, "So, off you go!"

"What do you mean?" I asked him.

"What do you need me for now?"

Friends who spent years struggling through analysis never forgave me for that. It was as if I'd taken a speed course. But I didn't go to him for analysis; I went because I wanted a real relationship and now I'd gotten one. Mission accomplished.

When Louis and I sometimes talked about having children, he'd say, "Children are a gift you give yourself." But basically, I was looking for reasons not to have a child. Much of this I ascribe to hefty social changes swirling at the time, primarily the Women's Movement. It was exploding all around us, shaking everything up and inside out. It put the brakes on the traditional choices. One of the iconic images of that period was a Pop Art cartoon by Roy Lichtenstein of a woman in distress, clutching her face, exclaiming, "I CAN'T BELIEVE IT. I FORGOT TO HAVE CHILDREN!" Bingo. Women were pushing the fertility envelope, and many missed their chance. Would I be one of them? There was a sudden increase in adoptions. A friend who'd had her husband get a vasectomy now asked him to reverse it. At lunch at a trendy East Side bistro, a friend said, "You know, in Berkeley, women eat their placentas. Yep, they scramble it with eggs."

When I was about thirty-five, I'd written in my journal:

On an aptitude test for motherhood, I would be ranked low on the scale. I am more qualified to be a father.

Snow White, Rapunzel, Sleeping Beauty. Brenda Starr—at least she had a job and didn't just sit or sleep *waiting*. Waiting for her Prince to come and save her from making her own decisions, taking some control of her own life. My, how we were trained to wait.

Beauty is terrifying. Life smiles upon you. Everything comes to you—you have done nothing to deserve it. Little to discourage it. Guilt and confusion for being the favored one.

The ticking was louder every day. How was I able to shut it out? By now people were almost rude. "Where's the kid?!" "Are you guys going to wait forever?!" Maybe I was. My great friend Tessa, mother extraordinaire of five, kept saying, "Candy, they give your life meaning! You don't feel complete unless you're with them." Say what? I had no idea what Tessa was saying to me. My mother, to her credit, never asked when she might be a grandmother.

My good friend Rusty Unger wrote me:

Today is Halloween. Amanda [her daughter] told me sorrowfully that this may be her last year of trick-or-treating. I guess there's a cutoff date for being a kid among her friends, and suddenly one year it's considered childish, like believing in Santa Claus. . . . I'm sad, too, about Amanda growing out of it—oh the peer pressure to grow up—and also that she lost her last baby tooth in August. The Tooth Fairy is dead. Boo hoo. Listen, I, personally, hope you have a baby, and if you don't like it and change your mind, I could make a deal with you. I will take the baby if you support it. You could visit any time you chose. Think about it.

At thirty-eight, I went back to the analyst. "What are you back here for?" he wanted to know. "I'm resisting having a baby," I told him. We began again. We had several intense sessions. I'd leave the office and sit on the planter outside, waiting for my head to clear.

At thirty-nine, I stopped using birth control. I don't think I even told Louis what I'd done; I had such ambivalence. Besides, what were the odds of getting pregnant at thirty-nine?

I got pregnant very soon after. Louis and I were visiting Cuote in Munich and I began to feel slightly nauseated. I was mostly silent in the hour and a half that we drove from Munich to Salzburg. I told him there that I was pregnant. He looked like I had hit him with a mallet. It would take him a moment to adjust. He had, after all, been blindsided. I had a chilling thought. Once he'd had his other two children, his relationship with their mothers ended. Would that happen to me?

Back in New York, the doctor confirmed my suspicion with a blood test. Then he rolled his cycs. "Wait until you have an adolescent and you're going through menopause. If you can survive that, you can survive anything. You're having hot flashes and you're at your most vulnerable and all they can think about is themselves. It's a nightmare." Then he excused himself to take a call from his teenage daughter.

I hoped I'd have a boy. I'm not sure why; maybe because my mother and I had had such a fraught relationship, I figured a girl would come back to punish me for it.

From the moment the doctor confirmed it, I was in a state of anxiety. I got the postpartum depression over with early by having it prepartum. Anxiety suffocated me like an old wet blanket; I was finding it difficult to bond with this upstart in my womb. I looked at it like an alien invader, an internal trooper come to wreak terror on my life as I knew it. My life with Louis.

At dinners, friends swapped adolescent horror stories. Kids committed to mental hospitals. Drug rehab centers. Women reminisced about finally reclaiming their houses and tranquility. "It was a time of great liberation. The children were gone. I didn't have a housekeeper. It was one of the best times of my life; I had the house all to myself."

"Elderly primigravida." Translation: pregnant geezer, knocked up for the first time. I was now an urban statistic. That was my official medical diagnosis, and one that flourished in the 1980s.

I went to Doubleday Books, looking for books on pregnancy. There were none to be found. There was every conceivable book on feminism, the differences between men and women, AIDS, sisterhood, brotherhood—but none on babyhood. In Manhattan in 1985, apparently, it was an obsolete issue.

In my second month, I went shopping and, curiously, bought a pair of pants that would be too small before I'd paid for them. A case of denial?

Calder prints decorated the white walls of the small Upper East Side office of my New York obstetrician-gynecologist. Vivaldi's *Four Seasons* played softly. An anxious woman approached the nurse at the desk. "I'm forty and I don't have a child yet. I also don't have a boyfriend. I thought of just having one anyway, but I don't think I'm up to being a single parent." The nurse smiled reassuringly. "We have a lot of late-in-life births. Most of the women love it and can't wait to have another."

Since I was working a lot in LA that year, I needed a West Coast doctor as well. The Beverly Hills ob-gyn's office was a stark contrast to the one in New York. The waiting room was as big as a city block. A fleet of nurses bustled back and forth. Urgent messages crackled in the air: "Mrs. Poitier's housekeeper needs an appointment." Muzak blared "The Spanish Flea." My nurse frowned as I stepped on the scale. I'd put on eight pounds in three weeks. "The first trimester, you're not eating for two, you're eating nutritionally for one. This is excessive weight gain," she warned me. I tried to look penitent.

I was led into a darkened room, cool gel spread on my growing belly. The first sonogram. The fetus of course looked like a prawn. It seemed like the heartbeat was sending out little pulses of light. It beat quickly, like a hummingbird. My chest tightened and my eyes filmed over. I was surprised at my relative calm. They gave me a Polaroid in a card: Baby's First Picture.

Next I was seated in an office as a nurse popped in a videotape for me to watch: "Your Pregnancy." It opened with a sleek black Porsche pulling up to Cedars-Sinai hospital. A gorgeous couple gets out, the woman slim and blond and tan and perfect, a tiny bulge under her Laura Ashley. The man, brown-haired, tall and trim, muscular and athletic in his Lacoste shirt and khakis. They glide inside, obviously very much in love. We cut to a doctor, one from the practice, who introduces the four partners. They speak in turn into the camera surely, slowly, clearly. They have been well coached. They tell you about what you will experience and how to eat and no recreational drugs. We see the couple over the nine months as her stomach swells becomingly, but not her feet or face. It is like a Disney nature film. We see her with her feet up on an ottoman, her husband massaging them. He brings her a Perrier. I have no recollection of the actual birth, but I assume it too was wreathed in a glowing halo.

I went straight from the checkup to the market. I blamed the doctors' early warnings: "Nausea is sometimes the sign of a healthy pregnancy. Keep your stomach full. Carry hard candies and crackers." This advice was a fatal mistake to someone like me. I packed my pockets with every conceivable candy, including twelve rolls of Life Savers. Each time I left the house it was like going on a pack trip. All I thought of was food and reasons to eat it. A few months along, I was presenting at the Oscars when I ran into Farrah Fawcett backstage—around seven months pregnant herself and glowing. I was wearing a Versace chain-mail bronze dress that highlighted my stomach. She looked me up and down. "Candy, you should try the tummy control panty hose." I was so past that.

"Elderly primigravida" meant amniocentesis.

My friend Connie Freiberg went with me for the procedure, armed with chocolate-covered marshmallows. Connie, whom I met in the eighth grade at Westlake School for Girls in Los Angeles, is my oldest friend, to the point of being family. In the waiting room, we joined a kind of instant sorority of older mothers-to-be. All anxious. The husbands sitting there sheepishly seemed to fade from view. One woman said, "My ears are burning, I'm so nervous." Another woman's eyes filled up with tears. One expectant mother walked out of the office and our heads lifted collectively. "Piece of cake," she declared. The next one to go in for the test was wiping her forehead and shaking. She'd been through this before. "I know what to expect this time. I'll never forget the feeling of the puncture. It was like a needle puncturing a stiff rubber raft. That's why I brought my husband this time around."

"We don't need to hear this," I said; I was terrified. There was going to be something wrong, I was convinced. Once again, I was worried I couldn't love a baby as much as a dog.

A stern and officious nurse led me in for a pre-interview. She asked me a number of questions designed, I guess, to avoid malpractice suits while informing me what the test would determine and warning me what it would not. What I was worried about, of course, was Down syndrome, but through her encouragement, I now worried about deafness, diabetes, blindness, dwarfism, scoliosis, and mental retardation. When it came time for the actual procedure, I was a crying wreck. Connie held my cold, clammy hand. We watched the doctor locate the fetus on the screen. It was jumping jerkily: hiccups. The doctor pressed on my stomach and the fetus scooted out of the way. As the needle was inserted, it registered as a tiny dot of light on the screen. The fetus was well out of range. It felt exactly like a needle puncturing a stiff rubber raft. Eerie, stressful, but not painful. I watched the amniotic fluid fill the syringe. It was clear, no blood, and looked like chicken broth. Just having the test over, I felt almost buoyant—incredibly relieved.

I had a dream that night: The amniocentesis showed a seven-pound boy. Wow, he was big for four months! But I was thrilled. The next night, another dream: The baby was just born. It seemed to be a boy. Very wet and tiny. I lay down, my face inches from his. "Hi," I whispered. "Hi," he whispered back. I was ecstatic and amazed.

I was sure it would be a boy, which would be a

relief. I knew that the mother-daughter dynamic was incredibly charged; a boy would be easier to raise. I began working on boys' names. Lucas? Diego? Quincy? Casper?

I didn't want anyone to know until I knew the results of my amnio. I was suddenly incredibly superstitious. I told only two close friends, my mom, and my brother that I was pregnant. My mother looked stunned and her eyes filled with tears. She'd given up having a grandchild by me and was waiting for one by my brother. She'd endured decades of that tedious question, "When are you going to be a grandmother?"

I had dinner with an old friend, one I'd often discussed children with. I had talked about my ambivalence about motherhood. During a lull in the conversation he asked, almost rhetorically, "Are you going to have a baby?"

"I *am* going to have a baby."

He started to weep.

I found out the sex of the commando as I was scrambling eggs, as it were, in the kitchen in our apartment in New York City. The doctor's office called and said the test results had come back; would I like to know the sex of my baby? It was an impromptu moment, to say the least. I was alone over the stove. Louis and I were not seated together in the doctor's office, facing him behind his desk. There was no drum roll. But what was the point of waiting for an artificially orchestrated ritual?

On my wacky maternal grandmother's side, there were two sets of twins, so the odds of my having them were high. I wanted twins. There was none of today's high-tech in vitro stuff, so twins were uncommon then. But while I looked like I was having twins, it was a single occupancy. The nurse told me, "You've having a healthy girl."

Obviously, since this was going to be my first child at the advanced age of thirty-nine, I gave a great deal of thought to the sacred rite of naming. The first one that came to mind was Chloe. Hard as it may be to imagine, Chloe was an unusual name in 1985. There was Chloe perfume and I knew of two or three young girls with that name, but, by and large, it was not much used. I thought it was lovely, feminine, and unpretentious—and it made the transition into French quite neatly. Still, I asked opinions, and even when I didn't, they were offered. "What about Victoria?" asked my oldest friend Tessa, who was English. Nope. Samantha, said Ann. "She could be Sam." No.

I asked the father-to-be. After a long pause, he said, "Cynthia?" Seriously? Cynthia? Really? That's the best you can come up with? I turned to my stepdaughter, Justine, who wasn't too thrilled about this whole thing anyway, and asked, "How 'bout you?"

"Henrietta?"

What was this, a conspiracy?

Clearly, I was on my own. Eloise was my second choice; I loved Clementine too. India? Isabelle? Perhaps I'd call her Annie, with "Animal" as a nickname. Or Minnie, with "Minimal." Chloe had found a nook in my brain and I stuck with that one. Just Chloe. No umlaut. No accent. Just neat.

Chloe's boyfriend, Graham, recently looked up the usage of the name "Chloe" in 1985. That year it languished near the bottom of the list. Toward the end of the year and into the next, however, it spiked to near the top. It was suddenly the name du jour. Chloe had caught fire. There were announcements when we had Chloe and that may have contributed to it a little bit. The other night, we were having dinner and Chloe said, "I wish I had a name that wasn't so popular." "Well, you *did!*" I said. "It was an unusual name when we gave it to you." Not so much now. Watching *Ray Donovan* this year, I noted a nubile teenage hooker named Chloe, which seemed to indicate that the exclusivity of the name had waned. And Chloe said that when she gave her name at Starbucks, it was usually spelled on the cup with a K. Thank you, Kardashians.

So in the end, it was Chloe. I'd recently bought an Arabian filly. I decided to name her Chloe as a placeholder, as if to tell the whole world,

"That's my daughter's name; I have a filly to prove it." An ugly filly, as it turned out, with warts on her muzzle, but still. No one else could take it. The name was mine.

Louis asked if her middle name could be Françoise after his mother. As my mother's name was Frances and she was very much alive, that worked perfectly. Chloe Françoise Malle.

It was the last day of shooting for a TV movie of the week when the *New York Post* ran an item: "Great Expectations: New Addition in the Fall," making the announcement for me. The cat was out of the bag.

In some ways it was a relief. I couldn't stop eating. I craved ice cream in particular, which was unfortunate. Yet there was no panic when I got on the scale. I was under a spell.

I recorded a typical diet from the movie set where I was working:

5:30 a.m.: a whole papaya
6:30 a.m.: huevos rancheros
7:30 a.m.: chocolate donut
9:30 a.m.: three taquitos with guacamole
11:00 a.m.: chicken noodle soup
1:00 p.m.: tuna salad, chicken, rice pudding,
* ice-cream sandwich, Jell-O, chocolate milk*
4:00 p.m.: hot chocolate
6:00 p.m.: bowl of chili
8:00 p.m.: chow mein and fried rice

At the three-month checkup, the doctor warned me, "You've put on your entire weight gain in your first trimester." At five and a half months, I was already up fifty-four pounds. With each weigh-in, the nurses warned: "Excessive weight gain." "I know, I know." People started to pat my stomach. The doctor. The dry cleaner. Strangers. I was being treated like a sacred vessel carrying precious cargo.

It was difficult to put on my shoes; I finished red in the face. The extra weight pulled me down, cut all my energy and stamina. I wheezed and panted. Yoga was hopeless. Bike riding up a hill was impossible. Still, I was fascinated by what was happening, by the phenomenon that had invaded and occupied my body.

And apprehensive. Such ambivalence. How complicated the future seemed. I was constantly confronting my limitations. Impatience. Intolerance. How could I be a mom? How to work it out? Would I be okay? And Louis and I. Would *we* be okay? Louis had emerged from his earlier ambivalence and was now embracing the idea of our child together, whom he'd nicknamed "Mortimer Snerd" after the hayseed dummy who was Charlie McCarthy's sidekick in my father's ventriloquist act. And the baby? Who has chosen to be our baby? What would she teach me?

I stopped calling my mother "Frances" suddenly, finding it fresh and disrespectful. If my daughter called me "Candice," I would hate it.

In LA, I began attending prenatal exercise classes at Jane Fonda's Workout Studio. We stretched and bent to a disco version of the triumphal march in *Aida* and a disco *Nutcracker Suite*. "You know," the instructor told us, "I didn't know till the other day that this was classical music." She had us lie down on our mats. "Relax your mind. Relax the insides of your body. Relax your baby," she advised. I started crying. All this feeling rising up and tears spilling down my cheeks. Was it fear? Was it feeling? Was it the approaching reality of the experience? The experience I'd awaited, avoided, for so long? Childhood's end: enter Motherhood.

My dinners with women friends stoked my ambivalence: "I put on thirty pounds the first three months—more than my entire allotted weight," one said. My heart leapt. "I love my son, but motherhood isn't all it's cracked up to be," she added. My heart sank.

"But if you don't, you'll be like all our friends without children—always worrying about what resort to go to," said another.

"I never worried about resorts until I *had* children," a third retorted. "Now it's all I do."

"It's the best," a fourth declared, persuasively.

Yet another woman showed off her very small child's very grand résumé. "Don't you want one like this?" Oh God. "I had an orgasm giving birth," declared another. Enough.

Mom gave me a baby shower at Le Restaurant, a chic French bistro in West Hollywood. There were about twenty-five women there, all Mom's age. "I haven't been to a shower in forty years!" one told me. They were adorable and they brought fantastic gifts. Chic baby outfits from Nieman's, including a sailor hat and striped maillot T-shirt. An Asprey's engraved silver frame. An Edwardian pearl-handled rattle. Mom had them serve pink Champagne. I wore a white silk tent dress, which I filled out nicely. Everyone chattered about my pregnancy, which at that time was considered a medical miracle. At thirty-nine! My brother capped it off by arriving with a four-foot-tall stuffed white bear, so huge that all I could see was his feet sticking out from underneath. It was a lovely celebration of the invader.

Louis's latest film, *Alamo Bay*, was released. It depicted a bloody clash between Texas fishermen and the immigrant Vietnamese who fished and shrimped beside them. Vincent Canby of the *New York Times* released a devastating review, calling the movie "almost shamefully clumsy and superficial," and "manufactured 'art.' " "Watching it is an unhappy experience that never becomes illuminating," he wrote.

Louis was absolutely devastated by what felt like an especially personal attack. He'd had two or three major periods of depression before, demons and darkness that he battled. The Canby panning sent him into a spiral. His black mood blanketed the apartment. It was hard for him to come out from under it, so he fled to a spa in France to recover.

There is a necessary selfishness for an artist, yet Louis could have astonishing bursts of generosity. The fact that he took himself off to France to recover on his own while I was pregnant was an act of self-reliance—brave in its way. We'd talk on the phone a couple times a day, send faxes.

He tried to immerse himself in new projects, including one with his dear friend, playwright John Guare, to little avail. He announced, "Okay, I'm going to make movies in France. They have no interest in my work here anymore." He wrote me from Le Coual:

The same austere and melancholic house from where I wrote you, a little more than 5 years ago, that first Easter. I wanted to tell you how happy you'd made me, how much I thought of you in the solitude of Le Coual, how I knew our love was the first love, the only love.

I would repeat the same letter, Candy, the same words. And yet lots have happened in those 5 years. It was Easter then, the end of winter. Spring was to come, a very late spring in my life, but what hopes, enthusiasm, certitude something was happening that had not happened before, ever, ever.

Through these 5 years, we had more splendid springs, long hot summers, hard winters. It was a beautiful voyage, my love, as much as work, yours, mine, hasn't been in the middle. It seems to be work's fate, and revenge of sorts, to try to bring down a relationship as exhilarating as ours.

What I am trying to tell you? I love you, more, I need you, more, want to be with you, more. This child, our child, you're bearing, delivering the promise, our love made flesh, I want to think of nothing else, and you, with you. But you're in L.A. Telephone is hard, as usual, because it's abstract, it lacks the feeling, the looking, the touching and I just spent 2 weeks pretending my professional life was going on the same, with John at his best and his worst and discussing a project I can't even get interested in. There is something dead in me, something has been hurt deep, and I can't even reach it dig it out and try to get rid of it. Hopes I had—still naïve, after all these years—have been shattered for good. Yet I am not weak enough to claim injustice. What I need is silence, first a moment of pure silence, and then to be with you, and the kids this summer, and wait for Mortimer. Or else move on, find something to do, anything, move on, be frustrated and possibly enjoy it (the worst of me). Here I am now, mentally prostrated, angry at myself, weak, tempted absurdly by drastic changes. Physically, the body hurts too, it's in bad shape too.

What am I trying to say? Let's get together my love, not for 3 days or a week-end, between planes, but for time, experience quiet, isolation, silence, together. And talk, about things, about the future. And let's love each other, let me enjoy what I miss so much when I am away from you, this unique combination of heart and intelligence, of strength and vulnerability, you. And I'll be cured and I'll be rid of the boring past, recent failures, old frustrations, and we can laugh again, try to organize the future, with time and a distance, the distance love gives to everything. I love you, miss you, need you. Let's have this moment of retreat together, just us together.

L.

With Louis away in Paris, I attended most of my Lamaze classes alone, the only single mother among five other couples. A male doctor taught them. "The purpose of these classes is to have as natural a birth as possible," he told us. I wasn't sure this was a great idea; every story I'd heard from a woman who'd had natural childbirth made it sound like a nightmare.

Louis came back in time for the last class, entering the room just as the instructor was inserting a baby doll into a foam rubber pelvis. He blanched. At one of the classes they showed us a movie of an episiotomy in close-up. That was it. I was going to do drugs, no question—no natural child-birth, in spite of Lamaze. I quietly encouraged the other mothers to go for epidurals too.

I took the hospital tour with a group of Upper East Side couples and me, the lone representative of the no man's land of Central Park South. The maternity ward was painted battleship gray. Really? Must we give birth in rooms that resembled a mental hospital? "Is it possible we could have it painted before our due dates?" someone asked. A butter yellow perhaps? They would be happy to pay. Peach? Something neutral, non-gender-specific. It was New York, after all. The women were, however, thwarted in their mission. The staff smiled patronizingly. We passed a sign: "No placenta to be thrown in garbage ever." Was this a common faux pas?

By September, one of the hottest Septembers on record, I'd hit 175 pounds. My brother, Kris, said, "You're twenty-five pounds away from two hundred. I say go for it!" I took a stroll through Central Park. A horse-drawn carriage driver pointed me out to tourists sitting in the back: "That used to be Candice Bergen."

I became fixated on the end of something. The end of my life as a person with no responsibilities. The end of complete mobility. As one who prided herself on traveling light, I thought, this is the last time I'll be flying anywhere with only a carry-on. Every small act seemed a premature mourning: This is the last time I'll be spending Sunday morning in bed with the *New York Times*. As the books predicted, it was an emotional roller coaster. I was edgy. Sleepier than I had ever been in my life. Narcoleptic, lethargic, given to flights of fancy and hallucinations. When I was in my fifth month, my mother, unable to restrain herself any longer, had given me a pair of tiny pink feetie pajamas. I'd hung them over the back of a chair and the feet protruded, lifelike, as if there was someone in them. I stared at them from the bed, where I spent most of my time now. It was getting realer.

I got sick. A bad sore throat. Infected ears. Awake at night, breathing badly. It was my first time sick since the pregnancy. How could I take antibiotics? What if I had pneumonia? The medicine might harm the baby, but without it, could I die? What about the baby? I stared at the pajamas on the chair at the foot of the bed, the tiny lifelike feet. Oh God. What if those feet were never filled? Oh God, the baby.

At the ear, nose, and throat doctor's office the next morning, he medicated conservatively, checking with the ob-gyn. He was unusually conciliatory and concerned. "I'm not just thinking of you," he said. "I'm thinking of the baby."

Me too. Me too.

A month before my due date I woke at six o'clock in the morning to a long, low, rumbling noise followed by the windows rattling. I knew it couldn't be an earthquake—that was one of the few reassuring things about life in New York City. Nuclear testing in Connecticut? What seemed most likely was that it was a huge spaceship; it sounded like the ones in *Close Encounters*. In my sleepy state, I reasoned that the spaceship was cruising over Central Park for the express purpose of kidnapping my unborn baby. I must protect my baby. Louis stirred beside me.

"Did you hear that?" I asked.

He had; I was relieved not to have imagined it. "What was it?" he asked.

"I think it was a spaceship," I told him. Louis looked at me and just rolled over and went back to sleep. Later in the morning, the news reported it was an earthquake—3.8 on the Richter scale. My baby was safe.

And she stayed safe, despite being weeks overdue, three epidurals, and a cesarean section. Now the drama of the birth was behind me and a healthy Chloe was in my arms. The ambivalence about motherhood, the premature mourning of losing my old life, were swept away in the moment I looked into her fierce blue eyes.

She and I stayed in the hospital for three days. Until Chloe's birth, my purest moments of bliss had been Louis and my wedding day in France, which was a level of complete happiness, fullness, and contentment I'd never known. The days following Chloe's birth were a hundred times that.

Nurses walked me through nursing her. Put her on my breast. The hospital arranged for a candlelit "Stork Dinner." Louis and I beamed at each other across a linen tablecloth spread with a sad steak and a withered baked potato. So sweet. I snuck in a Rigaud scented green candle and kept it burning in the room. When my mom and an old family friend arrived two days after the birth, Louis met them for dinner at Petrossian, sliding giddily into the mink-trimmed banquette. They all toasted with Champagne, over the moon.

My hospital room was a perfect sanctuary. I held Chloe in my arms and gazed outside the window. The park was wet and the trees bare. I was in thrall to my daughter, who owned me from the first second.

My idyll was interrupted only once. I was nursing the baby when a big burly bearded guy with a shirt unbuttoned to the navel and gold chains nesting in his chest hair suddenly strode into the room. He was apparently a fan who'd heard I was in the hospital and decided to pay a welcome call. The moment I looked up, he turned and walked back out.

Herbert Allen, a lifelong friend, came to the hospital and brought me a cassette player and a tape of Spike Jones singing "Chloe (Song of the Swamp)." I pressed the Play button. The song was classic Jones, all shrill claxons and bells and clashes and clatters. "Through the black of night / I've got to go where you are." "Chlooooooo—eee . . . I've got to go where you are." It was everything I felt.

❧ 6 ❧

"Come in, please, we're just getting started." The hostess for the day's event was whippet-thin and wore a chartreuse minidress; enormous earrings dangled from her lobes. I scanned her midsection; no trace of her baby weight remained. The other guests—all anxious, responsible parents in their late thirties—were likewise dressed in hyperchic attire. I was dressed entirely Ralph: a navy open-necked gabardine shirt, skinny croc belt, pleated khaki slacks, and moccasins. I'd managed to drop the sixty pounds I'd gained with Chloe. The Tribeca loft was high-end, hip, done up in black-and-white 1950s furniture with leopard skin prints. Keith Jarrett wafted through the stereo. The intercom buzzed and our hostess let in two more people, lugging four huge duffel bags. The baby CPR course was about to begin.

It was five couples, all parents of newborns, and me, a singleton: a by-now familiar arrangement. Louis was in Paris. An assistant with the shades and mustache of a dealer from *Miami Vice* unzipped the duffels and handed us each our own rubber baby doll. "Now we're going to learn infant CPR," our instructor told us. All of us intently lined up our baby dolls on the dining room table as instructed and began administering mouth-to-mouth breathing. It was hard not to pass out from anxiety.

I scribbled notes on how to deal with the direst of medical emergencies:

"If not breathing, open airway."

"Call 911. Say, 'My baby's not breathing'—it's their first priority."

"Often child vomits, turn to side, scoop out vomit, continue rescue breathing."

"If stomach rises with breathing, you're breathing too hard. If just stomach rises, you may have forgotten to clear the airway." Surely the medics would have arrived before I had to determine whether I was overinflating my child or failing to diagnose a blocked trachea?

"Dangerous objects: pencils, scissors, forks." I wrote it all down as though it would never occur to me not to give three-month-old Chloe a pair of gleaming shears.

Drowning. Choking. My notes grew to fourteen pages. Poisons. Burns. Fires. "Fire in house. Get out. Baby's lungs are small; danger of smoke." "Watch out for glass doors." Heimlich maneuvers. Use two fingers for compression under rib cage. Head injuries. "Bruising behind ears and under eyes: problem."

Danger lurked everywhere: "Watch for glass tables." "Watch hot-water setting." "Lids on chests." The most benign objects were hidden death traps: "Check pacifiers." "NO: Ribbons on toys. Toy telephones. Ties on clothing. Phone cords. Drape cords. *No cords.* No plastic bags anywhere. No rubber balloons. WATCH OUT FOR BUTTONS."

The infant CPR was by far the most terrifying prospect. "Check carotid artery for pulse." "Drag under arms to phone to call for help." "Sternum must give way—1½ inches. You will do damage to ribs." Could they possibly expect parents paralyzed with fear to do any of this?

My handwriting trembled: "Bleeding: Direct pressure. If bandage soaked with blood, leave and put more on top."

It was clear: I could and would plug every socket, cover the glass table with a kilim rug, wrap every table leg with foam and tape. If Chloe made it to her first birthday, it would be a miracle.

With her blue-white skin and black, greasy hair, Chloe looked like a baby from a far-distant continent. People would say, "Oh. She looks Tibetan!" or "Oh, an Inuit baby!" Nora Ephron sent our first of six copies of *Goodnight Moon* with a lovely note: "For Chloe: Welcome. Here are our favorite records and favorite book. We hope you all like them. With love from Nora and Jacob and Max." Lorne Michaels sent over a Moses basket with a note that said, "This is Chloe's first E Ride. Hope she enjoys it." Teri Garr gave her a black tuxedo onesie, which made her look like an elderly waiter with a bad toupee. A bouquet of baby's breath came with a note: "Dearest Chloe, Happy Birthday every day!" from Dick Avedon. Mike Nichols sent over a sterling silver Tiffany cup and a note:

Dear Chloe:

This is for you to drink out of as soon as you get off the bottle. Bang it on the table as much as you want because you might as well get used to being privileged early.

Your godfather, who loves you,
Mike.

I still have the note that Carrie Fisher, whose birthday was Chloe's original due date, sent along with her gift:

Mama Malle,

At first I was very hurt that Chloe Françoise decided that my birthday [October 21] wasn't good enough for her. But after spending several days sobbing in an isolation tank listening to Brenda Lee albums, I emerged refreshed and resigned. I now see that Chloe had to have her own birthday and that finally it has less to do with me than I originally thought. I have found this to be the case many times during my life, so it was a break-through of a more or less mundane variety. But enough about me (. . .) and back to Chloe.

First, there was the perfume, then the clothing line and now at long (unbelievably long) last, the child. I see her eclipsing not only the fragrance and most of the clothes, but anything she casts her shadow on—as soon as she's big enough to have her own shadow —or start her own clothing line or throw off a marketable scent.

From the man that brought us *Murmur of the Heart* and the woman that brought us *The Group*—their combined efforts now bring us a kind of "Murmur of the Group"—Miss Chloe Françoise Malle. Child of the eighties, adolescent of the nineties, turn-of-the-century woman.

This has been a maternal message from Miss Pishy at the nonnuclear star wars message center.

Little,
Carrie

We had our first Christmas in New York City when Chloe was seven weeks old, dressed in her red velour Christmas onesie by our twinkling tree in the cozy back of our apartment. Louis and I would spend days burrowed inside our cocoon, boiling milk bottles, sterilizing nipples, and eating Chinese from Shun Lee while snow fell outside.

Louis, of course, had much more experience with babies than I did. He was the relaxed one; I was the hypervigilant mother. I would hear an ambulance forty blocks away and run downstairs, sure it was Chloe, her cry sounded so much like a siren. Louis retreated to his office downstairs in our building. One afternoon, soon after getting home from the hospital, I called him, crying. Still recovering from my cesarean, I had to be careful with the stairs. "Could you please bring me a cup of tea?" "Oh my darling, I thought your mother would do that," he said. "But she's gone out to lunch!" I wailed.

A friend told me, "May your daughter bring you all the joy you brought your mother." Was that a blessing or a curse?

When I'd visited Jane Goodall in Tanzania in 1975, she and I observed chimpanzees for more than ten days. The mother is the fixed parent; the father quickly takes off. The child is dependent on and bonded with the mother, from whom it learns all of life's fundamental lessons. My lesson was clear: Louis might come and go, but I was never going to leave my child for more than a week. I would try to be present, because my parents had traveled often. When they'd come back after weeks away, I wouldn't recognize them and would burst into tears. This was not going to happen here.

While I would have a nanny or a housekeeper, I was adamant that I'd be Chloe's primary caretaker. Until I was ten or eleven, I'd had a wonderful Dutch nanny, Dena, with whom I was very close. Dee and I slept in the same room after saying our prayers. We'd drift off while listening to *The Shadow* and *The Lone Ranger* on the radio. I could tell her anything, go to her if I was sad or frightened. She was the maternal presence in my life; my very young mother was more of an older sister. But I was Chloe's mother; her main maternal influence would be me.

I vowed I wasn't going to overreact to petty, superficial things, such as spilling or breakage. I was going to be more like those mothers in Spielberg movies, exhibiting infinite patience and good humor while my beloved little ones fled the house with a tiny alien or sculpted their mashed potatoes into Devil's Tower.

Most important, I was going to make sure my child knew and heard that I loved her "relentlessly," because while my parents loved me, they never told me so. That was common for families of that generation. I was of the generation where parents of a certain means basically didn't verbalize affection or demonstrate it. We were not huggers. My father, being Swedish, was even less demonstrative. For me, the elephant in the room was being unable to say "I love you" because I'd never heard it. These were three loaded words for me. I was never able to tell my parents that I loved them until quite late in their lives because I'd never heard that from them. I wasn't able to comfortably tell my mother that I loved her until I reached my thirties. I would put it in letters, but saying it face-to-face was overwhelming. Pure terror. I wouldn't repeat that pattern with my own daughter.

Chloe would be my first priority by miles.

It seemed that Chloe was determined to foil my plans from the start. She was always prickly, a very cute cactus. If I was nursing her and our housekeeper came in and started talking, Chloe would stop, turn her head, and glower until she left. People were floored. From her first moments, she was so particular and so present—hyper-present. The baby nurse would have to take days off because she was so exhausted by The Baby Who Never Slept. She eventually quit. The slightest sound, barely audible to the human ear, would startle Chloe. She tyrannized the household because you had to maintain absolute silence. She would fall asleep in the carriage as I pushed her around Central Park, but the second the wheels stopped turning, she'd wake up and start screaming. She'd have a meltdown every evening, which made putting her to bed a nightmare; she would not let up. The only way to get her to sleep was to hold her in your arms. The second you got up to pee, alarms sounded. She had colic, which kept her crying for hours on cnd. It was exhausting. Louis and I would look at each other cross-eyed.

Getting Chloe dressed was another nightmare. Because she was born in the dead of winter, we had to bundle her up until just her nose would show to get some fresh air. Everyone braced themselves for the wardrobing of The Cactus. Visitors would spend a few minutes with her and exclaim, "Whoa, she's a mittful."

Louis declared me *une mère excessive.* He wrote in his journal, "Candice . . . absolute mother, excessive mother, admirable mother." I don't think I slept that first year. (Actually, I don't think I slept for five years.) He told reporters, "I'm just one poor man living with two strong-willed women—my wife and daughter."

The adrenaline jolt you get from the second you give birth makes caffeine look petty. We discovered that Chloe had kidney reflux, so periodically she had to have a procedure where they ran dye through her kidney to see if the condition had corrected itself. The first time they gave me a sedative to give to her. (The smarter thing would have been to give one to me.) She passed out cold. We quickly took her in a taxi to the hospital, where the second they laid her on the operating table, she woke up and started crying hysterically. In my efforts to comfort her, I violated the sterile field. The doctors weren't so patient with me when we had to repeat the procedure in Paris the following year. "We like to take the babies away from the parents," a nurse informed me coolly in French as I sobbed. Louis said, "Darling, you're overreacting," but he was crying too.

Chloe would routinely wake up at 5:30 a.m. If we traveled to LA, it was even worse; there with the time change she'd wake at 2:30 a.m. and we'd have to start our day. There were moments I was ready to give up.

The truth was that Chloe was not a bonder. You'd reach into her crib to comfort her as she cried, but she'd push you away. She wasn't an affectionate baby. She was more than aloof, which was hard because I was so in love with her. She'd cry, but push me away if I came in to comfort her. It was as if she was trying to say, "Get off my case. I don't want any help. I can do it myself." I took to singing Jerome Kern's "A Fine Romance" to her, the baby who "won't nestle."

One of my friends with two daughters said, "Always give her as much time as you can to talk with her and to just have conversations with her." I imagined the day I was going to have this dialogue with her: "Chloe, we all have work to do in life. Yours is to work on patience. To learn to control your temper, to find flexibility, to always balance your ferocity with love." In the meantime, however, I began a plan to gentle the animal. I'd dance with her to Sade's "The Sweetest Taboo" while looking out at the park. We'd listen to it over and over. I'd glide and swoop with her under the white sparkly lights hung on my ficus until she quieted. Every night when I put her to bed, I'd sing her a simple song I made up: "I love you, Chloe, I love your eyes, I love your nose, I love your fingers, I love your toes . . ." Over and over, for half an hour. She'd go into a trance. It was my attempt to civilize her.

As she got a little older, she would touch the parts of her body as I sang them. "I love your earlobes and your elbows." Older still, she would ask me to sing the I Yuv You song. The lyrics got more abstract: "I love your heart. I love your spirit." She would lie perfectly still, listening and gently stroking her pillow.

The first year I was mostly content to be in the cocoon with Chloe, our friend Beryl, who became our housekeeper, and our Welsh nanny, Ingrid, whom I had met when she was working for Mick Jagger and Jerry Hall, and who quickly became part of our family. We burrowed into the study of our apartment, where I could spend hours holding Chloe and looking out over the park.

Chloe was a potent, tiny spirit who had clearly been fighting to get here; I was purely transportation for her. For me, that first year was extremely emotional, as if thirty-nine years of suppressed feelings were suddenly spilling out of me. After having been terrified of it for so long, I never felt for a second that I didn't want to have the responsibility after she was born, even in her difficult first year.

Louis took Justine to Kenya for ten days; he had wanted me to join them, but I didn't want to leave Chloe. He sent her back a postcard:

Big hugs to the little *crétine*.
    Dear *petite crétine*, We're going to miss you and your mommy. I wish you could pat those elephants with us. Lots of love, Papi, Big Big Kisses

With Louis gone, it was just the old-fashioned comfort of women quilting around the fire, taking care of the baby. A sewing circle, particularly cozy in the wintertime. A circle Louis felt left out of.

"I feel as if you don't notice me if I'm in the house now," Louis told me after returning from a trip. He'd felt such tenderness from me before; now I paid him scant attention.

There was something a little combative between Louis and Chloe. A father-daughter mano a mano; she was too much like him. Watching Chloe's frequent meltdowns, I asked Louis's sister Catherine, "Did Louis have this kind of anger?" "*Oui, il avait des colères, des grande colères.*" "Oh yes, he had a huge temper." He was very loving with her—he declared her "*toujours cute*"—but the competitiveness leaked out in small slights. He would call her "dumbbell." "Hey, dumbbell, come here." "*Crétine.*" A flash of memory; hadn't my own beloved father called me "Monstro," after the devouring whale in *Pinocchio*?

"Let's take a trip," Louis pleaded. "Let's go somewhere for three weeks. Let's go to Brazil, just the two of us, up the Amazon." He wanted to try to recapture what we'd had. I just looked at him. Leave my baby for three weeks? Was he insane? I asked my mother. She said, "Well, we left you for six weeks and didn't think a thing about it."

Louis finally convinced me to go away for my fortieth birthday. He wanted to take me to

Washington, DC, to celebrate together, away from Chloe for the first time since her birth six months earlier. For two days before we left, I burst into tears at odd moments. An allegedly sympathetic friend consoled me: "It must be hard even to leave a passive little thing for the first time." I was indignant. Passive! There was *nothing* passive about this baby. As Louis and I walked down the train platform, I was sobbing. I continued to sob the whole trip down to DC. I was irrationally enraged at Louis for separating me from Chloe. I had become a lunatic.

Once we got to DC, however, I regained my sanity and we had a lovely weekend, just the two of us. It was good to reclaim each other, to rediscover the intimacy.

When Chloe was seven months old, Louis and I decided to take her on a carousel ride in Central Park. I carefully selected the horse with the same intensity as I had when I was eight, choosing my own first mount. I wanted her to have the perfect horse—ears forward, not back; a neck arched and graceful, not thin and straining; and a magnificent mane and tail in a color to catch her eye. Aha! A white horse with a gold mane and tail. Perfect. I got on. Louis put her in front of me and mounted a horse behind us. The Central Park carousel is fairly sinister, walled in 1930s institutional brick more appropriate for a house of detention, with ghoulish clowns suspended from pilasters. Yet the music was Urban Cheery: "Raindrops Keep Falling On My Head," "Downtown." We were off in a soft rolling movement, up and down, while tears streamed down my face. I couldn't believe it. Here I was on the merry-go-round I loved so much as a child, holding my own seven-month-old baby, who sat silently alert, like an animal in the forest, studying the new sights, sounds, motion, and trying to make sense of it. I was overwhelmed with this wonderful creature, ecstatic on our white and gold horse.

We took Chloe to France shortly after that. Because she was such a spiky baby, she dominated the household. Her room was at the head of the creaky stairs in our house and everyone was petrified to climb them. One squeak was enough to set her off. It was like living with a tiny terrorist. Because she was so clearly the first priority, it distanced Louis and me, even though we were together in the house for the whole summer.

Because Louis would be gone so often, I chose Chloe's godparents with particular care. I asked Tessa Kennedy, my first woman friend, to be Chloe's godmother. Tessa, an Englishwoman, has five children and I never saw her get flustered or lose her temper. She took to her new role with vigor. She exclaimed over how communicative Chloe was at a few months old and she made gorgeous Victorian shadow boxes with lace, doilies, flowers, and photos of Chloe with family and friends. In a turn that would have done Maria von Trapp proud, she even made Chloe her first Easter dress out of an old pair of floral chintz drapes. We had Chloe christened at Runnymede, England, near Tessa's home.

I chose my brother, Kris, and my old friend Mike Nichols to be godfathers. Mike relished the role and served with distinction. He'd personally pick out handmade outfits for her, gave her a gold pendant of the Owl of Knowledge set with a topaz, her birthstone, for college graduation, and later an exquisite pair of antique topaz earrings. More important, he took on her intellectual development. Her first substantial library was courtesy of Mike: a first edition of *Catcher in the Rye* and a complete set of *The Adventures of Sherlock Holmes*.

But the most wonderfully surprising and welcome support came from Mom. My mother lost about ten years when Chloe was born. In a way, she was reborn. She was a fabulous grandmother; Chloe gave her a meaning in life that I had not. Mom had been so young when she'd had me, only twenty-three. I don't think she was ready for the rigors of motherhood. When my brother Kris came along fifteen years after me, she was a more confident, relaxed mother. She'd been thirty-nine at the time, just like me. By the time Chloe was born, Mom and I had remade our own relationship, complete with closeness and family dinners. Chloe became the centerpiece of our gatherings. Mom was a natural grandmother—very attentive, even worshipful of Chloe—and they had a fantastic time together. The mother who could be so irascible with me never lost her temper with this querulous child.

I recorded the challenges of her first year in Chloe's baby book. Under "Things that made me sad," I wrote "people talking when I ate, not eating, not being held, going to sleep, any noise, hearing 'no,' not getting my way." Baby's first word? "I barked at all animals in greeting, especially dogs." Chloe's favorite toy wasn't a cuddly stuffed animal but a rubber snake, which she wore looped around her neck as she hissed.

After I'd been home with Chloe for a while, I got a call from my agent. Did I want to do the movie of *Mayflower Madam*? I'd turned down a number of Movies of the Week and the occasional feature. Now it felt like the right time to return. *Mayflower* was a valid project with some heft; the book had been a huge bestseller and I wanted to work. I said yes.

The main part of the shoot was in Atlanta. I was scared and happy, wildly ambivalent—I didn't want to be away from Chloe, but I'd missed working. And here, on the set, *I* was being treated like the baby: picked up, dropped off, room-serviced, catered to. Scrambled egg sandwiches in the makeup trailer, coffee light, no sugar.

I'd missed the hubbub on a set, dodging the cables, makeup touch-ups, doughnuts. I missed my Winnebago, the ultimate refuge from adulthood. I missed the laughter, the raunchy dopiness, the raucous high spirits.

Of course I missed it; I grew up around it, *in it.* I'd made movies since I was nineteen. It had now been a year of pregnancy plus a year of baby and no work of any kind.

The first day of shooting I was nervous; I'd forgotten how scripts are constantly rewritten. I would barely learn the lines on the blue pages when in would come the new salmon-colored pages, then the new sage, followed by goldenrod mustard. It wasn't good.

One more thing I'd forgotten: the scrutiny. I'd been leading a normal life in New York, paying little attention to how I looked. Now a camera crew was screwing up their faces as they lit my close-ups. The director of photography discreetly called for more flags, the black oblong pieces of cardboard meant to shade the aging parts of my face and my crepey neck. Suddenly there were more flags than at the opening ceremony of the Olympics. Nets and cutters and key lights and eye lights were called in to shade my neck, lighten the circles under my eyes. They lit and relit, always discreetly. But for the first time, I noticed it. I was self-conscious, aware of looking forty. The makeup woman doing my eyes held up the hoods of flesh gingerly with one hand to shade under them with the other. I started thinking of plastic surgery. My eyelids. My breasts. My thighs. Why did I suddenly care now when I never did before? I was in better shape than I had been on other jobs. Was it because I saw my face, my body changing? How fast would it go? How far was I prepared to go to stop it? Was this what it meant to be forty in films?

Yet it was great fun to get back in the game. People seemed to like what I was doing. Ingrid kept watch over Chloe while I was on the set. I'd call between scenes to see how she was. "Oh, she's fine," Ingrid said. "Are you *sure?*" I was finding that the having-it-all thing was way more complicated than the women who seemed to have it all made it sound. I saw increasingly that I yearned for a big traditional family, a long dinner table, lots of kids while I railed at all the travel Louis and I were doing, at how fragmented our family was. I longed for the kind of family closeness I saw in movies starring loud, boisterous, sprawling Italian families, perhaps because I had known nothing like them. But I could barely manage a single child. How could Louis and I make this work?

Chloe had her first birthday at my mother's house in Beverly Hills. She shared that with her close friend Anna Kennedy, born on the same date. We had Silly Billy—the clown later featured in *Capturing the Friedmans*—making her a crown and blowing up balloons.

It was a miracle. Chloe had made it through her first year. And so had I.

❈ 7 ❈

Au Revoir Les Enfants was Louis's most personal movie by far; at age fifty-five, he'd only just felt ready to write it and shoot it. It was based on his own experience as an eleven-year-old attending a Jesuit boarding school outside Paris during the war. The headmaster, Père Jacques, had taken in three Jewish schoolboys, giving them Christian names to protect them from the Gestapo. When their true identities were later revealed, the boys and the headmaster were sent off to Auschwitz and Mauthausen-Gusen concentration camps, where they later died. (Yad Vashem, the Holocaust memorial in Israel, later recognized Père Jacques's heroic actions.) This was the story Louis was protecting and nurturing and always had in the back of his mind.

Louis wrote the screenplay in his study in Le Coual. It was his favorite room. Filled with files and scripts and books and shelves of movies, hung with Indian art, the study was a round tower room on the third floor off the salon where we all gathered to watch films. It was there that Louis read the screenplay to Justine and me when he finished it. We were both in tears by the end, and so proud of him, moved that he had gotten this cornerstone of a life experience down on paper, that he had realized it so perfectly.

While he was preparing to shoot, Louis and I went to see the school he'd attended in the winter because that was when the story was set; he'd never forgotten the intense chill. Sure enough, it was bitterly cold. The grounds were very bleak and spare amid the raw, freezing weather.

Preparing for the film, Louis was firing on all cylinders, alive and enthusiastic. He did the casting in Paris. He was very confident when he met the boy who would play Julien, his counterpart in the film, who in fact looked very much like Louis when he was small. Once he started shooting, I went to visit the set at St. John of the Cross, a French Catholic boarding school near Fontainebleau, a hamlet south of Paris. Suddenly the frigid air of the lycée came alive, the schoolyard filled with kids playing in their uniforms—wool shorts, kneesocks, dark sweaters over their shirts—Jesuits walking around in their brown robes, bare feet in sandals. It was wonderful to see Louis so engaged. In the town I bought an electric kettle, mugs, tea bags, and honey and set up a tea tray for him in his tiny hotel room, put flowers in a vase. It was his home away from home, after all.

The film was a critical and commercial triumph. When it showed at the 1987 Venice Film Festival, where it won the Golden Lion for Best Film, Louis got a ten-minute standing ovation. It was the first time that had happened; that an ovation went on and on. He kept standing up, sitting down, standing up, sitting down. We were both in tears at the end of that screening, overwhelmed. Then it happened again in France. Louis won seven Césars, the French Oscar, including ones for Best Director, Best Film, and Best Writing. (Such an ugly award; created by the sculptor César Baldaccini, it looked like a compacted car in gold and weighed about forty pounds.) It was a huge win.

Au Revoir Les Enfants was nominated for two Academy Awards, for Best Foreign Language Film and Best Original Screenplay. Even in those days, the frenzy before the Oscars was unbelievable. Louis was by far the odds-on favorite. He'd been nominated many times before, for *Murmur of the Heart*; *Lacombe, Lucien*; *Atlantic City*. He'd won an Oscar for Best Documentary for *Le Monde du Silence*—"The Silent World," the film he'd codirected when he was twenty-three with Jacques Cousteau—but I knew how badly he wanted acknowledgment for this movie after the brutal reviews he'd received on his last two films, *Alamo Bay* and *Crackers*. We'd brought Cuote and JuJu to LA for the ceremony. He was almost out of his seat to accept the Oscar when Faye Dunaway and James Garner announced that *Babette's Feast* had won Best Foreign Language Film. It knocked the wind out of us. We felt bushwhacked.

That was the year that Cher won Best Actress for *Moonstruck*—and thanked her hair and makeup people but not her director, Norman Jewison. "What is this country, where they remember to thank hair and makeup but not the director?" Louis wanted to know.

The mood in the house was black for a week. We barely spoke while feeling humiliated for taking it so seriously. Louis took the kids and returned to Europe to lick his wounds; he had to get out of LA.

⚜ 8 ⚜

That year there was to be a ball. An authentic ball, not some hoo-hah thrown by Paris Hilton at the Plaza. It was to be held at a sixteenth-century château an hour outside of Paris, Château de Courances. It belonged to an aristocratic family that Louis had known since childhood.

A ball gown was needed and it was arranged that I could borrow one from Christian Lacroix.

Chloe was then two and I took her with me to the Lacroix atelier for the fitting. The assistant brought in a magnificent, brilliantly colored strapless gown. It was in a watered silk in a mottled pattern of tangerine, turquoise, canary yellow, and deep fuchsia. A Fauvist palette, incredibly vibrant, embroidered with flowers and paillettes. They set about making it fit while Chloe played happily underneath the vast skirt. Christian Lacroix stuck his head in to say hello and see how the dress looked. He added matching four-inch statement earrings and a fuchsia satin stole. The dress looked fantastic, and frankly, so did I.

The night of the ball, Louis and I had some trouble batting the bouffant billowing skirt into our little BMW. He finally packed me in and off we went, arriving at the château forty minutes later. Once we were through the gatehouse, we saw an enormous courtyard stretching before us. It was lit entirely by kerosene lanterns. They lined the tops of the walls and the staircase to the entrance. There were hundreds of them; it was breathtaking. Vicomtesse Jacqueline de Ribes was ascending the stairs ahead of us. Then came Louis and me in my rental.

The interior was entirely candlelit, with wood paneling and wooden planked floors largely emptied of furniture for the evening. An enfilade led to a ballroom where a Brazilian band was playing soft sambas. Understated. Refined beyond belief. The women had arranged themselves in languid, elegant forms. And they held those carefully assumed positions with no apparent strain. They were Frenchwomen, after all, and strain was not becoming. I was intensely uncomfortable, clearly an interloper, while Louis was giddy, happy at seeing childhood friends, delighted to catch up. Rarely had I seen him so at ease. I, on the other hand, was watching the waiters, who were frantically scurrying about, following orders given sotto voce by the hosts.

If my life had hung in the balance, I could not have found a scintilla of vulgarity in the vast ballroom. Not a coarse speck. And it was all uniformly muted. They set the volume knob to Aristocratic, not American, and maintained it all evening. Across from me stood a console table lit, of course, by heavy silver candelabra; next to it, a group of men and women were talking discreetly, laughing gaily when suddenly, there was a soft but definite flare of light. A woman's hair had caught fire. Mothlike, she had drifted too close to the flames. If it had been me or any of my American friends, I promise, there would have been shrieking. There would have been swearing. There would have been hell to pay.

But this was *la belle France*. The vibe was one of extreme modulation, absolute discretion. Already this woman had threatened to upset the balance by bursting into flames, but she rose nobly to the occasion by stepping nimbly away from the candelabra and quietly patting out the pyre on her head. The French would rather go elegantly to their death than indiscreetly cause a scene.

A beautifully dressed woman approached Louis and they kissed hello. She turned to me and said, *"Je suis Philippine."* Odd, I thought, she doesn't look Philippine. Mostly because she *wasn't,* of course; she was Baroness Philippine de Rothschild, social doyenne. *Quel faux pas.*

There was dancing. Louis was doing his peculiar energetic hopping while holding my wrist and pumping it up and down. He was so goddamned happy there, like an alum attending a school reunion. After midnight, the Triumphal March from *Aida* was piped outside and there was a magnificent fireworks display in the garden synchronized to the Puccini score. People were draped languidly on the terrace, artfully arranged along the balconies to watch *le spectacle.* Young well-born ladies, balancing cigarette holders in hands in long evening gloves, exhaled plumes of smoke into the night, silhouetted against the light show behind them.

I farted discreetly under my magnificent gown. It was my secret.

I was always constricted into acting like an adult in France. France is a very muted, low-volume place—Paris especially. They're grown-ups there, very elegant grown-ups, very controlled. They don't seem to react the same way emotionally; they have a distaste for sentimental qualities. They find Americans incredibly vulgar, loud, and overstated. They are not wrong in this. In a restaurant, you'd know immediately when an American party entered the room; the volume would go up several decibels. Whenever I was in Paris with Louis, I would take much more time getting dressed, wearing more feminine clothes in more muted colors, but I was always at a loss, always struggling to find the right note. I knew enough not to even try at dinner parties. In any case, my French early on wasn't good enough for confident conversation.

Louis was from a very old French family, pancultural people who would often greet each other with a "Namaste"; they were always very welcoming to me. When Louis would see my brother, Kris, he'd reach out to shake hands; Kris would grab him in a big bear hug.

We had an eccentric apartment on the Isle de la Cité. It was so small there was no room for Chloe, so we wedged her crib into the hall right up against the upholstered walls. Our nanny, Ingrid, slept in the room upstairs, which looked out onto the spires of Notre Dame and the Eiffel Tower beyond.

By the age of two, Chloe had shed her spikiness

and become very affectionate. She was startlingly energetic, as committed a multitasker as Louis. She rarely did only one thing at a time. I'd watch her drink her bottle with one hand while stacking blocks with the other. She was physically fearless, always climbing over furniture and up the drapes. When I took her to the park, she'd join the fray without a backward glance. I would steer her by the neck, gently holding that joystick and turning her in the direction I wanted us to go, so she wouldn't dart off. Louis described her in his journal as "an admirable wild child, climber of trees, acrobat, the crazy queen of Le Coual." She had a unique ability to occupy herself.

Thank heavens she was a good traveler, because she spent a good deal of her time on airplanes, shuttling from New York to LA to visit my mother and brother, and, of course, Paris, where she fit right in. She looked French, whatever that means. She was a blue-eyed brunette, with a sauciness and a sparkle that elicited a *"Qu'elle est vive!"* from the French. Her hair was kept in a pixie cut and I thought she looked very chic, very Leslie-Caron-as-Lili. When people started saying, "Oh, what a handsome son you have!" I knew it was time to grow it out.

The French don't love children, not like the Italians, but it's great fun to have a child in France. Your baby is an extension of your chic self; it is very much about presentation. In the

French countryside, I could sometimes get away with Goodwill clothing for Chloe, but even in a tiny shop near Le Coual, hundreds of miles from Paris, the saleslady would come out with a tiny striped maillot, saying *"Ça a beaucoup de chic."* It's in their DNA. In Paris I'd make much more of an effort, dressing Chloe in her nicest outfits. She had fantastic bright green suede shoes and would hold her feet up and inspect them in her stroller. I'd put her in red-and-white-striped jerseys, blue denim overalls, red high-top sneakers with zippers up the side. Again, *beaucoup de chic.*

Even the baby food in Paris is chic. The food purees were of Michelin four-fork rating, almost like foie gras, incredibly refined.

I'd wheel Chloe's stroller through the bird and flower market among the rows of parakeets, canaries, lovebirds. We'd cross the river to the animal market where we'd pass cages stacked on the sidewalks for four or five blocks with goats, piglets, geese, puppies, kittens. I always had to restrain myself from bringing any home.

We wandered the flea markets at Clignancourt, the antiques dealers at Vernaison in the Marché aux Puces de St. Ouen with their exquisite old clocks and toys, the magnificent marquetry tables. Wedged into the middle of the market was Chez Louisette, a charming little bistro open on two sides where we sat and ate couscous at long communal tables. A trio of very old Muppets—men with matted toupees and dyed moustaches and eyebrows, very Bert and Ernie—played accordions energetically while an equally aged chanteuse in an evening gown (at lunch) belted out old Piaf standards. It was heaven.

We'd go to the Tuileries for pony rides, take in the Punch and Judy puppet show, ride the carousel in the Jardin du Luxembourg, or rent ancient miniature sailboats and float them in the pond.

Louis took us to the spectacular rose gardens at La Bagatelle, drove us to Versailles to show Chloe the Hall of Mirrors and the Le Nôtre gardens. He took us to a favorite bistro on the Place des Vosges, where we sat outside and ordered a beefsteak for Chloe, who always loved meat. We watched in awe as this petite four-year-old ate a rare steak the size of a life raft. Lou Lou also took us to the Île Saint-Louis to wait in line at Berthillon so Chloe could taste the best ice cream in the world.

When friends came to the city, I'd take them on the dinner cruise on the bateaux-mouches, the tourist barges that toured up and down the Seine. It always surprised me how elegant everything was. There was a harpist on board, playing quietly while we drank wine and nibbled melon, smoked salmon, quail tournedos, and *pour le dessert, feuillantines au chocolat.* It was lovely; you didn't feel like a schmuck.

Chloe spent her second Christmas in Paris at Louis's parents' home. It was a big, beautiful apartment overlooking the Seine in a turn-of-the-century building with a cage elevator. There was a large Degas ballerina pastel over the mantel, an Aubusson tapestry, Louis XVI fauteuils, and threadbare, priceless carpets. It was a typical *haute bourgeoise* apartment, furnished only with antiques and singularly uncomfortable. Chloe was barely waddling; she got as far as the salon, heard the conversational buzz, took in the spectacle— guests chattering away, the tinkling of glasses, the huge spread of hors d'oeuvres—and without stopping, promptly turned around and headed back out the front door. It was all too much. I scooped her up and bore her away.

It was so bitterly cold that winter that chunks of ice were floating by on the Seine and snow was blowing horizontally; the city was wound tight as a drum. Several months earlier there had been some terrorist attacks, bombs placed in trash cans outside department stores, in the lobby of a movie theater on the Champs-Elysées, and the post office of the Hôtel de Ville. Chloe and I had been there in the morning; that afternoon it was bombed. You couldn't leave a package unattended anywhere; people would scream at you to pick it up. Ingrid, Chloe, and I decided to make a break for it.

It was against this backdrop that we headed for

the airport. Louis took the car with our luggage; I grabbed a taxi with Ingrid and Chloe so we could check in. We went skidding through the icy streets. When we got to De Gaulle Airport, I saw Louis waving at us from the curb. His head was bandaged and bloody. It turned out that he'd slipped and hit his head on a baggage cart, slicing his forehead open. The airport was swarming with Special Ops forces shouldering machine guns; they wanted to get Louis out of sight before passengers assumed he'd been the target of a terrorist attack and the crowd got spooked. Ingrid, Chloe, and I were hustled onto the plane, the wings were de-iced, and we sped home to New York City, which seemed positively balmy with temperatures in the thirties.

For her first few years, Chloe spent almost all her Christmases in Paris or at Le Coual. When she was five, Mom got her a tiny Chanel-like suit—red with black and white braid down the front and gold buttons, which she wore with black tights and Mary Janes. She wore this outfit to the Paris Opéra to see the ballet. Louis got us tickets, then reservations on Christmas Eve at Jules Verne, the restaurant on the Eiffel Tower. It was freezing cold, but it's lovely to be in Paris at Christmastime because you remember how Christmas began. It's still a religious holiday in this predominantly Catholic country; unlike in

America, the orgy of buying and gift-giving is conspicuously absent. As usual, elegant French restraint prevails.

At midnight we went to Christmas mass at Notre Dame. The square in front of the cathedral featured a living crèche complete with camels, a holiday *son et lumière.* Angels lit with pale blue spotlights trumpeted from the balcony above the portals, and one glided gently down on a wire to land in front of the crèche. The mass was accompanied by magnificent music that culminated at midnight with a deep chorus of bells that thrummed in the air.

Sometimes we'd celebrate Christmas Eve with Alexandra, Justine's mother, who lived on the Bois de Vincennes—the "lungs of Paris"—on the outskirts of the city, a huge park with sprawling meadows, forests, and, in good weather, a giant lake speckled with people in paddleboats. Alexandra lived in a small but charming three-story house to which she'd added a winter garden, a Victorian sunroom of mullioned glass with a stove inside to warm it; this is where she served a fantastic Moroccan pigeon pie.

Christmas at Le Coual generally centered around the kitchen. You passed a huge blazing fire in the entry as you came into the house. The first time we brought Chloe, one year old, for Christmas and walked up the stone steps, Armande, our caretaker, smiled as she opened the door to the kitchen, which was lit only by a roaring fire and the candles on a large Christmas tree. I'd never seen a tree lit by candles except in paintings and illustrations; it was a Dickens tale brought to life, so beautiful I burst into tears. Le Coual was very raw in winter, and we'd huddle in the kitchen, which had its own fireplace. We opened a few presents on Christmas Eve; the next morning was an equally low-key affair with very few gifts. Chloe was delighted when Justine and Cuote joined us.

Summers, on the other hand, we were always out of doors. We would pack up huge picnic baskets and drive to a spot on the river that was perfect for swimming. We had to wade across rocks below a little waterfall and once we reached the other side, we left our baskets on the bank and swam for an hour in the cool, deep water. Then we would unpack our lunch and eat it before heading back home.

We also shopped at the local markets. One day, Louis and I brought Chloe to the section of the big farmer's market that sold live poultry such as chickens and geese. She chose two baby chicks, a yellow one and a black one, named them Pinchy and Tweety, and, with her cousin Jackson, proceeded to give them "flying lessons." I looked up from the sink in the kitchen and saw yellow and black puffs of feathers as she and Jackson tossed them back and forth. Somehow the chicks survived. Then they'd put them on a raft in the pool and "teach them to swim." The next summer, they got her back. Hearing her shriek, we looked up as she came running into the garden from the barnyard, sobbing, "Pinchy's attacking me!"

We loved to play badminton on the lawn outside the kitchen. I made the outlines of the court with a bag of flour. We had swimming races. And we painted caves.

Le Coual was in the region of France where several prehistoric caves had been discovered. The cave nearest us, Pech Merle, had been found by two teenagers. It was huge and the paintings inside were in pristine condition. The caves were so cold that people donned parkas before descending into them. Visitors walk past stalactites and then enter an enormous cavern where thousands of years ago our human ancestors painted clear, realistic pictures of animals in blacks and burnt reds.

There was a tiny cave on the property of Le Coual. Really tiny, only big enough for two or three people. I decided we should paint it. In honor of Pech Merle, we called it Pech Malle. We brought paints, brushes, and bottles of water and hiked to the cave, where we decorated the walls with dinosaurs and butterflies. We couldn't wait for it to be rediscovered.

4

Murphy: Mike Wallace in a Dress

After living in New York City for years, I had begun to miss smoggy southern California. Louis was scathing when LA was mentioned. Yet I am that rare thing: a native Angeleno. Even though I railed against the dopiness of it, the obliviousness, I missed it. I became unexpectedly emotional when I returned for short visits, bursting into tears at random times. Also, to be frank, I missed working. I'd worked since I was nineteen, and now, since the birth of my daughter, I'd barely worked in over three years. As desperately in love with Chloe as I was, I *needed* to work. I might have been going a little crazy. Louis could tell.

There was a script for a television pilot circulating. No one at my agency thought to submit me for it except for one lowly new agent. He was a southern boy named Bryan Lourd: refined, attractive, very bright. (So bright he is now co-chair of CAA, one of the most powerful agencies in Los Angeles.) Bryan submitted my name close to the end of the casting process and sent me the script. I left it by the bed for a week and a half. I didn't watch much TV, unless you counted *Sesame Street* and *Fraggle Rock*. The only show I was aware of with strong female roles was *Designing Women*, which was sharply written and performed. And at that time, 1988, in the show-biz caste system, television hovered close to the bottom.

Bryan called to noodge me, "You know the script I sent you? You really should read it; they need an answer." I was leaving for New York the next day and took it with me on the plane. When Chloe went down for a nap, I started it; it was as good as any comedy I'd ever read. It was also, surprisingly, perfect for me.

No one else would have thought that (except Bryan), but I knew. I had just had a funny role in a comedy called *Starting Over* with Burt Reynolds and the late Jill Clayburgh. In one scene, I had to sing a song that I had supposedly written to try to seduce my ex-husband, played by Burt. I was supposed to be obliviously off-key—a wincing performance to witness. No winking at the camera allowed. Alan Pakula, the director, pushed me not to hold back. "You should sing with no holds barred. Don't try to hide any vocal defects—just embrace them." With that in mind, the singing off-key just happened naturally. To me, it was heaven because I finally got the courage to make a fool of myself—and that was a major liberation. The scene got huge laughs, which was music to my ears, plus I got an Academy Award nomination for Best Supporting Actress; I got the news while on my second date with Louis. (Meryl Streep won for *Kramer vs. Kramer*.)

And at the end of the pilot script, the character, named Murphy Brown, went home to her empty townhouse, put Aretha on the sound system, started opening her mail, and began singing along to "Natural Woman" at the top of her lungs. She is caught by her house painter, Eldin, who's working in the kitchen. Be still my heart; it was written for me.

The lead was a television news reporter. She was big, she was brassy, she was fearless. Smart, fast-paced, and funny, the dialogue was similar to the great comedies of the 1940s, sparky and spiky. There was something in the writing of the Murphy character that hooked me, as she eventually hooked many women. Is it that she was, in many ways, who we wished we could be as women? Successful in a field dominated by men. Free of the need to please. Impolitic, impolite, yet in some weird way, irresistible?

In those days we had pay phones on planes; I grabbed it, called Bryan, and said, "This is one of the best comedies I've ever read. I hope it's not too late. What do I have to do?"

The character of Murphy Brown, a spiky, wise-cracking iconoclast who worked for *FYI*, a fictional television newsmagazine, had come to writer-producer Diane English fully formed as she was driving on the Hollywood Freeway. Murphy made her entrance stepping off the elevator at the offices of *FYI*, a nighttime newsmagazine, after a month of rehab at Betty Ford. Did it have to be a *month* at *Betty Ford?* The network wanted to know. Why couldn't she be returning after a *week* at a *spa?* And did she have to be *forty?* Why couldn't she be *thirty* . . . and played by Heather Locklear? Diane, a committed feminist, pushed back: the whole point of Murphy was that she had crossed forty and was at the top of her profession but decidedly flawed, an alcoholic. She refused to let the network defang the show.

Diane flew to New York to meet me. I opened the door to find a strikingly appealing woman: direct blue eyes, light brown bobbed hair, fair skin, slim, probably five-six or five-seven. Very Anglo-Saxon, very alert, confident. Her manner was open and warm; I liked her at once. We read through the script together. It was very comfortable. Plus we wore the same lipstick—French Fawn—and the same perfume. It was kismet.

The next step: CBS flew me to LA to audition for the network. Diane and I met at her office at Warner Bros. to read the script with director Barnet Kellman. Then, playing the Motown that would become a Murphy trademark, Diane drove me to CBS.

We entered the office of the president of the network and shook hands with him and the head of casting. After a few minutes of small talk, he pressed a remote and electric drapes whirred shut across the windows. With the harsh overhead light, it was like being in an interrogation room—not the ideal atmosphere for comedy. We'd rehearsed beforehand with Barnet in Diane's office and it had gone fairly well. Now it didn't. I choked; the audition tanked. CBS had been right in their earlier suspicion: I didn't have "comedy chops," and now they were free to make an offer to Heather Locklear. After I'd finished the reading and slunk out of the office, the network president turned to Diane: "I don't think she can do it."

Diane English was convinced I could and so was I. Diane backs down for no man. She took the president back to his office and said, "My husband [Joel Shukovsky, also her creative partner at the time] and I have as much invested in this as you do. We are convinced she can do this and we feel very strongly about casting her." He came out looking sheepish. Walking up to me, he stuck out his hand and said, smiling tightly, "Congratulations, Murphy." I had the job. Soon afterward, he was fired from the network. Later he took me out to dinner to apologize. They sat us near the kitchen, where the door kept whacking him in the shoulder.

On February 18, 1988, I received a lovely note from Diane and Joel on Warner Bros. stationery: "Dear Candice, We can't tell you how excited we are about you being Murphy! Other actresses are throwing themselves into the ocean—it's horrible."

I didn't know how TV worked. If I did the pilot and they picked it up, I knew it might go for five episodes or five years. Everybody told me, "The odds of any pilot going for five years are slim to none." I took them at their word and signed a contract for five years.

The character, surprisingly, fit me like a glove. I was instantly comfortable with the writing. Diane had created a complex, original, bratty, endearing, feisty, take-no-prisoners woman. And more surprisingly, a woman who cared not a whit what others thought of her. I think this is what women loved about Murphy; it's what I loved playing that role. There was not an ounce of submission, not a drop of passivity, no suggestion of shrivel. Murphy was fierce and principled. She had passion—especially for her work, which, at that time, was dominated by men and where she gave no quarter. We all wanted to be her. That character gave me permission to be my brattiest, bawdiest self.

My father was schizophrenic in that same way. Fully Swedish, incredibly buttoned-down, no one would have guessed he was in entertainment, much less vaudeville. He was always quiet, respectful, introverted. But if he was with friends or had Charlie McCarthy with him, out would come his inner vaudevillian and he would be incredibly risqué. He belonged to a men's group called the Rancheros Visitadores. They would go on weekend horseback rides and camp out and tell stories and fart around a campfire. My father always brought the house down doing routines with Charlie and making incredibly bawdy jokes. Then he would button everything up again and come home like the enormously dignified man he was. Playing Murphy was like channeling my inner Charlie.

The casting was a huge part of the show's magic. I read with several different actors, but when Faith Ford came into the office, looking like she was hot out of the Louisiana swamp, it seemed inevitable that we'd found our Corky Sherwood. She wore a blue suit and heels, her hair tied back with a ribbon. At the end of her audition, as she was gathering her handbag, she said, "And this is how Corky would dance!" She proceeded to do a dainty frug while spinning her hands in tight little circles and bopping her head to music only she could hear. It was very funny and perfectly in character; Faith was a natural comedienne. She was twenty-two or twenty-three when we started; I watched her grow up.

I called her the Swamp Queen. She'd come in with stories about her momma and daddy and their huntin' camp in the bayou, shootin' gators. You just looked at her agape; how could such a person exist in Burbank? She was so authentic:

southern and completely feminine, sexy and bawdy. I'd consult her about the best makeup and hair people. My dressing room was across from the cast table: "Faith, what should I order for lunch?" "You want the Southwest Salad." "Faith, what should I wear?" All the guys had a crush on Faith but she had a boyfriend, who eventually became a husband. She was pure catnip to guys. I saw it over and over. They all wanted her, she was flirtatious in a lighthearted way, but also maternal, and she could cook like a demon. She'd come to the set with little pecan tarts that would make you faint or pots of gumbo for lunch. She became our cast nutritionist. She'd hollow out bagels, mash up the hard-boiled eggs from the craft table with some tomatoes and the scooped-out bread, add a touch of Dijon and mayo, and refill the bagels with the mixture. She made me one of these stuffed bagels every morning; I would start drooling on my drive in. In fact, that is still one of my favorite breakfasts.

I absolutely love Faithie. She's very smart and I learned early never to underestimate her. She was a natural entrepreneur: She wrote a cookbook. She planned a restaurant called Jambalaya. Now she's in Louisiana getting a TV studio under way, liaising with the governor.

I read with a couple of Frank Fontanas, *FYI*'s investigative journalist, including one I'd seen making ends meet bartending at a party, but Joe

Regalbuto was by far the most appealing. He was a highly experienced character actor who'd also taught acting. He knew and respected his craft and had superior social skills; he was kind and charming. Since *Murphy Brown*, he's gone on to direct many TV series besides acting on the stage.

Charles Kimbrough, who was cast as starchy Jim Dial, senior correspondent of *FYI*, was the only adult in our cast; he really suffered the rest of us fools. He was highly intelligent and cultivated —a mature man, older than the rest of us by a few years. Charlie had a wonderful voice and sang beautifully. He'd starred in Sondheim works on Broadway: *Sunday in the Park with George* and *Company*; he was a Sondheim stalwart. Charlie was at a rocky point in his life when he was cast, staying in a depressing temporary rental complex for actors and divorced husbands, so *Murphy* gave him a base and let him earn real money for the first time. He called me "Sis" and I adored him.

I had the most comedy chemistry with Grant Shaud, a Catholic kid from Philadelphia who played the baby-faced Miles Silverberg, the Jewish nebbish sent over by the network to torment the journalists as *FYI*'s producer. He would be greeted by Murphy's latest assistant chiming out, "Oh, Mr. Silverberg, you look so very grown up in your little blue blazer!" Grant's dream was to be a dramatic actor—Al Pacino was his god—but his gift was for comedy, and he took it very seriously. He'd been flown in at the last minute to read for the part of Miles. He arrived with nothing—no suitcase, just these weird New York City boots with grommets. Grant was planning to fly right back to New York after the audition, so he hadn't even brought a change of clothes. He hadn't planned on nailing the audition and getting the part right away. They were a week away from shooting. He quickly bought underwear and socks and moved straight into the same depressing rental complex as Charlie until he could find something better.

Bobby Pastorelli was from a parallel universe full of bookies and hookers and big guys in black leather from Jersey. He played Eldin Bernecky, the excessively creative house painter who never left Murphy's townhouse. Later his character would become a father figure to Avery, Murphy's son.

Eldin was a huge audience favorite. I thought he'd fallen out of a tree. He was a real Italian from New Jersey, a true goombah. He was authentic. He loved to ruffle feathers, but he was always protective of me, very loving and dear. He used to bring his Vegas bookie to the set. He'd pull up in his 1960s pink Cadillac convertible with a friend who was a hooker or an addict or both. Bobby had trouble with drugs; there was a dark side. The third week, he came to the stage for rehearsal clearly stoned. Diane and Joel took him aside and said, "If this happens again, you're gone." It never happened again, at least not onstage.

Diane English had a dinner at her house in Malibu Canyon to introduce the cast to one another the night before we started work on the pilot. Nobody said there would be a reading, but we had all brought our scripts; I couldn't wait. I'd never felt this kind of confidence in a script.

We draped ourselves across the couches and chairs in Diane's living room and started reading the script after dinner. It was so raucous that Diane later said, "My walls are still cracked." It was thrilling to hear the script come to life. The smarts, the wit. After meeting Corky for the first time, Murphy quipped, "She thinks Camus is a soap."

The pilot opened with Murphy stepping out of the elevator after her month in rehab, announcing, "I'm BAAAAA-AAACK!!!" She meets her baby-faced producer, Miles Silverberg, and chafes at being under his command: "I'm sorry, Mr. Silverberg, if it appears I'm being rude to you. It's just that I can't help thinking about the fact that while I got maced at the Democratic Convention of '68, you were wondering if you'd ever meet Adam West." She comes home to Eldin Bernecky, crowing, "You know, thirty million people watched me on television tonight," to which an unfazed Eldin says, "Yeah? I won ten bucks at lotto!" The episode closed with Murphy singing along to Aretha Franklin belting "Natural Woman," Murphy exuberantly off-key and fearless. It was excruciating for everyone but me.

Rehearsing the pilot, I felt as if I'd been shot out of a cannon. I had barely watched a half-hour comedy, much less shot one. Everything was incredibly fast-paced and intense. We had to shoot an early draft of the script because we were in the middle of a writers' strike and Diane wasn't permitted to rewrite the pilot. We packed the studio audience with friends and got lots of laughs —big ones. When we finished shooting the last scene, with Murphy getting caught out by Eldin, Barnet called "Cut!" and I burst into tears.

The pilot got high word of mouth among network people and advertisers. There was buzz. Once it went on the air, it got wonderful reviews. We were a hit from the get-go. The press, on whom the show was based, loved it; the fact that it was rooted in current events made it even more appealing. Bill Zehme, interviewing me for *Rolling Stone*, described me as a "testosterone phosphate, a zesty ballbuster who stomps through doors, rattling hinges loose, trailing a wake of high-octane wisecracks . . . a hornier, thornier version of Rosalind Russell in *His Girl Friday*; she is Linda Ellerbee as glamour-puss; she is, simply put, Hard Candy."

Murphy Brown was on opposite Monday Night Football. The NFL was untouchable in terms of viewing habits. One of the first signs that our audience was growing beyond women was when one of the producers told us, "You know, you guys are eating into our lead here. We didn't expect that." So we were nibbling at the feet of the NFL broadcasts. They were never in any danger from us, but they were looking over their shoulders from time to time.

It was the first time I'd thrown myself into something with such abandon and joy.

Murphy was a kind of dybbuk: profane, in-your-face, fearless. She'd take on anyone. This was very far from me as a person, although the character inevitably bled into me. I became a much more aggressive driver, for example; Louis was terrified of being in the car with me. Being Murphy freed me to express that sarcastic side of my personality, which only those people closest to me knew existed. My pal Peter Hyams told me, "Now the whole world will know what the rest of us have always known—which is that you are a total asshole." I told Bill Zehme that the great thing about playing Murphy was that I didn't have time to be polite anymore, to say things I didn't mean. My friend, director Peter Davis, wrote me a mash note after the pilot aired:

Dear Candy, . . .

Maybe my favorite thing was [your character] hanging up on the Secretary of State to talk to the house painter—until the end. The end, with you miming the words to the record, the record in effect ventriloquizing you, made me shiver. You have to have waited, in some corner of yourself, your whole life, to do that.

Ventriloquizing? Was I becoming my own Charlie McCarthy?

What I had going for me was the element of surprise. No one ever expected me to be funny, not least because of my glacial Nordic looks and affect. I'd mostly been reviled in my acting career; I'd given many bad performances in many bad movies. The Oscar nomination for *Starting Over* was an anomaly; basically I'd had fifteen years of bad notices by the time Murphy came along in 1988.

Now, at last, I was getting some respect. The fact that the title of the pilot episode was "Respect" just felt prophetic.

People would credit me with Murphy Brown's intelligence and wit, which were of course not mine; they were Diane's and our writers'. I envied Murphy's supreme self-confidence. I loved that she'd been able to drink guys under the table. Like many women at the time, I wanted to be Murphy Brown.

Murphy Brown quickly became established. It was in the top five shows and a huge critical hit as well. We were credited with returning CBS to its place as the Tiffany Network and making the network number one again after a long fallow period. It was like Champagne—very, very heady stuff.

The power of the show became clear when the then-president of CBS Entertainment gave a press conference. In extolling Diane English's creative freedom, he made an offhand reference to my horrible audition. This apparently did not sit well with upper management. I received a three-page letter of contrition. Then came the final paragraph. It was a doozy:

> Candice, please indulge me in what might be purple apology. In the middle of the Dordogne region of France there is a town called Rocamadour. I do not know if you have ever been there, but it is the end stop of where the reproached of the church would finish their journey of penitence, sack-clothed, chafed, and starving. On their knees, they would have to ascend hundreds upon hundreds of coarse granite steps under flagellation, surrounded by murals of death to reach the pinnacle of this stone cliff monastery. If they reached the top, forgiveness and freedom would be given. I view what I have done to you as a great sin.

As God is my witness, I never intended it. But it is done. If there is a modern equivalent to Rocamadour, I will find it. And when on top, I will sing your praises and exalt you. You are gifted, professional and quintessentially beautiful. I am truly sorry for what I have done.

For the first time of my life, at age forty-one, I had a regular job: I knew where I was going to be for seven months a year, which was vital for Chloe, who had just started school. I'd seen the children who are a product of unpredictable parental absences. It was incredibly hard on kids, and I wanted to avoid it.

When it seemed clear that I'd be working steadily in LA, it made sense to buy a house. Louis and Connie spotted it first. "You're really going to love it," Connie said. "It's the perfect house for you." She knew I responded to eccentric and unusual houses. This was one you could put in your pocket. I loved that it was up in the hills because I had grown up high on a hill; I was happiest where you could go on great walks and see coyotes and owls and deer, the occasional snake. Louis loved it too. As much as he could love anything in Los Angeles.

The house was charming, very light and open, one story. It was set in a eucalyptus grove, with a lovely little pool and pool house. The prettiest, coziest house, with two bedrooms plus a maid's room and a living room. No dining room. With designer Karin Blake, we bleached the floors and painted everything white; made it into a cottage. I added a conservatory room onto the back, with a copy of a long quilting table that could seat twelve or fourteen, and that was where we'd have our Thanksgiving and Christmas and family dinners. Best of all, Kris and Mom lived within five minutes of our little house.

Kris was now known as Uncle Zooey, since I'd randomly called him "Zooey" when he was little. "Uncle Zooey" morphed into "Unka Zoo" to "Zoo." And there it stayed. Everyone was helping, so Chloe had as normal a family life as we could manage. It was cozy, reliable—what I thought was healthy for a child. And healthy for me.

What was not normal was Louis being mostly absent while we lived in LA. He came to stay every two or three weeks from Paris or New York, except for summers when we were all together for three months. I would often come to New York on my week off each month, but it was always a strain. There was an inevitable period of adjustment, starting with the nine-hour time change if he came from France. It took Chloe a few days to lower her guard, and by the time she did, he was off again. Our daily rhythm was thrown off and Louis was moving so constantly, he could rarely establish one.

● ● ●

Diane English and her writers were the backbone of the show. In television, writer-producers are king—queen, in this case. There was a magic to the pilot script and almost every script that followed was thrilling to read and great fun to play. The references were always smart. Diane had a high opinion of *Murphy*'s viewers: "We expect them to know Indira Gandhi, Golda Meir, and Margaret Mead." She had an ear for dialogue and could write men as convincingly as women. The writing staff on *Murphy*, who numbered about eight, were not only talented comedy writers; they had to be more informed and sophisticated than most because *Murphy* was a news show set in Washington, DC. They might spend an entire hour on a single joke, sometimes two hours.

Diane and the writers were fully responsible for what came out of Murphy's mouth, but the producers let me have a lot of input into the rest of her character. I always saw myself as Murphy's guardian in that I didn't want her to tip over into utter obnoxiousness. It was important that she somehow redeem herself by the end of each episode.

It was also important to me that her work space reflect her sense of humor, so our prop man, Larry Dolan, and I put toys all over Murphy's office. Larry put a Siamese fighting fish into a fishbowl and hung a little green Ninja Turtle on the rim, peering inside. We did actual shoots of fake magazine covers so we could decorate Murphy's office walls with photos of her on the covers of *Time*, *Life*, and *Newsweek* talking to international figures like the pope. (We hired a pope impersonator in a white beanie and cassock and gold crucifix to stand next to me in the garden at Warner Bros. to give the photo shoot a kind of Mediterranean feeling.) Eventually, the mock *Time* and *Newsweek* covers were replaced by real ones.

It also mattered to me that Murphy, a successful, ambitious woman, have a certain style, so I got very involved with her wardrobe. While I didn't have the time—I had a small child and a big role—I just did it and didn't ask anyone, not even the costume designer, whose tastes were very different from my own. I was friends with many designers. I went to Ralph Lauren, Donna Karan, Isaac Mizrahi, Todd Oldham (he made fantastic whimsical shirts embroidered with tassels and appliqués), Robert Lee Morris for handbags and jewelry. His earrings and cuffs looked great with Donna Karan. Occasionally, I'd go next door to men's wardrobe and pull out old leather bomber jackets and caps for when Murphy was dressing down. During hiatus, I'd go alone to the sample sales, order at wholesale. During the first season, the costume designer politely ignored it. After the first season, it was clear that Murphy had become a certain style icon. Then they were interviewing him on TV. He began coming with me to the designers and we'd order from their showrooms on Seventh Avenue. Each show had four to six outfit changes and each season had some twenty-two episodes—a lot of wardrobe. I'd wear my own shoes, then we'd buy the ones I liked. Good shoes are very important to the look of an outfit and I didn't want inexpensive ones. Then the costume designer started getting witty vintage pins: Felix the Cat. Bakelite.

I wanted every outfit to be an event. And in a way, they were. Women loved what Murphy wore. When I wanted to wear a baseball cap with a high ponytail, we couldn't find one with an opening in the back, so Judy McGivney, our wardrobe woman, made one by cutting a hole in the back. A couple of months after the show aired, you could buy them in any store. Now they're standard.

I felt strongly that Murphy lived with a certain level of taste. Her townhouse almost became another character on the show, especially as Eldin's grandiose plans for it evolved over the seasons. Originally Diane and our set designer, Roy Christopher, envisioned it as very modern, monochromatic, with beiges, taupes, and sisal. Nobody asked, but that didn't work for me. I wanted it to have character and family history.

Pieces of furniture from when the family was still intact. Roy looked at photos of my loft in *Architectural Digest*. He then took the set to a double-height living room with bookshelves and a gallery on the second floor. He added Persian carpets, a standing Tiffany lamp like my own, and a handsome burgundy striped sofa that anchored the living room. He painted the walls hunter green. People were always writing to find out where they could buy the sofa or how they could get the lamp (a copy of a real Tiffany lamp, which in fact they rented—for ten years). Pieces from the set were in high demand.

Chloe and I settled into our schedule. She would generally awaken sweetly but vocally about five thirty—on a good day. The kid was peppy. This was always tough to get used to the morning after tape nights, since I'd get to bed at one in the morning. I rarely went out for dinner during the week because I was learning my lines after I put Chloe to bed. I didn't have a nanny living in with us, which was a deliberate choice on my part. With Louis dividing his time now between New York, Paris, and LA, he was absent a good deal, so it was just us girls. This, of course, made me sublimely happy. I would get up, make us breakfast on trays, and bring them into the bedroom, where we would watch Winnie the Pooh cartoons and read books till eight thirty; then I would drive her down the hill to the preschool in Coldwater Canyon. From there, I would head back over the canyon to work on Stage Four of Warner Bros. Studios in Burbank.

Half-hour schedules are by far the most humane, a combination of mostly bankers' hours with the vibe of live theater and the adrenaline of bank robberies. I'd drive car pool twice a week, arrive by nine thirty, and, most days, head home by about five o'clock.

I had rarely *watched* a sitcom in my life, much less shot one, and for most of the first season, I was in a state of shock. It was a complete out-of-body experience, a dramatically different format: four-camera film before a live audience. My pupils were always dilated to the size of platters; I was just holding on for dear life. Chloe was my top priority, but during the first year, Warner Bros. wanted me to publicize the show relentlessly. Every time I had fifteen minutes free on the set or on weekends, I was expected to be doing publicity. It was intense and tough on everyone.

The time constraints of putting on a live show in five days are huge. There's the pressure of learning lines, which on *Murphy* were many. Murphy was in every scene for ten years with big blocks of dialogue, which was a lot to learn in four days; her character drove the show. The scripts were longer than other half-hour scripts because we played it with breakneck pacing that would duplicate the energy of an East Coast newsroom. Our director for the first four years, Barnet Kellman, saw to that. He'd gone to Yale Drama School, directed plays in New York, and was whip-smart, intense, and witty. The *Murphy* set crackled with electricity. Barnet established that immediately and got a real sense of movement, the way an actual newsroom would run. He brought the urgency of hovering deadlines, people rocketing in and out of doors, faxing, typing, doing.

It was a lot to do in five days, like a little play each week. You began the week with a read-through of the script for the week ahead, which would be given to you, hopefully, when you left after the taping Friday night. Sometimes it would be delivered to your door on Saturday or Sunday.

During the table read on Monday morning, the cast, writers, and department heads would sit around a long T-shaped table with our scripts and read the week's show out loud in front of a few people from the network and studio. They left us alone and were always very supportive. After the read-through, I'd have a look in Women's Wardrobe at what I'd be wearing in the show. I'd try the outfits on at lunchtime and decide. Then, doughnut in hand, I'd go back to the stage and start rehearsing the show, scene by scene, with the rest of the cast.

It takes a village to make a TV show—a big

village. Okay, a small town. The writers kept insane hours, getting home at 2:00 or 3:00 a.m. routinely, and sometimes not at all. They were very well paid, let me tell you. And very tired. High pay, high toll.

We saw less of our writers as the week wore on because they were in another building, chained to their typewriters or doing table sessions, where all the writers would order Chinese food and go over each line in the script and punch it up: adding jokes, trimming, fine-tuning, sharpening references, incorporating news events as they happened close to Shoot Day. When a script was outstanding, the Monday morning table reads were raucous and the writers were beaming at the laughs their jokes got.

We'd be allowed to hold our scripts for rehearsals the first few days. By Thursday, our dialogue coach, Beverly Dixon, sat with us as we gathered in my dressing room on breaks and ran lines. Beverly would correct us when we "went up"—forgot our lines. Barnet called it the "White Rabbit"—that moment in a scene when your eyes widened in terror as you realized you had no idea what you were supposed to say. Beverly would cue our lines and correct the most minute mistakes. There was absolutely no improv. If a guest tried, we'd just look at them: *You schmuck.* We were grateful for such crackling good scripts and the writers expected them to be said as written. Exactly as written. Even semicolons were to be observed. I would usually stay later to drill lines since I had the bulk of them. I had to memorize long pages of exposition to deliver while the many cameras swooped around me. Sometimes I'd have tears streaming down my cheeks if I had a particularly dialogue-heavy show or because a writer had a rhythm I found hard to memorize. I put some of Murphy's lines inside a coffee mug on the set once, then forgot and poured coffee on them. Diane's scripts had a distinct rhythm I could absorb quickly. I learned to run my lines while sitting on a hard chair in my kitchen so I wouldn't fall asleep.

Thursdays were long days because that was camera-blocking day. Almost all half-hour shows then were shot with four cameras. Each camera is assigned to get specific shots or follow specific people during a scene. These shots are rehearsed all day on Thursday, with the operators seated at their cameras and the grips behind, pushing and guiding the cameras in a kind of silent hippo ballet, gliding quietly in front of the set and somehow never slamming into each other. That these crews didn't crash constantly, moving within a small space on the stage to cover their subjects, was astounding.

Barnet drilled us on our pacing and taught me some basics of comedy. *P*'s and *K*'s are funny—they make a clipped, popping sound. The number

7 is a funnier number than 4 or 5. I couldn't have asked for a better comedy clinic.

On Thursday night my muscles would be tight as a drum. I'd have someone come up to the house and work on my shoulders, neck, and back while I studied my lines.

Fridays were the longest days. No car pool for me. We arrived at nine in the morning and went into Hair and Makeup. We then went into a run-through in front of the writers with the camera crews around ten o'clock. If the writers felt we needed any rewrites or if any jokes needed punching up, they'd scurry back to their Writers' Room. The original scripts always started out on white paper; you didn't dare memorize them before Wednesday lest they be rewritten twice more by Friday. Throughout the week, any rewrites were announced with color changes: first pink, then blue, yellow, salmon, mint, goldenrod, buff. If you got to goldenrod, you knew the show was in trouble. Dinner was served in the empty sound stage across the street on the Warner lot. All the crew, cast, extras, writers, hair and makeup people, and wardrobe staff would serve themselves from long tables filled with food. We'd eat fast because we had to get back into makeup for touch-ups, then get into our first wardrobe changes before the cast did a speed drill in the makeup room. This was a fast-paced reading not for performance or timing, just to lock the lines in place before show time. The studio audience of 250 people would be seated, the cast would be introduced, and then we were off. Shooting started at 7:00 p.m. and usually went till 11:30 or even past midnight. Audiences were generally sophisticated and responsive. We loved getting the laughs, I can't tell you how much. It made my heart go pitty-pat.

I'd usually get home well after midnight. Our nanny—Patsy, later Delia—would leave and I'd pour myself a drink and sit on the wicker rocker on our patio to decompress. For the first few years, I'd make a greyhound—vodka and grapefruit juice on the rocks. I'd gotten started on them by a nutritionist from Malibu. He'd seen my puffy eyes—"No more grape for you! If you're going to drink, drink pure vodka—Absolut or any of the fine vodkas. You're allergic to grapes." So that put a real dent in my wine drinking with my French husband and promoted me to a raging alcoholic. To unwind, I'd take my drink outside and listen to the coyotes yipping. Then I'd join Chloe, who would be sleeping in my bed.

Kris and Connie would come up every Saturday morning. We'd make French toast together, then Kris would take Chloe on a little adventure—usually hiking up the hill behind the house—so I could sleep in. Once they got stung by a swarm of wasps whose nest they came across and came back screaming bloody murder. Kris was stung twelve times. He'd wrapped Chloe inside his jacket so she wasn't stung at all. He fell on the grenade. Sunday nights, we'd have an early family dinner at Orso. Chloe sat discreetly on the floor and played with her rabbit house and rabbit dolls while we waited for our pizza. Sometimes it would be Trader Vic's, or Chasen's, where I introduced Chloe to Dorothy Lamour, whom Chloe knew from the Bob Hope and Bing Crosby "road movies." Dorothy had swapped her sarong for a muumuu.

Other members of the cast would spend the whole weekend in bed after a show; we were zapped. But when you have a four-year-old, there's no time to be zapped. For a humane schedule, it was exhausting. It took us eight days to do the single pilot show; the other episodes took five days. (I learned much later that *Friends* would do a show in two or three days, same with *Will & Grace*, including read-throughs. So it was really two and a quarter days' actual work per episode. Were we idiots?) I'd often lose six or eight pounds during my first month back because I was moving all day, with only about fifteen minutes to sit down at lunch.

With all that pressure, the cast and I were constantly pulling practical jokes on each other to blow off steam. Because we *needed* to blow off steam. At least I did. I was completely juvenile, balancing a bucket of powder on top of Murphy's door so it would dump on Barnet's head; of course it fell on someone else. We'd go at each other with Super Soakers. Once we had a Silly String attack, which aggrieved one of our writers, a complete health nut, who complained that he'd been covered in "highly toxic" material. In one script, Chris Rich, who played the preternaturally handsome journalist Miller Redfield for a three-show arc, was supposed to run around the back of an elevator on the *FYI* set. I inveigled Larry, our prop guy, to build a wall of cartons so Chris would have to crash through it, for which I received a well-earned "Candice, fuck you!" The camera crew, the part of the crew we were closest with since we worked with them two days a week, were all fantastic guys. Funny, smart, hard-working—and a great audience for some of our bawdier moments. I would routinely flip the camera guys off; that was just my hello of the day. Bobby Pastorelli called me his "Little Pap Smear." (I called him my "Little Scrotum.")

Grant and I would always break each other up. One Friday shoot night, the script had Murphy in a minimum security prison for not revealing her journalism source. I was knitting an endless scarf in a seedy robe. Miles Silverberg arrives to visit Murphy, who looks up and asks, "Grandpa, is that you?" It took us twenty minutes to get through it without laughing.

Joe Regalbuto launched his career as a director

with an episode of *Murphy Brown*. During rehearsals, his director's note to me was, "Just have fun with it," which is the lamest, most cliché direction you can give. On shoot night of his directorial debut, I sent for Joe to come to my trailer. It was urgent. He opened the door to find me writhing and moaning on my couch. "Joe," I gasped. "I'm so sorry, but I've gotten a stomach flu. I don't think I can make it." He blanched, grabbed his head, and said, "Oh my God! Oh my God! This is terrible! What can we do? What do you need?" At which point I held up a sign that said, JUST HAVE FUN WITH IT, ASSHOLE!

A few years into the show, the entire cast, crew, and writers were told to appear at a conference room during lunch break. Some 150 people were gathered when in swept this corporate lawyer wearing a cloak of gravitas like the Emperor Ming in *Flash Gordon*—authority personified. Sexual harassment lawsuits were flaring into fashion and everyone was suing their bosses for real and imagined improprieties, overstepping the line routinely. It was irrelevant if you trusted your regular coworkers. But if someone new to the cast or crew heard inappropriate language on the set, they could report you. "Once someone files a claim, you're toast," he told us. He was deadly serious, very savvy, and knew he was addressing comedy writers about a topic that was their bread and butter. If a man told a woman that she looked nice in that blouse, for example, he said, that's all you needed to bring a lawsuit. The temperature lowered about thirty degrees. The lawyer made it clear that the boundaries had little wiggle room. We felt like we were being punished for a crime we hadn't committed.

That meeting put a huge dent in the free-wheeling atmosphere on set. I switched to flipping the camera guys off with my index finger, which was worse, but nobody knew.

As the show skyrocketed in popularity, every-one would be recognized on the street except for Grant, who in real life didn't look like a nebbish or wear glasses. In fact, the glasses so defined his part that the writers made him wear them for Monday table reads so they could see the character. Grant and Joe were pals. Whenever they'd go out together, everyone would recognize Joe—"Hey, Frank, how ya doing?"— and ignore Grant. "I feel like his little gay lover," he moaned, because without his navy blazer, khakis, and tortoise-shelled glasses, he was a completely different guy.

Besides my mother, brother, and great friend Connie, the people on *Murphy Brown* were my support system. The crew I loved. They were the nicest, most cheerful, smart, hardest-working crew, and every morning you'd walk into this vast cocoon of people. I'd always conveniently forget that their livelihood depended on me, but they always seemed so happy to see me and I was especially close to the cast; we even took ski trips together.

Bob Daly and Terry Semel were the heads of the studio while I was there. Bob Daly and I had an annual lunch in the commissary. I loved working at Warner Bros. It was a huge, historic studio lot with beautiful gardens and fountains and an ethic of hard work and generosity. Our stage was across the street from Clint Eastwood's office bungalow. It was strongly advised not to park in his parking space. He was known to pull up, see his personal space taken (usually temporarily by a messenger, poor bastard), fish out a baseball bat, smash the window, then leave a check to reimburse the driver for replacing it.

A few years later, *ER* moved into the stage on our corner. They had Krispy Kreme doughnuts flown in from somewhere. This was a perk we envied. But our schedule was infinitely better. Hour-long shows like *ER* are almost unbearable in the length of their days, which can run to sixteen or eighteen hours for the crews. As the season progressed, crew members just willed themselves to get through each day.

We had a magnificent craft service on the *Murphy* set, where the food was spread out for the cast and crew. It was, unfortunately, right in front of my trailer, which meant I fell into the doughnuts whenever I came in or out. Whenever Faith wasn't there to police my eating, I'd whip up my favorite doughnut combo: a cinnamon sugar doughnut, cut in half horizontally and then popped in the toaster oven until the sugar started to caramelize and the top was crispy and golden brown.

For the ten years I did that show, my life revolved around a darkened sound stage. It was like living in a cushy Habitrail. During the winter months, I'd arrive in the morning and when I'd come out to go home, it would be dark. I was so focused on the work, I wasn't even aware of the impact it had on me. Despite the fact that *Murphy Brown* revolved around a newsmagazine, it was a struggle to keep up with current events. I'd carry the *New York Times Book Review* back and forth on the plane between LA and New York and never read it. I was lucky to read a magazine, much less a book. I was very conscious that my frame of reference had shrunk. I was out of the loop at dinner parties.

Yet there was such reassurance in having a steady job. You'd know in May if the show was going to be picked up for the next season. For me, having a young child, the job security was incredible. And I never wanted it to end; doing *Murphy Brown* was insanely fun. When the writing was good, as it was for the first years of *Murphy* and on and off after, it was a giddy, joyous experience. I was the most comfortable and confident I'd ever been. The part was a godsend—an absolutely fantastic role that completely suited me. To spend five days a week with people you loved being with, doing work you always dreamt of doing, and having it so well received was really a dream. My friends were all happy for me; it was unusual for a woman my age to get that role and that success.

Our guest stars were actors with distinguished classical careers who could also do comedy with ease and skill, legendary actors such as Colleen Dewhurst, who played Murphy's mom, Avery. We had *huge* guest stars, like Elizabeth Taylor, Julia Roberts, Bette Midler, John F. Kennedy Jr., Rosie O'Donnell, Martin Sheen. Julia Roberts played herself in the penultimate episode, confessing an unrequited crush on Frank Fontana. Bette played one of Murphy's many secretaries. Even the actors playing small parts on the show were insanely talented. It was humbling because every actor who was hired to do even a few lines was vastly over-qualified. They sang like birds. They danced like gods. They hit a joke out of the park. These people could act and dance and sing circles around me, yet they were mostly unemployed; jobs were hard to come by.

In Season 3, Aretha Franklin, the Queen of Soul herself, came on the show. Aretha doesn't fly; she drove with her entourage in her bus from Detroit to New York City, where we mocked up a set to look like the *FYI* studio. In the scene, she looks Murphy up and down dismissively. I sat on a piano bench next to her and chimed in while she played and sang "Natural Woman." For me, this was an exquisite blend of thrill and terror. She finished her anthem, said good-bye, boarded her bus, and left. She said very little; she was, after all, The Queen.

In 2012, when I was in a play on Broadway, I was in Orso having supper and Aretha arrived, followed by her retinue. She crossed the room slowly, like a ship of state, as people froze with their forks in midair. I gave her a big grin; she nodded regally and swept past. But Aretha, it's me!

A running joke on the show was that Murphy was such a horrific boss to work for that every week they'd have to find her a new secretary. Sally Field played a memory-challenged secretary. Paul Reubens—aka Pee-wee Herman—played a conniving secretary lured away by the end of the episode to a studio position. Craig Bierko, a bona fide Broadway star and my future *Boston Legal* costar, led the band of former secretaries who kidnapped Murphy Brown and held her for a ransom no one paid. Annabelle Gurwitch played an Eliza Doolittle secretary à la *My Fair Lady*. Michael Richards channeled his Kramer from *Seinfeld* to take his position behind the desk.

When Murphy was briefly jailed for refusing to reveal a source, she was made a secretary to the prison warden—and naturally proved to be a lousy one. Every now and then I'll work with someone and they'll tell me, "I was Secretary 34" or "I played the Hitler secretary." Bette Midler played Murphy's ninety-third and final secretary.

Early in our relationship, Louis and I had decided that I would never star in one of his films. Marriage was demanding enough; we feared the demands of a director on an actress would be asking too much of a marriage. I knew he respected the work I was doing on the show. I still have the envelope on which he scrawled, "My darling, I love you, I love you, I love you. And I am fiercely proud of your talent. Le monkey." I was delighted when Louis agreed to star in a single episode of *Murphy Brown* during Season 6. The writers came up with this idea: Murphy has decided to play a "small but pivotal role" in Louis Malle's new film. She then storms the set to insist on changes to protect her "journalistic integrity." Louis loved the idea and wrote the producers: "Thank you for a very funny scene, very well written. I'll do my best not to embarrass you guys—and the wife. As far as I am concerned, I am beyond ridicule." He flew in from Paris two days before to do it. He was very game about learning his lines on the plane but arrived exhausted and completely jet-lagged.

Everybody on the show had great respect and affection for Louis. I tried to get him to relax for his line readings and in the end he was great. At the end of the scene, Murphy asks, "Are you *firing* me?" "Bingo," Louis says. Murphy stalks off, and Louis proclaims, "What a nightmare. Can you imagine being married to that woman?" He got a huge laugh.

Even though a half-hour, four-camera show is the best TV schedule, it's all-consuming. From the second we started the season to the day we wrapped to go on hiatus, it was like getting on a train you couldn't get off. One week off a month wasn't enough to get over the depth of exhaustion. I spent every moment of that week volunteering at Chloe's school, catching up with friends, and going to doctor's appointments. Sometimes I'd fly to New York to give dinners with old friends at my apartment: John Guare and Adele Chatfield-Taylor, Bette Midler and Martin von Haselberg, Richard Avedon.

We'd wrap the season at the end of March and have four months off; production on the new season began at the end of July. During my time off, Louis, Chloe, and I would go to Paris and Le Coual. The French didn't understand or like Murphy. She was loud and bossy, unfeminine. She was American. Frenchwomen have a mystery about them and are much more veiled in their strength. It would be very unusual for a French-woman to raise her voice or lose control. They behave with dignity at all times until they implode and collapse. Murphy would yell and have tantrums. She made her position known.

I was overwhelmed when I got nominated for an Emmy that first year, having grown so accustomed to critical abuse. Would people be voting for my leap into the comedy void? My willingness to appear foolish, brassy, imposing, pushy?

I'd won the Golden Globe a few months earlier. I was wearing my friend Ali MacGraw's black strapless Halston. In those days you didn't have stylists; people didn't give you clothes—you winged it. I wore my friend Anne Sterling's pearl choker. For the Emmys, I was looking through *Town & Country* and I spotted a Bill Blass dress that I thought would be great. It was a strapless gown with a top in muted metallic gold and the bottom was metallic leopard print. It was a stunning, simple dress. I called Bill, whom I'd known socially for years, and he connected me with his PR people. As it happened, the sample size fit me. Those were the days. The hair and makeup people got me in drag. I had written a short speech because I believe in preparing for those shows. It's self-indulgent not to—spare us. When they announced my name, I told the audience, "Call it karma, call it kismet, but it's all Diane English."

When I got home the night I won the Emmy, I put the statuette on the chest at the foot of the bed. It was mine, all mine. I brought it to work the next day. The writers were all wearing T-shirts that said SWAT TEAM because in my acceptance speech, I'd thanked "our SWAT team of writers." It took a couple of days for the atmosphere with the cast to right itself, because we all knew I shouldn't have won this thing. The cast knew my shortcomings; they were limitless.

Congratulations poured in from friends and coworkers, but the letter I treasured most came from Kris:

So My Pal,

To keep it brief, I honestly never had a doubt but now that it's official, congratulations (with tears in my eyes). Your little brother loves you more than any other could love his big sister. You now have your Emmy and as I sit here with Chloe sleeping in my arms watching *Sleeping Beauty* I realize that you have it all and always have.

> I love you my pal
> Unk Zoo

After the first Emmy, my management wasn't happy about my salary, which was very low that

185

first year. While I'd signed a contract with Warner Bros. agreeing not to renegotiate for two years, my agent urged noncompliance. My lawyer complained to me, "You're not crazy enough. It always goes better when the client is crazy and won't show up for work."

I was amused when *Star Magazine* ran a story about my alleged contract demands:

> Candice Bergen has given producers her list of requirements for staying on *Murphy Brown* next season—and a chef who will make her favorite chili every day tops the list. "Chili is Candy's favorite food, and she gets really upset when it's not there," says a set insider. "She yells during a rehearsal or taping, 'Where's my chili?' if something else is being served. She's been running over to the *Maverick* set next door and eating their chili," adds the insider. . . . "And Candice has demanded, in return for signing a new contract with the show, that she gets chili all the time."

Chili aside, not to show up would be a breach of contract. I couldn't do that to the cast or the crew. What I valued most were my relationships on the set; I loved those people and I couldn't imagine pulling a diva. In ten years, I was never *late* for work, much less absent. I always scheduled getting sick on my off week. I'm always surprised when actors don't show up as a renegotiation ploy; it seems like such a betrayal, but it always works. Not my style. In any case, I was very well paid after the first two years when my contract came up for renewal.

I won the Emmy the second year as well. Then the fourth. Then two more, making it five, the most for one person for playing the same role in Emmy history. Paul "Pee-wee Herman" Reubens sent me a telegram: "You must be running out of mantel space. Congratulations!" In 1995, after seven years on the show, I withdrew my name from competition in part because Helen Hunt was starring in *Mad About You* and she deserved to win. I could also sense a shift, a slightly veiled hostility emanating from the Emmy audience every time I won after that first year. *Her again?* But the real reason was the damage it did to my relationships on the set. The Monday after my fifth Emmy, everyone was very reserved. The cast was distant and polite. Normally, our rapport was fantastic—bawdy, raunchy, affectionate. For about a week, shields went up. It was an ensemble cast, we worked together and we worked hard, yet I was the one getting the recognition. In some fairness to myself, I was not only in every scene, I was the *engine* of the scene, driving it, so it was a lot to manage. Learning the lion's share of the lines, nailing the performance level. (Whenever I suggested they give me a scene off, the answer was always "No. The show is called *Murphy Brown*.") My fellow cast members, whom I loved, were equally if not more deserving, but they were generally not nominated. It was awkward.

After a couple of years, I stole a sign—CAMP NACEWSEY ("Yes We Can" spelled backward)—from a show about some corporate retreat and hung it over the sofa in my Warner Bros. dressing room.

"Yes We Can." A lovely slogan. And we did.

⚜ 10 ⚜

I continued to marvel at the intensity of Chloe's desire to grow herself up. She was easily frustrated until she got to the age when she was able to express herself. Once she'd drawn something, a furious scrawl. "Yook!" she said, handing it proudly to me.

"Oh, honey, what is it, a salad?"

"It's a EAGLE," she said indignantly, taking it back.

I loved reading to Chloe. Once she was struggling to pronounce *The Wind in the Willows*, which we were reading at the time. "Da Windizza Wizzle" was the best she could manage. It was agitating to her; you could see that her brain was far ahead of her motor skills, and for years she couldn't articulate her thoughts. She was fiercely focused on mastering communication skills, keenly proud when she prevailed. Her strength of will and drive to succeed were moving to me. Enid Blyton's Famous Five books were later favorites, as was Roald Dahl's *BFG*. (We still call farts "whizzpoppers.")

As she got older and better able to articulate things, her frustration subsided. I recorded her progress in my journal:

Jan '89 LA

Chloe is now four. We talk about "stuff" now. Stories. The past. Le Coual. Always Le Coual. Me and Kris in Africa. In Yosemite. And she inevitably asks, "Was I there?"

"No, you weren't born yet."

"Where was I?"

A pause. "You were waiting. You were a star in the sky waiting to come to us."

A pause. She is chewing on that one. "I want my pa [which is what she called her pacifier]."

Another time. Again. "Was I there?"

"No, not yet. It was long before you were born."

"Where was I?"

Okay, here goes. "Chloe, it's difficult to explain."

She stares out the car window, frowning in thought. "Maybe someone else knows."

I consult a friend, Georgeann, a supermom. "What do I say here?"

"Tell her she was a dream in your heart."

"Okay, that's very nice but I don't think she'll buy it."

"Was I there?"

"No, not yet. It was long before you were born."

"Where was I?"

"You were a dream in my heart."

Beat. "But where *was* I?"

Jan '89 LA

Chloe trying on my heels, my sweater, clomping in the shoes, the sweater trailing like a train. "They fit!" she shouts. The power struggle begins. "Now, I'm the mommy and you're the baby. . . ."

July '89 Le Coual

I have never pushed her. I have tried desperately to hang onto the now occasional mispronunciations: "Foon" for "spoon." "Weeb" for "leaf." "Yat" for "that." "Gigynic" for "gigantic." But she is also saying things like, "Then I realized it was complicated." Furrowing her brow, frowning in effort to remember a word—"What's yat word? Jealous!"

She has become a fashion maven, looking at *Cinderella* and *Gigi* for the long dresses. "She looks beautiful in yat dress, but I'm *not* happy she's wearing gloves." Fairy tales have become mere fashion vehicles. When she was two, she waddled up to me, reached toward my face, and said, "I *love* your earrings!"

She surprises me with a broad Southern accent from time to time. "Ah think we'ah gonna have a lil pahty."

Chloe began to accumulate nicknames: Le French Fry. The Peach Pit. Poochnik. Mike Nichols, her godfather, dubbed her Clovis. When Chloe's inevitable princess phase hit, I bought big sheets of white poster board; one of the few things I can do is draw. We'd sit at the table on the patio and I'd draw princesses to order: "Hair up or down?" "Braid or chignon?" There was always a crown. "Do you want the dress to be strapless? Long sleeves? Puff sleeves? What color?" Pink with turquoise was the usual choice. I'd draw it, she'd paint it. We'd glue on decorations—hard candies and mini-marshmallows on the skirt with feathers, sequins, and glitter—then cut them out. It was our Saturday project.

She reads every book on Cinderella, but only for the fashion. She loves long ball gowns. She designs them, makes them on her Barbie.

She tells stories of princesses and princes that are only about what they wear. There is no suggestion of plot. "The prince was wearing a gold T-shirt, and gold tights and shoes." "Princess Aurora was wearing a gold dress covered with marshmallows and lollipops and chocolate candy and sash-fires."

"Sash-fires?"

"The blue stones," she said. Duh. "What are the green ones?" she asked.

"Emeralds."

"Yes, and emeralds and rubies and did I forget anything?"

"Lollipops?"

"I said lollipops. Oh—pearls! And she had a gold crown and rubies stuck to her head with lots of tiny sticky pieces of tape."

Chloe was always a great traveler, thank god, and she loved LA from the start. We visited often, because my family and so many of my friends were there. Whenever we were in town, we'd stay at Carrie Fisher's house, a whimsical log house set in an oak forest. I'd known Carrie since she was eight years old because she used to live next door to my friend Connie, who used to babysit her. Carrie's mom, Debbie Reynolds, had married Harry Karl, and they had a huge house in Beverly Hills that looked like a mausoleum. We'd go over there for dinner and Carrie would always be in her room reading.

Carrie's house was the perfect house for kids. It had a swing in the master bedroom, a parrot named Joan, and a Jack Russell terrier named Buddy. She had her own skee-ball machine. Chloe thought Carrie's house *was* California, and she always wanted to go there. "Califoooornia doing?" she'd ask repeatedly.

It was wonderful being back with Mom and Kris. Becoming a grandmother transformed my mom. I used to call my grandmother Nana. Kris called her Nanoo, and as she got crazier and crazier, I started calling her Bananoo. Chloe called my mother Franoo, for Frances. Mom assumed an Auntie Mame persona—the furthest thing from who she was. Her instincts were great with my whirlwind daughter. She'd pick us up at the airport and say, "Let's stop at the park so she can burn off some steam." She never lost her temper with Chloe. She bought her wonderful clothes and sometimes we'd dress for tea. Mom would arrive with a big lavender picture hat and gloves and pearls. I'd put on a hat with a veil and Delia, Chloe's nanny, would serve scones and jam and tea out on the patio. We were high-toned ladies who held our teacups with two fingers and spoke with veddy English accents. Chloe adored it and so did we.

On shoot nights, which were Fridays and went late, Chloe would stay in the guest room at Mom's. They'd have sleepovers where Mom would put on old mambo and cha-cha records and show Chloe the steps. She'd take out her vintage hats, black mink muffs, and costume jewelry and they'd play dress-up.

Kris—aka "Unka Zoo"—immediately stepped in as a surrogate father for Chloe in Louis's frequent absences. He showed no restraint. Of course, Chloe loved Barbies and she had quite a collection. My brother, however, raised the Barbie bar one Christmas when he went to Toys-R-Us and got Chloe two special edition Bob Mackie Barbies. They were "special" because they wore outfits designed by costume designer Bob Mackie himself and some of the outfits were inspired by the beaded, theatrical numbers he created for Cher in her concert act. In other words, these Barbies were every American girl's or drag queen's dream. The Barbies kept coming in; I found fuchsia and purple Barbie stilettos in every jacket pocket. We had all the hideous fuchsia furniture; we even had a pink Barbie plane. Once when Chloe was cradling the dolls in her arms, stroking their towering chignons, I asked her what she was going to name these new additions to her Barbie family. She stared ahead solemnly, then announced, "Ontasha and Herbin."

I got Chloe a bright yellow fighter jet as a corrective. It didn't take.

The year Chloe started preschool, the *Exxon Valdez* had its huge oil spill in Prudhoe Bay, Alaska. I told Chloe about it on the way to school. She listened with her focused, furrowed brow and then went into her classroom and got up in front of her grade and fervently told everyone about the environmental disaster. Then she burst into tears.

One morning I came in to wake Chloe after she'd been up most of the night sick. I asked her if she wanted to stay home. She stretched her arms in the air and said, "No! I am the Mighty One! I CAN DO IT!"

The first couple of years of *Murphy*, Chloe visited the set only two or three times. I deliberately kept work and home separate; I didn't want my daughter to have that sense of entitlement that was common to kids of celebrities. Chloe thought I worked in an office with a lot of cameras. Her only question about work was why everyone had different names on and off the job. We never watched the show together. Whenever she walked by the TV while Louis and I were watching the show, she just assumed it was home movies from work. (In fact, Chloe still has seen only the rare episode. She was an early *Lucy* convert and stayed that way.) In her prekindergarten class, when the teacher asked the kids what their mommies did, Chloe replied, "She's just my mommy."

Louis was there for Chloe's first family picnic at school. It was totally exotic to him. One father came up, slapped him on the back, and said, "Hi, I'm Bart, I'm head of Indian Princesses Club"—a kind of Brownies offshoot—"and I want to know if you want to bring Chloe on a father-daughter camping trip." Louis looked at him blankly; he knew more about *East* Indians. After that, I usually went alone to parent-teacher conferences and other school functions, or I brought Kris with me.

The next year was kindergarten. On Parents Night we all filed in and sat on the little chairs. It was just after the United States had launched its war against Iraq, and as the teacher began to describe the children's curriculum for that year, I raised my hand, ever the firebrand, and asked if she'd be teaching the kids about the Gulf War. There was a collective gasp as the other parents looked at me with horror. The teacher paled and said softly, "We're working on colors."

In the lower grades, parental participation was encouraged, and I encountered the Special Forces Moms. These were another, hardier breed of moms; everything became an Op. They had multiple kids, they drove vans, they made crafts, they baked cakes. The only thing they didn't do was humor. They took their job as moms with deadly seriousness. Otherwise, how would they get it all done? They wore functional clothes, flat shoes, bobbed hair, no makeup. In November, they bore down the path with trays of cupcakes decorated (by them) with turkeys, Pilgrims, and pumpkins. They walked fast, briskly; they were not to be trifled with. They waited in car pool lines with thermoses and yogurts and takeout salads. They wasted no time; they were hard-core. They were pros.

There were other breeds of mom in LA as well. The perfectly made-up, bed-head, Spandex-legginged, designer cross trainer–wearing kind. The hungry, recently divorced kind. And they were on the hunt. They were fully enhanced and injected, their pouts preceded them by a few inches, coming from or going to the gym. Their school project was Husband #2.

I worried about Chloe growing up in the culture—or lack of it—of LA. In second grade, Chloe had to write a tiny paragraph about what she wanted to be when she grew up. I looked at the other essays on the bulletin board. "I want to have a Corvette." "I want to have a really nice car." "I want to live in Vegas." "I want beautiful clothes." How do you keep the LA insanity to a low hum?

Louis and I tried to keep Chloe grounded. We took her to one five-year-old's party in Beverly Hills. The parents had bought a snow machine, covered the lawn in snow, and given the little guests hats and mittens. The fanciest party we ever did for Chloe was her sixth, when we took Chloe and her friends to Disney Studios for a private screening of *Snow White*. We went back to our house for lunch on the patio, and a young woman dressed as Snow White appeared and played with the girls.

Chloe was never taken to public events, except for the opening of *The Little Mermaid* at El Capitan Theatre on Hollywood Boulevard, which had been restored and opened for the occasion. There was a stage show before the screening with sparkling, dancing mermaids and lobsters. I almost wept at how excited Chloe was. We got tons of invitations to events, but Chloe never even knew about them. I think, for all the time we spent in LA, she was photographed once. I knew that kind of attention spun children's heads around because I'd had it with my father. It turned kids into spoiled, attention-craving critters. It was not healthy for children and we tried to avoid it.

⁓{ 11 }⁓

It was autumn. Chloe and I headed home to New York for Thanksgiving week. That's when I had a vision that we needed a cat. Chloe should have an animal in her life.

Perhaps because I was an only child who lived on top of a mountain above Beverly Hills and used to play by myself, I'd take my dogs everywhere—we'd hike the hills, make forts, I'd use my slingshot. My best friends were dogs. How people do or don't relate to dogs says a lot to me. I feel sorry for the ones who don't; I think they're missing a huge part of their own humanity. If someone is really squeamish around dogs—"Get it away!"—it's hard for me to get over that. When Chloe was only months old, I'd push her in her stroller in the park and get down on my knees at the sight of anything at the end of a leash. "Look, Chloe, it's a *dog!*" She was programmed from the start.

Now Chloe had just turned four. Enough of my begging dog owners to stop for a second so we could pat their dog. Enough of "renting" Carrie Fisher's Jack Russell terrier, Buddy. My mission was for her to bond with animals—that's a spiritual hallmark.

Getting a pet while we lived in LA was pure

provocation. I was subversively planting a flag, making a statement that we'd be staying a while now that *Murphy Brown* was shooting. Chloe had a half brother and half sister, but she was essentially an only child; I wanted to enhance our family presence in LA.

Our building in New York didn't allow dogs, but a cat was doable. Besides, Louis wasn't at all a dog guy; I tried not to hold this against him. I went to look for an Abyssinian cat; I knew they were the most doglike of felines. There was a pet store on the Upper East Side that specialized in exotic cats, so I went to see what they had. The shop was quirky—filled with cats all roaming free, climbing, grooming, clawing, stalking, doing their cat stuff. I looked around, talked to the owner, and left. Two doors down was another pet store; I couldn't resist. I walked in and that is when I found Lois.

Lois was a random mix of basset hound and some kind of wire-haired terrier. She'd come from a farm in Pennsylvania; she should have been a rescue. She was *the* cutest puppy I'd ever seen. She was irresistible. In no time she was mine. I bought her for $300, grabbed her, and hopped in a cab home. This was insane from every angle. Not only were dogs not allowed in our building; we were flying back to LA in a few days. Who was going to take care of a PUPPY!!?? What was I thinking?

I enclosed Lois in our little kitchen. That afternoon, when Chloe came home with Ingrid, her nanny, I said, "I have a surprise for you!" and brought her into the kitchen where Lois wriggled. "Her name is Lois," I said. There'd been a *Murphy* episode with a character named Lois. *What a great name for a dog,* I thought.

Chloe looked stunned. Overwhelmed. "Could we call her Lois*ina?*" She wanted to feminize the name.

"Of course," I said.

Chloe then shortened the puppy's name to Seener. I always called her Lois.

A few days later we put Lois in a crate and flew back to LA on MGM Grand. MGM Grand was a tiny, high-end airline that had only two planes that went between LA and NYC. The cabin was designed in Art Deco, all dove grays and lavenders. There was a bar and a lounge in the front, faux Lalique glass dividers, plus a few comfy seats. There were four individual cabins with four seats that could be made into beds; you could pull the curtains and have total privacy. Lois flew with Chloe and me in our cabin. Passengers peeked in to see Lois, saying, "That is *the* cutest puppy!"

Of course, it was chaos. One morning, I had dressed Chloe for school and given her breakfast. We were about to leave when Lois got out the door and fell into the shallow end of the pool. I jumped in with my flannel slacks and tasseled loafers and pulled her out. That was a late morning.

Nobody knew that Lois would grow into a sixty-pound dog with no legs. She resembled a furry stretch limo, her back built like a swaying suspension bridge. She was a pistol as a puppy, into everything, a real terror. She chewed the table legs; I had to wrap them. She made simply eating a potato chip hysterical. She'd fly on the Warner jet, delicately nibbling salmon on bites of bagel. On landing, she had to back out of the plane because it was too narrow for her to turn around in.

Lois was indeed Chloe's sibling growing up. She'd never jump up on Chloe when she was little, innately respectful of her small size. She loved children and was very protective of Chloe and her friends. They hung out together constantly, and Lois accompanied Kris and Chloe on hikes. She was the most affectionate dog with the best sense of humor and she loved to sit in your lap, although lifting her up wasn't easy. She was the perfect companion.

Every day around four, Lois would go into the living room and camp out by the front door to wait for Chloe to come home from school: this was her purpose in life. One evening as Chloe was taking her dish to the sink, I caught her casually flipping a half-eaten slice of pizza into Lois's bowl. As if. Another time I wrapped a leftover piece of steak in Saran wrap with a Post-it on which I'd written, "Steak for Lois or Chloe." To this day, Chloe has not forgiven me my sense of priority.

Lois gave huge hellos. Huge. You could have gone to the market for a quart of milk, but when you got back, she would sob and weep and wail for ten minutes. She was a big talker, very vocal. She would jump into the armchair where you had settled and put her paws on your shoulders, looking at the ceiling while you scratched her chest. Then she would moan. Indifference was not part of her doggy DNA.

There was a big, comfy armchair in the bedroom; it was Lois's. No one else's. If someone came to the house for the first time and sat in Lois's chair, she would sit and stare at you until you were asked to please move to the other, less comfortable chair. Lois, being so low to the ground, found the height of the chair daunting. She would first stand in front of it in contemplation, then slowly rock back and forth to launch herself up into it. She would then circle a couple of times to flatten the cushion, and finally, with a huge sigh of relief, lie down. She'd sleep lying upside down on her back, with her head hanging backward over the edge of the chair. Her lips would fall away from her mouth, revealing her teeth and gums, her ears dangling like furry pendants. People spotting her in this position for the first time were sure she had died.

When Louis was away, Chloe would sleep in my bed. In the morning, on the weekends, Chloe and I would snuggle in bed and Lois would jump up and wail her morning greeting. Then we would bring breakfast on trays and have breakfast in bed and watch Disney cartoons. The perfect morning.

On Valentine's Day, Lois trotted around with a heart sticker Chloe had stuck on her forehead. Another day, Chloe painted eyebrows above her eyes and emerald earrings on her ears.

Lois loved snow. After a few inches of fresh powder in Sun Valley, she could be tracked by the tip of her tail trotting down the drive. The rest of her was invisible. When Chloe was ice skating, Lois bounded onto the rink and followed her around until she was evicted. That was probably the only time a dog had been on that ice rink.

Early on in our Lois-ship, I spotted Lois happily chugging down the hall with chunks of fur missing from her back. She was followed by Chloe holding her play scissors in one hand and batches of hair in the other.

"What's happening?" I asked.

"We're doing the letter *F* at school," Chloe proudly said, holding up her hand. "Fuh, fuh, FUR!!!" She brought it to school in a baggie the next day as a phonetic example.

Connie and Chloe were walking Lois up a little street in our neighborhood. Chloe and Lois disappeared for a minute. When they came back, Connie asked Chloe, "Did Lois do caca?"

"Yes!" Chloe said. "And so did I!"

"Oh God, no," Connie moaned. "Where!"

"In yat yard!"

We accumulated cats because we lived up in the hills where unwanted cats or kittens were often abandoned. Soon they were ours and became Lucy and Ethel, Fred and Furball, and Pearl. I don't generally love cats, but they hold my interest; they add texture to a home. Not many cats have a sense of humor, but the ones that do, I love. I'd come home wired from work and need to decompress. I'd flop on the bed, slap a cat onto my stomach, and that took the edge off. Ethel, a big, dumb cat, liked to drink out of the goldfish bowl we kept on the counter in the kitchen, which didn't seem to bother Bergen, the goldfish, but which appalled guests who were eating inches away.

All the cats bonded with Chloe, especially Pearl, our calico rescue, who would run to Chloe's side whenever she cried. Pearl would jump up on her lap, put her paws on Chloe's shoulders, and nuzzle her. Whenever we'd come back after time away, the cats would run to the gate and hug Chloe. Unfortunately, our neighborhood also had coyotes and owls; our cat mortality rate was high.

When Chloe bathed at night, the animals would gather tubside and talk about their day. I would usually come home at this time and we all sat around her in the bath, the cats on the edge of the tub, Lois lying below on the bath mat, communing, while Chloe sang and played.

Chloe and I had established a real beachhead.

❦ 12 ❦

My rising celebrity redefined Louis and me. It changed the weight in our relationship. The elevation of my status after *Murphy Brown* debuted in November 1988 was instantaneous. A month later, Louis and I went to a press screening. Louis was tense. Dark. Oppressive. A black hole sucking in everything in its path. There was a line of photographers. Louis scowled, pretended not to hear people. He took offense at imaginary slights. "They were talking to *you,* not me. They don't even see me." I vowed never to go to an event again with him. It was too tough. Too tense.

We went home and I reheated a dinner. Then I forgot the drink I'd gone to get him. I quickly laid the table. Louis deserved better. Is this one of the ways I might lose him? Would I look back and say, "If only I'd cooked more. If only I'd taken more care."

So, suddenly, I roused myself, hoping it wasn't too late. I made meals, organized dinners at home with friends; I took more care.

Before *Murphy Brown*, people would ask Louis, "Why don't you and Candy work together?" Afterward they would say, "I don't think you can afford her." Louis knew that *Murphy Brown* was a dream job for me. He was so proud; he'd read the script and found it extremely well written, perfect for me. He knew it would be a strain on us, obviously, but he knew I had to do it. I think he hoped the pilot wouldn't be picked up.

Certainly we never predicted how difficult the show would be for us. The first five years of our marriage worked wonderfully because it was just the two of us. He was always great about reporting in if he was going to be late. He was really present, and we were very much in love.

Then I had Chloe, and she became the love of my life. I was obsessed. In a sense, I'd betrayed him. I had fallen in love with someone else and it was head over heels. Then I took on an almost full-time job, which restricted us even more. Louis now had a newly successful wife . . . and less of her attention. His letters expressed love, pride, and ambivalence.

My darling,

This is just to tell you how much I miss you, how much I miss *la petite crétine*. After this great great summer we spent together, it is very hard for me to think of life without the 2 of you. Most of last winter we were together and now I am looking to the next months of separation, split by these occasional visits, with fear and some anguish.

There is nothing we can do about it, it's just hard, much harder than 2 years ago, I don't know why. Yes, I know why. Our bond, between the 3 of us, is getting so strong, I feel like something essential of myself is missing when I am away from you.

I want to work faster and come back to you as quickly as possible as often as possible. I want to work with you. I want to get up in the morning, close to you, against you in the bed, then get Chloe her breakfast and have those great chats with her.

I love you,

L

My tidy, organized husband was tired of dog hair all over his jackets, of cats popping out of closets and showers. "What is happening?" he pleaded. It's a long flight from Paris to LA, and he'd be exhausted. His first words would be, "How long are you going to be doing this?"

My darling,

I was so sad to leave and didn't know how to deal with it. I wanted to hold you in my arms but didn't want to give you my cold. Well, it's all been difficult and confusing and messy, but remember that we are so well together sometimes and if it's difficult, it's because I miss you very much when I am away and even when we are together sometimes. When your season is over, when I'll be less tense about the future, we will have great time together again. I had a good time these past 2 weeks, and it has been tough to pack again. That's all. I love you.

Louis was perpetually on Paris time; I was on LA time. It took a week for us to get on the same schedule, and by that time, he'd be on his way back to France. It was asking too much. Louis and I both recognized that it was the perfect solution for Chloe to be where her grandmother and uncle were, to have LA as a home base. We felt torn. Louis wanted us all to move to Paris, where Justine and Louis's family were. I couldn't bear the thought of being away from my family in LA.

Murphy also gave me a sense of self-definition. In April 1989, the end of the show's first season, Chloe and I flew to New York; I was finished with the show until the end of July or early August.

I immediately fell into a depression. It was disorienting to suddenly not be working. To have little but free time where, days ago, I didn't have a second. And I missed the people on the show, the energy, the drive and camaraderie. I missed the work and what the work made me into: an energetic, accomplished, successful, funny, self-confident *(newly* self-confident) woman. I missed Murphy.

I was ashamed at the debt I owed to the show and my dependency on it. I was amazed at the incredible luck of it. For two weeks I was restless, edgy, at sea. Then I readjusted.

A good part of this depression seemed to fasten on to the desire to have another child. My forty-second birthday was days away. If, in fact, it was still possible, this was the last possible time. I was getting fixated. I couldn't do it, I knew. On many counts. I didn't have enough time now; it was all I could do to return phone calls, much less have a baby.

It would torpedo the show, no question.

I was jealous of pregnant women, women with big families, with small babies. Chloe was now a little girl—every day more articulate and self-possessed. I saw how soon it would pass, and I hated it.

I was weeding out her baby things—books and toys and clothes and potties. I couldn't yet face taking out the crib. I could hardly bear to throw anything away at all. Stubbornly I hung on to a few outfits I had had when I was pregnant. Who knew? It was impossible but still . . .

I got up the nerve to talk to Louis about it—how sad I was not to have another, how Chloe was growing up. I burst into tears immediately, and to my surprise he agreed. "It would be great. *She* is so great." His sadness showed at Justine and Cuote being grown and almost gone. In a minute, Chloe would be too. He'd thought about it, often.

This was a great comfort and relief, and for a moment I was ecstatic at the notion of having another baby. Then the practical came into play. After all, it was only when I had some free time after seven months of *no* free time that I thought about it. It was only when I was, for once, not bone-tired that I could imagine as much. This was, in part, a hysterical pregnancy of the recently unemploycd.

Two years later, the *National Enquirer* ran a headline blaring, "Candice Bergen Baby Crisis." Inside was the "untold story" of "Candice Bergen's Heartache: She Can't Have Another Baby."

> Candice was particularly fond of singing, "I Got You Babe," as she fed Chloe her strained vegetables. . . . Candice's TV bosses have warned her that having a child could wreck her hit show. . . . They told Candice that to change her character, to make Murphy Brown

maternal, just wouldn't work out. It could wreck the show and destroy all that Candice has worked so hard to achieve. Candice was really upset, but she had to agree, revealed some insiders.

Although Candice feels terrible now, friends fear her anguish is going to grow much worse once time completely runs out for her to have a baby . . . friends are worried sick about how she's going to react when her dream finally crumbles to dust.

How wrong they were.

On May 9, my birthday, Chloe, then four, came into the bedroom to explain that she and Poppy had a surprise for me. "It's something you wear on your wrist."

I heard Louis downstairs saying, "Did you tell her the surprise?"

"I didn't tell her it was a *bracelet!*" she said loudly.

Later, Louis and Chloe presented me with a silver Taurus bracelet from Tiffany with "Happy birthday, Mommy, Chloe" engraved inside. I wept.

For the few months in New York between LA and France, I put Chloe into the Lycée Français in New York. There she was, at four years of age, in her uniform: white blouse with a Peter Pan collar, gray pleated skirt, and navy cardigan. Sometimes a yellow slicker. With her hair in its usual pixie cut, she looked enchanting. And after years of watching Lycée students going in and out and thinking if we had a child he or she would probably be a student there, now we did and suddenly *she* was going there—skipping through the mists of Gauloises, past teachers in snoods.

Chloe thrived there, so strong and self-confident. In one week she had five invitations—parties at pony farms, parties at pizza parlors, picnics at the carousel. A typical New York schedule.

One day, I picked her up and she said excitedly, "Mommy, there's a statue of you in the park!"

"What?"

She repeated it. I laughed and let it go. Then, as we headed toward Fifth Avenue, down 72nd Street, she pointed and squealed, "See!"

There, along the side of a bus stop, was a long photo of me, a *Murphy Brown* poster saying, "Who says comedy can't be pretty?"

"I *told* you," she said and skipped along.

Doing *Murphy Brown* was the first time I felt like I'd really won professionally, the first time I'd done one thing for a sustained amount of time. When I guest-hosted *Saturday Night Live* in 1975 and 1976, I thought, what I would give to be in this place where you could really learn to play comedy and the joy that gives you week in, week out. On *Murphy*, that's what I got. Every time the season ended and we'd go on hiatus, like a chameleon, my color would fade and I'd begin to blend into the rocks and all the vibrancy and certitude and hyperconfidence would dissipate over our three months off.

Come June we'd typically head out to Le Coual, where a torpor would generally overtake me. I recorded my malaise in my journal:

Well, here we are again and here I go again, sinking back into my traditional lethargy.

What I come up against, year after year here, is my almost *utter uselessness*. And I think over and over, Bergen women are not made of strong, resourceful stuff.

Mom came to visit for two weeks that summer. I was struck by her slow, endless rhythm. She did *everything* slowly. Eat. Walk. Dress. Get ready. It drove me nuts. She walked around the kitchen singing and weeping along with Sinatra while Ingrid and I fixed dinner. But Mom was a good sport, game for anything. *Et* voilà.

That summer Louis was starting a film, *May Fools*, with a French actress named Miou-Miou.

"Miou-Miou?" my mother said. "Isn't that the French sex kitten?" Great.

It had been almost ten years since we'd gotten married. It seemed a time for vigilance. Louis was trouble. He stayed out of trouble, I'm convinced, for a long time after we were married, but I'd heard stories about him for years before we met— that he would be with one woman but romancing another.

Louis would come home now from location seemingly remote, preoccupied with a strange new sexual energy. Uh-oh. I was tense, ready, antennae up and swiveling, alert to any noises in the forest. *Let's nip this in the bud.* He was distant on the phone—it was his first week shooting— and I could smell it. "How are the actors?" I asked, oh so casually.

"Michel [Piccoli] is great. Miou-Miou is great." Miou-Miou is great. God is great. Ten years are great. Would we see eleven? Why didn't I lose weight? Cook more. Work out. Read. Listen. All the moments I missed living alone, the way I wanted animals, California, work . . . When I faced it all ending, I was struck dumb. Panicked.

The anxiety grew. I was tenser with Louis on the phone. He didn't come home that weekend; he was cutting the film. And although I encouraged him to stay, knew he had a horrible deadline, I resented it, suspected it. The anxiety grew still more. What would I do?

Then Mom and I decided to visit the set, an old farmhouse an hour and a half away. We arrived at lunchtime. The French crew was eating at a long table on the porch. Then, as one, they stopped, turned around, and stared silently as we approached. Nobody spoke, nobody got up. There was a striking shift in the atmosphere. Mom looked at me. The temperature dropped by twenty degrees. Even Louis's brother Vincent, a producer on the movie, behaved bizarrely. Rude. Aloof. It was unbearably uncomfortable. I'd never felt so unwelcome. My stomach sank, the elevator missing the floor. And I knew—they were staring because *they knew*. It was obvious. He was having an affair with his leading lady and the wife had arrived. He was a Frenchman, it was France, such things were accepted.

The next day I visited the set again. I worked in the shadows, spying, scrutinizing every nuance, every peck on the cheek, checking for signs of intimacy. None. Surely he must have had affairs. I could meet him only in New York for one week every month. I think he felt I'd made a life elsewhere, which I had. Of course I felt betrayed, but if I hadn't had so much else in my life, the idea would have eaten at me more. And I'd contributed to the distance between us by falling in love with Chloe.

The next night I confronted Louis on the phone about the remote behavior. The cold, icy reception. Finally: "There's no other explanation than you're having an affair!"

"What!" And Louis exploded with laughter. "*Me!* An affair! I'm fifty-six years old!"

"And who's more attractive?"

"You must be joking!"

Such huffing and puffing. "That's ridiculous!" He denied it vehemently. I was furious to be laughed at in my agony but he couldn't believe my suspicion. He was so convincing in his denial that I believed him.

I was relieved. Deeply. And he explained. "But *you* were tense on the phone, not *me!*"

"I had my mother for two weeks!"

"Well, I knew that was part of it."

And so a narrow miss. Perhaps.

A few months later, on the anniversary of our first date, a letter from Louis:

March 6, 1990

My darling,

This is just to tell you how sorry I am not to be with you the next 17th of March, St. Patrick's Day. I remember the rain, the drunks, the long evening before it finally happened! These 10 years seem like 10 months, we've been through all kinds of moods but it has been great, very great. I feel like I finally got home, you gave me a sense of belonging, our love has been carrying us all along and it seems stronger and better 10 years later. I am hugging you, long and hard, you and our wonderful, miraculous little girl.

My everlasting love,
L.

The separations were very hard on us. My brother became the de facto father figure for Chloe in Louis's long absences, and Chloe worshipped him. When Louis came home, they instinctively both concealed the depth of their relationship and downplayed the connection between them so as to not hurt him.

She'd become such a force. She told Connie about an encounter with a boy she'd had a bit of a crush on.

"Can you be yourself when you're around someone like that?" Connie wanted to know.

Chloe gave her a disbelieving look. "I'm my *extra* self!"

Chloe learned to protect herself from the sudden appearance and disappearance of her father. She put an invisible governor on her feelings, kept her distance from him. The first few days he was back were always the hardest. When Chloe and I were alone in LA, which was often, we had our rituals. She'd sleep with me, and we'd have Date Nights where we'd get our dinner on trays, light the fire, and watch *Sleeping Beauty* or *Cinderella* and have Lois and the cats on the bed and it was bliss. Louis's arrival always interrupted the Two of Us.

Chloe resented Louis's sudden reappearances; he had to win her over every time. He was totally hands-on whenever he was there—teaching Chloe to ride a bike, taking her to Sea World, standing her on his shoulders while they were playing together in the pool, then tossing her into the air. She loved that. One Christmas he spent six hours putting together a Playmobil pirate ship for her; it was the only thing she'd seen and she'd wanted it desperately. Her next Playmobil crush, two years later, was a Victorian dollhouse and she got it on her sixth birthday. I bought a low, six-foot-long white worktable and we set it up in front of the window in her room. The options were endless: coaches and horses, children and nannies, cooks, kettles, and dogs. Chloe would play with it for hours. At the time there was a dollhouse museum in LA, and it was truly spectacular. There was a Tara from *Gone with the Wind*, an eighteenth-century Japanese palace, a White House. The uber dollhouse, however, was on the grounds of Windsor Castle. It was Queen Mary's dollhouse that she had played with as a little girl. Chloe's godmother, Tessa Kennedy, took us to see it, and it was a knockout. It had a wine cellar with tiny bottles with French labels. There was a weensy garden hose outside in the back. There were ivory hairbrushes less than half an inch long with real bristles. It was a dollhouse as a work of art.

As she got older, Chloe wanted a real dollhouse, so I went to a dollhouse store in LA. The choices were astounding; I chose a three-story Victorian number. It took as long to pick out the wallpaper, flooring, and carpets for this dollhouse as it had for my own house. Chloe and I furnished its three stories for the parents, two children, cook, and maid who resided there. Weensy salami and hams rested on the kitchen table; there were serving dishes of peas and carrots and tiny silver settings with forks and knives in the dining room. Miniature bunny slippers painted white with pink ears nestled beside the little girl's bed in the nursery on the third floor. A wreath hung on the front door and garlands of holly festooned the mantel. There was a Christmas tree in the salon and stockings on the mantel. The interior was electrified with chandeliers and Victorian gas lamps with glass bulbs. There was even toilet paper in the bathroom! This was the miniature world in which Chloe and I could get lost for hours. And then, in Chloe's eyes, in would come Louis to interrupt our idyll and ruin the fun. Chloe would stomp off in a temper and I'd find a note tucked under my pillow:

Dear Mama,

All I wanted was one simple night with you. I wouldn't of rathered a million things for the doll house. But Poppy ruined it there was no time. Love Chloe

As hard as Louis's reentries were, the last few days were hardest because most of her defenses had come down and then he would leave to return to New York and Paris. Home was never LA, where he was sure they put something in the water.

When Chloe was seven, she had to have surgery to correct the reflux affecting her kidneys. The operation was successful, but the next thirty-six hours in the hospital were horrible. Chloe was furious. When a nurse came in to remove her catheter, Chloe snapped at her: "You must be joking!" The tension between Louis and me was extreme during all this because the thought of Chloe having surgery left me tight as a drum. The surgery was only part of it, of course; living apart, endless commuting on Louis's part, constant jet lag—all because I had a job and we had a home in LA—was taking too high a toll. That Louis had been supportive of my doing the show was staggering in its generosity; he had to have known what it would cost. That I didn't was self-serving denial.

When I first signed up for *Murphy Brown*, it was for five years; then we'd negotiate year to year after that. After year 6, Louis asked, "When are you going to stop?" I wouldn't give an answer. I would point to our daughter and say, "It's great for Chloe. She has a fixed point and fixed people in her life." Louis knew that the quality of the show was exceptional and unusual. He knew it was great for me, but it continued to cost us and our relationship.

❧ 13 ☙

Murphy Brown went from commenting on the culture to becoming embedded in it. The faked magazine covers on Murphy's office walls came true when real-life politicians like Newt Gingrich started calling and asking for walk-ons. Journalists loved *Murphy* because it was such a plugged-in, politically attuned, sharp-witted show. It had an insider's perspective and respect for the job, and journalists appreciated that. And, okay, its sensibilities were liberal. But it presented issues fairly and objectively, and usually from both sides. Journalists like Walter Cronkite, Katie Couric, Mike Wallace, Connie Chung, Larry King, and Wolf Blitzer appeared as themselves on the show. We got our own *MAD* magazine satire: "Murky Brown."

Then the show became enveloped by the culture. Murphy Brown decided to have a baby.

My favorite episode, "Birth 101," was the final episode of Diane English's tenure. This was the episode where Murphy gives birth.

Single motherhood for Murphy had been Diane's idea. It was the fourth season, and Diane was looking for new ways to explore the character. The producers consulted a Magic 8 Ball to see if this was a good idea, but kept getting "Ask Again Later." Diane, eight producers, and myself all had dinner in the private room at Mr. Chow's to discuss it. We talked out all the possibilities. The plotline could torpedo the show; it had never been successfully done. As Diane later told an interviewer, "The decision to give Murphy a baby was a big one. Our show was founded on the idea that we were writing a show about a very strong, successful, single woman, and we had legions of single women watching us. . . . What [is] the biggest challenge we can give to this character . . . who hasn't made room in her life for a pet, a man?"

The idea behind it was that Murphy as a mom would provide grist for the comedy mill as the prickly Murphy adjusted to the demands of balancing a newborn with a hard-driving career. It was always a tricky balance to get Murphy to redeem herself by the end of every episode, not to be too selfish or too ego-driven. That was my mission. She was in danger of becoming a caricature—the man-eater who's simply unable to be with a man. Diane thought that if it was her ex-husband who got Murphy pregnant, there'd be not only an emotional through-line, but it would sit a little easier.

Giving Murphy a baby was a completely different kind of tightrope walk. "My God, Murphy, it's a modern medical miracle!" Corky said, joking about Murphy's withered, dried-up eggs. Murphy had her baby when she was forty-four. We knew there was a lot of viewer interest in the pregnancy plotline. The episode with Murphy's baby shower—attended by Katie Couric, Joan Lunden, and Paula Zahn, among others—had more than 36 million viewers.

Diane English wrote "Birth 101," the episode where Murphy would give birth, with Korby Siamis, a key staff writer who'd just become a first-time mother. *Entertainment Weekly* sat all the cast members down for an interview that would run the week the episode aired. We knew the plotline had its detractors. Faith Ford told the reporter, "I happen to know that half the state of Louisiana no longer watches my show; my mother teaches in a Catholic school and reminds me of that." My close friend Herbert Allen warned me, "You be careful. You're sending a message here, and it's not going to be good for young women."

Diane English tried to convey how strongly

viewers connected to the show: "We wrote this line that said Murphy's lawn was such a mess and had so much garbage on it that it looked like a goat exploded. The next week, I'm not kidding, we got this serious letter from a group of goat herders, a very impassioned letter, saying goats don't eat garbage and they get a bad rap, with twenty to thirty signatures. 'And I was watching the show and I was very upset, and *you can imagine my pain!*' We have a collection of them at this point—short people, goats. . . . We always say this in unison when we're about to read one of those [letters]: *You can imagine my pain!*"

Filming the episode was very emotional for me because it brought back all those memories of giving birth to Chloe, who was now seven. I cried through several takes. Still, "Birth 101" gave me great opportunities for broad physical comedy, grabbing Miles and Frank and knocking their heads together across my hospital bed, calling them "sperm for brains," screaming for drugs. Miles was walking Murphy up and down the hall of the hospital when she stopped and gripped the railing during another contraction; he dove underneath her as if to catch the baby. When Murphy's in her hospital bed about to give birth, Jim was looking at the monitor, yelling, "She's gonna *blow!*" After the delivery, Murphy moaned, "Oh god, my body's making milk. It's like discovering you can get bacon out of your elbow."

The end of the episode was Frank's video of Murphy holding the baby with tears in her eyes while singing "Natural Woman," smiling in a way we've never seen before. Singing to the baby was the only idea I ever had for the show. Diane had wanted to write a speech for Murphy, but in the pilot, the character had sung "Natural Woman" horribly. I wanted to sing it again but mean it—which is what we did.

A reporter ran into Diane right after we shot the episode. "Are you thinking at all about the repercussions of this when it goes on the air?" he asked her. "No, why would there be any repercussions?" she told him. "It's 1992."

In its preview of the episode, which aired Monday, May 18, 1992, the *New York Times* wrote that my character would "give birth to a boy in what is expected to be the most public delivery since Lucy Ricardo had little Ricky in 1953." That very morning I was at the University of Pennsylvania getting an honorary doctorate from the school that had politely asked me to move on after I'd flunked painting and opera. As I told the *Philadelphia Inquirer*, "I always did respect them for that; that was a very strong lesson. But then they kept asking me for donations and I didn't give. I said, 'Come on, guys. Fair is fair.' "

The doctoral candidates walked in a processional across campus to the stadium where graduation was held and where I'd been home-coming queen decades earlier. I was seated between an atomic scientist and a geothermal engineer. My introduction referred to me as "the queen regnant of sophisticated comedy" and tactfully referred to "the quarter century since you departed the University of Pennsylvania." Later I said, "I'm here as a supreme gesture of goodwill and perhaps a tad of publicity. This is probably more time I've spent in Philadelphia than the two years I was in school."

"Birth 101" aired that night and was watched by some 38 million viewers.

Returning to New York the next morning, I walked into the lobby of my apartment building and saw on the reception desk the headlines on the front page of a leading tabloid: "Murphy Has Baby, Quayle Has Cow" The *New York Daily News* was perhaps less classy: "Quayle to Murphy Brown: You Tramp." The *New York Post* blared, "Dan Rips Murphy Brown." Predictably, the *New York Times* was more discreet. There was a photo of Murphy holding the baby on the center of the front page—above the fold. The headline read: "Views on Single Motherhood Are Multiple at White House."

Vice President Dan Quayle had been giving a speech out on the campaign trail. As Diane English later explained, he was basically on track at the beginning of his remarks. "Then he made the mistake of blaming the fall of Western civilization on this fictional character, and he hadn't seen the episode, so he was assuming it was all very frivolous and we were making fun of single motherhood." Quayle said, "It doesn't help matters when prime time TV has Murphy Brown—a character who supposedly epitomizes today's intelligent, highly paid, professional woman—mocking the importance of fathers by bearing a child alone, and calling it just another 'lifestyle choice.' "

The story was on every newscast, network and local. The next morning Quayle tried to qualify his earlier statement: "I have the greatest respect for single mothers. They are true heroes." The *Daily News* was more circumspect: "Oh, No, Danny Boy: White House in a Tizzy over 'Murphy Brown' Remark." *Newsday* mentioned "Quayle's War on Hollywood: Why He Bashed Murphy Brown."

Bush spokesman Marlin Fitzwater came out flailing. He told *USA Today*: "The glorification of the life of an unwed mother does not do good service to most unwed mothers who are not highly paid, glamorous anchorwomen," he railed. He corrected himself a few minutes later: "The *Murphy Brown* show [exhibits] pro-life values which we think are good."

It was clear that the media circus was taking on momentum with a vengeance.

THE *NEW YORK POST*, MAY 21, 1992:

David Letterman couldn't let Dan Quayle's latest stupid human trick go unchallenged. . . . "Top 10 Other Complaints About TV" (besides Murphy Brown's unwed motherhood). The list included (9) They never did tell us "Who's the Boss," (8) Even though you're screaming the answer at the top of your lungs, Pat and Vanna just ignore you, and (1) Not enough positive portrayals of really dumb guys.

THE *WASHINGTON POST*, MAY 21, 1992:

Vice President Quayle started a national debate with a Tuesday attack on television sitcom character Murphy Brown, and yesterday, instead of retreating, charged ahead with a fresh condemnation of Hollywood. "Hollywood thinks it's cute to glamorize illegitimacy," he told reporters. President Bush first tried to avoid the issue, then found himself pummeled with questions as he held a news conference with Canadian Prime Minister Brian Mulroney. Mulroney asked, somewhat plaintively, "Who's Murphy Brown?"

May 21, 1992, was also the night of the penultimate *Late Night with Johnny Carson* show.

Robin Williams had a field day with Quayle jokes, including one calling the vice president "one taco short of a combination plate." The next evening Johnny delivered his final monologue. He thanked Quayle "for making my final weeks so fruitful," then added: "Next question I get is what am I gonna do? Well, I have not really made any plans. But the events of this last week have helped me make a decision. I am going to join the cast of *Murphy Brown* and become a surrogate father to that kid."

Columnist Linda Winer wrote in New York *Newsday*, on May 22, 1992:

Come on. If the negative impact of Hollywood is to be traced seriously to any horrors on the streets today, it must start at the inhumane blow-'em-up thrills of violent movies by the administration's favorite big guy, Arnold Schwarzenegger. . . . Oddly enough, no one has mentioned my major concern about the plot twist—that, in this day, an educated TV newscaster failed to use a condom and practice safe sex in the brief affair that got her pregnant.

There was some history with Quayle, who was the frequent butt of jokes on the show. Diane English later described him as "the Sarah Palin of his time, minus the wit. His nonstop malapropisms were gifts from the comedy gods. . . . After four years of statements like 'I love California; I practically grew up in Phoenix,' it was like shooting fish in a barrel." She said, "We were so mortified that Dan Quayle was a heartbeat away from the presidency that we just felt it was our job to do a Dan Quayle joke every week. And so every week we did one. And after a while it was becoming too easy because he would say and do things we could not make up, so eventually we phased that out, but apparently it left quite an impression on him. He never forgot it." Small wonder he was made aware of the birth episode right away.

Diane's friend, CBS president Howard Stringer, told her, "Make one statement and then back off and let everyone else take up the debate." Diane said, "If the vice president thinks it's disgraceful for an unmarried woman to bear a child, and he believes that a woman cannot adequately raise a child without a father, then he'd better make sure abortion remains safe and legal." My publicist, Pat Kingsley, told me, "Candy, you should make a statement."

"Nope, I'm staying out of this one." I really just wanted to keep my head down. I was frankly overwhelmed. Columnist Ellen Goodman mistook my silence for serenity: "The only one who appeared to take the flap in stride was Candice Bergen. But then she grew up in a normal two-parent family with a wooden dummy as a sibling and a father who made his fame as a ventriloquist—on the radio."

A week later, the *New York Times* ran an article speculating whether I'd lose my lucrative contract with Sprint: "Sprint Faces an $80 Million Question, Thanks to Quayle." I'd been the telephone company's exclusive spokeswoman for two years by then. Should they drop me? Should they take a stand? One ad exec proposed, "Have Candice Bergen call Dan Quayle on her Sprint line, and that way you could have both views." Sprint kept me on for six more years.

The Pima County Board of Supervisors in Arizona declared a "Murphy Brown Day" to promote "compassion and tolerance" for single mothers and "celebrate choice, children, family and independence for women."

On June 1, 1992, columnist Lance Morrow wrote:

A *Murphy Brown* debate has gone layering up through a dozen levels of American life—political, moral, cultural, racial, even meta-physical. The exercise has seemed amazingly stupid, obscurely degrading and somehow important at the same time. . . . The uglier side of Quayle's mission begins to become apparent. One of Quayle's amazing but unlikable feats last week was metaphorically

232

to transform old Willie Horton into a beautiful blond fortyish WASP has-it-all knockout.

Because it was a campaign year, it was Topic A for six months. I'd open up the paper and never know if I'd find a political cartoon, like the one showing a fully armed Schwarzenegger with a "Bush/Quayle Spokesman" button pinned to his flak vest, brandishing his weaponry and mugging, "Vere is these Moofry Brown?" Or an op-ed piece on Murphy, Quayle, and "family values"—the first time that phrase had ever been used in connection with the show. In June, an article in the *New York Times* proclaimed, "Quayle Attacks a 'Cultural Elite,' Saying It Mocks Nation's Values." Quayle was quoted as saying that the reaction to his speech taught him that "to appeal to our country's enduring basic moral values is to invite the scorn and laughter of the elite culture. Talk about right and wrong, and they'll try to mock us in newsrooms, sitcom studios and faculty lounges across America. But in the heart of America, in the homes and workplaces and churches, the message is heard."

The Emmys aired at the end of August. I won again for playing Murphy. The first thing I said was, "I'd like to thank the vice president," as well as "the writers for their words and spelling them correctly"—a dig at Quayle's much-publicized misspelling of *potato,* to which he'd appended an

unfortunate *e*. *Time* magazine wrote that "the gang-stomping of Dan Quayle at the Emmy Awards ceremony . . . resembled a Rodney King beating by the Hollywood elite. . . . Quayle, TV's favored quipping boy . . . was the butt of what seemed like every third joke onstage." When the show itself won an Emmy, Diane English said in her acceptance speech: "I would like to thank our sponsors for hanging in there when it was getting really dangerous. I would also like to thank in particular all the single parents out there who, either by choice or necessity, are raising their kids alone. Don't let anybody tell you you're not a family. . . . As Murphy herself said, 'I couldn't possibly do a worse job raising a kid alone than the Reagans did with theirs.' "

Backstage after the Emmys, I told a *Los Angeles Times* reporter that I'd "become the patron saint of single moms. That's beyond anything the rational mind adjusts to. I don't think I'm prepared for the role, and I'd kind of like to get rid of it."

Then Bill Clinton adopted the issue in his campaign, bringing it up constantly. On September 21, 1992, I landed on the cover of *Time* under the headline "Hollywood & Politics: Murphy Brown for President."

The issue became Quayle's campaign platform. We learned later that the quote about Murphy Brown had been deleted from his original speech

by his speechwriter, who thought it was a red flag they didn't need. Quayle had reinserted it, which was very canny.

The whole thing was surreal. Then the atmosphere became very charged on the set. We got some death threats from right-wingers. I never saw them, but the studio sent the questionable letters to a security company run by Gavin de Becker, which monitored them. On shoot night the audience now had to pass through metal detectors. I was assigned full-time security. They were adorable ex-police, some injured in the line of duty. They couldn't have been sweeter. They were there when I would pull up in the morning and take my car. They'd walk me to and from lunch. Their code name for me was "Navigator," because I couldn't find my way out of a paper bag. Of course, the Warner lot is the safest place in California, so it was largely unnecessary.

I was very careful to check my rearview mirror when I drove home. If somebody was following me, I drove past my house and kept going until I lost them. A few times an odd woman who stalked me would be loitering outside my house, which was peculiar because I lived in a very out of the way neighborhood up in the canyons. It was very creepy, especially with Chloe. I reported the woman to the police, but there was nothing they could do. Security communicated with her and she backed off.

I absolutely agreed with Quayle's point that fathers are important, but his statement ignored the reality of the existence of single mothers. I have friends who think Murphy Brown's single motherhood was a very damaging message to send. We never intended it to be damaging. *Murphy Brown* was watched by a twenty- to forty-five-year-old demographic of well-educated people, but still . . . Years before, David Sheff had interviewed me for the cover story of December 1989 issue of *Playboy*—three full years before the infamous episode:

Murphy is at the top of her profession . . . she is, in a very realistic way, paying the price for it. I know many journalists, including television journalists, and I don't know any women in that position who haven't paid a very high price. Of course, we're doing a half-hour comedy, so the desperation is only hinted at, but it is noteworthy that the most meaningful relationship in Murphy Brown's life is with her house painter. The only complaint I've heard from a lot of women who really do what she does is that Murphy's life is not desperate enough. The women who really do what she does are so despondent that the landscape of their personal lives is so bleak. Murphy can hardly have a date.

Diane English departed at the end of Season 4. Our new executive producers were Gary Dontzig and Steve Peterman. New writers teed up Season 5 with an hour-long Murphy Brown premiere, "You Say Potatoe, I Say Potato," to address the controversy. There was a lot of public debate about how the show would handle it. The New Jersey *Star-Ledger* wrote, "It's the election-year equivalent of 'Who Shot J. R.?' How will the fictional Murphy Brown respond to the real-life Dan Quayle's comments about her unwed motherhood in the season premiere?" We shot several different versions of a few key scenes to help keep the premiere a secret, although the *National Enquirer* claimed it had been leaked a copy of the script. Consulting producer Korby Siamis told a reporter, "We're planning to have ourselves hypnotized so that we reveal the information in our heads only after being given a code word."

The new season opened with Murphy still in her pajamas, flailing around exhausted as she tried to take care of her baby, named Avery after Murphy's mother. Murphy was with her colleague Frank, watching Quayle's speech on TV, listening to him rail about how Murphy was "mocking the importance of fathers" and "glamorizing single motherhood."

"Glamorizing!" shouted an unshowered Murphy to Frank. "Do I *look* glamorous?" "Of course

237

not!" Frank shot back. "You look disgusting."

Another scene had Murphy surrounded by single parents and saying, "These are difficult times for our country, and in searching for the causes of our social ills, we could choose to blame the media, or the Congress, or an administration that's been in power for twelve years—or we could blame me."

Vice President Quayle tried to make amends— he sent Murphy's son, Avery, a baby present, a stuffed elephant, and a note that read: "Dear Baby Brown, I want to be one of the first to welcome you into the world. You may not realize it yet, but you've helped start an important discussion on ways to strengthen our traditional values." He never seemed to be able to stop being the punch line: The *Murphy Brown* staff issued a statement that said that "Baby Brown" already had several elephants—and stuffed donkeys, thank you very much. They planned to donate Quayle's gift to a homeless shelter.

Esquire made me "Woman of the Year" in 1992. The editors wrote:

> Candice's Murphy is telling us that it's okay for women to snap just as men do when the tension headache begins at the back of your neck . . . that just because she is not always sweetness and light does not mean women should be packed off to the Phyllis Schlafly

reeducation camp . . . that even the maligned medium of television has something potent to say about human affairs . . . and that Murphy (thanks to Candice) is sending a message of reason and maturity that is much needed in these hysteria-ridden times. Whose values, indeed.

The show was number one or two for the first few weeks when we came back. We'd gotten a 40 share of the audience—some 70 million viewers. Quayle never said anything to me directly, and to this day, we have never met. And of course, years later, Diane noted, when Rachel had Ross's baby on *Friends* without the benefit of marriage, no one made a peep.

I didn't want to send a message that as women we could easily have it all. It is *not* easy and there *are* sacrifices. Diane showed that with great acuity. Murphy had no personal life, zippo, until that fifth season when she became a mother.

Eldin Bernecky, house painter, became Avery's nanny. I didn't realize how difficult incorporating a baby into a show would be. Every time we had to shoot with the baby, I'd groan inwardly. *Oh God*. You're holding this very live baby who could blow at any second and trying to remember your lines; it was such a loaded situation. And of course the baby—babies, as Avery was played by twins—would cry, as babies do, so it was a strain.

Barnet Kellman had left by then, taking that specific crackling pace and electricity with him. The show never quite recaptured it.

I couldn't stand for Murphy to be an indifferent mother or an absent, overwhelmed mother. One script called for Murphy to come late to her son's birthday party. I couldn't bear it; it was just unacceptable to me. Diane was gone by then, so I went and complained about the script. "Murphy cannot continue her profession at the expense of her child. You cannot send that message to people." I couldn't stand that Murphy didn't cut back on her work after she'd had her child. We had lots of meetings and arguments about it. The trouble with me was that because I was a mom in real life, I found nothing humorous in being a bad mom on television. We'd negotiate on how far the show would go.

On June 12, 1998, six years after the initial kerfuffle and a month after the last episode ran, Lisa Schiffren, the speechwriter who'd written Quayle's infamous Murphy Brown speech, wrote an op-ed for the *New York Times*, claiming that our show glamorized single parenthood. Schiffren proposed a sitcom starring a married professional woman who quit her job to be a full-time stay-at-home mom when she realizes the nanny is neglecting her offspring. Schiffren implied that I was in full agreement with Quayle's points. This was too much. I broke my silence.

Los Angeles, June 19, 1998

To the Editor:

The first time my name appeared in the *New York Times* linked with Dan Quayle's—when he accused the character I played, Murphy Brown, of glamorizing out-of-wedlock pregnancy—I decided not to reply. I had no desire to heap ridicule and scorn on the Office of the Vice President, especially when Mr. Quayle seemed to be doing a fine job of that all by himself.

But this latest broadside from the Quayle camp is too much to let pass. Lisa Schiffren (op-ed, June 12), a former speechwriter for Mr. Quayle, misused several quotes from an interview I did with the *Los Angeles Times* to suggest that I was admitting that Mr. Quayle was a lone visionary whose speech had been right all along.

She quotes me as saying that family values "was the right theme to hammer home," that "I agreed with all of it except his references to the show," and that "the body of the speech was completely sound." Since that quote serves as the crux of her argument, let me print what she left out: "it was an arrogant and uninformed posture, but the body of the speech was completely sound."

In fact, Mr. Quayle hurled an accusation at a show he had never seen in an effort to turn it into a political Monday Night Football. At no point did *Murphy Brown* glamorize single motherhood or disparage the role of a father in raising a child. Ms. Schiffren is now a "full-time mother of two and an occasional writer." Not every woman has the luxury to make that choice. Perhaps next time she'll put her talent toward a candidate who would work to eliminate that problem.

Candice Bergen

Schiffren's response to my letter to the editor? "Being a full-time mom, I did not actually read the letter."

For ten years, I'd worked hard to humanize Murphy, to show sensitivity to others, to not have her be incessantly abrasive, to have her redeem herself by the end of each episode in whatever slight way. Murphy definitely had a monstrous side. She'd run over anyone to get a story, elbow anyone out of the way. My daughter was flat-out everything to me and I couldn't bear to send a negative message to girls and women.

We more than gave every holiday its due at our tiny house in the canyons of Beverly Hills.

We gave fantastic Easter parties. Chloe and I would shop for decorations at a party store near Paramount Studios where they had brightly colored swags and garlands, piñatas, Chinese lanterns in gay colors, and huge and tiny eggs. I would work like an Easter beaver to hang and drape and tack and then step back to admire my work. The patio was the first thing you saw when you came in the gate and you got a lot of bang for the buck. But the pièce de résistance was the Rabbit Suit. I asked Delia, Chloe's nanny, to ferret one out and she came back with a faux fur bunny costume complete with hood, ears, and mask. This was obviously kept secret from Chloe, who at age five very much believed in the Easter Bunny.

Usually, I would ask Paul, our friend and caterer, to get into rabbit drag. I would give the kids pastel-colored woven baskets filled with cellophane grass and herd them into Chloe's room so that the Easter Bunny, who was very shy, could hop out and hide the eggs. We had two zones, the Easy Egg zone, where eggs were put in plain sight, and the Advanced Egg Zone, where kids actually had to work to spot them. While the kids were chattering excitedly in Chloe's room, I would open the curtains just as Paul, in the bunny suit, hopped by the window carrying a basket of eggs. The kids would explode out Chloe's door and onto the lawn with shrieks and whoops while Paul tore in through the back door and changed out of his gear. The grand prize was a giant chocolate bunny wrapped in gold foil.

The patio filled with friends and kids and dogs. It was buoyant, giddy, and over the top. I loved it. Chloe loved it. Carrie Fisher came. Annette Bening brought her firstborn. Martin and Nancy Short brought their three, Meryl Streep brought a few of hers, Bob and Carole Daly brought Christopher. Bette Midler and Martin von Haselberg brought Sophie. Dorothy Lyman and my brother-in-law Vincent brought Chloe's cousin Jackson. Chloe's best friend, Shane, who lived around the corner, came with her parents, Dey and David Ladd. Karen Santo Domingo brought Carolina. The patio was bustling as we watched the kids collect their prizes and race to find the Golden Bunny.

Lois also gleefully joined in the Easter egg hunt. One year I ducked into the kitchen to get something and spotted her slinking furtively to her basket in the corner of the kitchen. When she heard me coming, she assumed her customary Freeze Position. Her strategy was to become completely immobile, sometimes with a paw raised midstep, eyes averted, in the hope that she would become invisible. This rarely worked. This time she looked up sheepishly. She'd found the Golden Bunny and had just started on the ears.

One year, Paul was unable to come and I asked a young woman who was helping serve to be the Easter Bunny. The kids were herded, as usual, into Chloe's room, and at the precise moment, I opened the curtain and there was the Bunny, carrying a big basket, hopping past my daughter's window. Unfortunately, a ponytail was visible sticking out the bottom of the hood. That was pretty much the end of the charade.

Because Halloween fell in the middle of a *Murphy* season, I would ask our wardrobe assistant to take me to the vast costume stage. Because our show was shot on the Warner lot and it was a big success, I had full access to this fantasyland, where rack upon rack of marvelous, funky outfits could be found. If they couldn't be found, they were made by the intrepid Judy McGivney. One year she made Chloe a peacock costume; another time it was a Chiquita Banana costume, complete with a turban filled with plastic fruit; and then she made a Lucy costume that included the short red curly wig conjured by our hairdresser, Judy Crown.

The year Chloe went as Chiquita Banana, I decided to go as Zorro and Judy came back with a perfect ensemble: broad-brimmed black hat, black mask, black shirt, cape, sword, and boots. Halloween was the day I was due to help serve lunch at John Thomas Dye, Chloe's middle school. I wore my Zorro costume. I drew a fine mustache with eyeliner pencil, put on the outfit, including the mask, and drove to Bel Air to the idyllic campus. On the way, I passed a truck with three Hispanic gardeners, who looked over, saw me, and gaped. I nodded, waved, and called, "Adios, amigos!" then drove off in a cloud of dust.

Lois loved to dress up, so I'd have doggie costume parties. One Halloween weekend, we had a dozen people and their kids for lunch. The only requirement was they had to bring a dog. In costume. Of course, we got some winners. A Chihuahua in a yarmulke, Barnet's golden retriever wearing a fleecy blanket on her back who came as a "wolf in sheep's clothing," a dog in a sombrero. Some brought presents for Lois: a Neiman's gift box with a stick, bones, beautifully wrapped, and a bright red hooded poncho. Dogs went home with party bags full of biscuits and chew sticks. It became an annual tradition that continued until Lois was twelve.

Lois had a section in my closet for her costumes, the favorite of which was her ball gown. This was something I had found in a catalog for dogs, before dog costumes became commonplace. It was a polyester pink dress with a skirt of tulle and pearls at the neck. Soon it became frayed from overuse, so Lois looked like Cinderella after the stepsisters got to her. Lois also wore Chloe's angel wings with her pink ballet tutu and a doggy tiara hooked onto her ears. This always got a big response from adults who opened the door to "Trick or Treat!" "Honey, come look at this! There's a dog fairy!"

When Chloe was eight, she had a goal. She wanted to collect the most candy on Halloween. I never said it was a noble goal, but she had it. She began searching for massive shopping bags, which we stored in the pantry. The bag she selected was almost half her size. A stiff paper one with sturdy handles.

She left the costume to me; she had bigger fish to fry. I once again went to the costume department to root around and quickly found a metallic amethyst fantasy outfit. The top was beaded and braided and the bottom had really wide harem pants. Sort of a Pulcinella costume. But the pièce de résistance was the turban we had made to go with it. Judy McGivney had found similar fabric and swathed it on a stiff hat form. She added a huge fake jewel at the center and an enormous purple plume to finish it, plus a glittery veil to loop under Chloe's chin. I have no idea what she was meant to look like, but it wouldn't be like anyone else.

Chloe paid scant attention to her finished costume because she had her focus on being at the head of the Trick or Treat pack. Getting the most candy was her main mission.

Louis made sure to be there for Halloween and we set out in a group for Santa Monica, where much was made of the holiday. There were houses with coffins in the entry halls from which Frankenstein's monster would pop up unexpectedly. There were wispy ghouls hanging from tree branches. In one driveway, there was an old vintage Cadillac convertible with the top down, piloted by skeletons in tuxedos. The neighborhood went all out and it was appreciated. We knew which streets were meant to be best and arrived early to get parking.

Louis wore a bat mask and I was dressed in my white rabbit suit, which I repurposed from our Easter egg hunts. We met our neighbors, Dey and David Ladd, and their daughter Shane. We planned our route. I was taking it very seriously, giving orders in my rabbit suit. Louis was slightly overwhelmed by it all. As long as he had lived in America, there were certain rituals that still stunned him. Halloween was one.

And they were off. A crazed group of girls wearing costumes du jour, with Chloe out ahead, determined to be in the lead. They launched assaults on house after house. Their bags were beginning to take on heft. So far, Chloe was way ahead in the candy count. Her eyes were glittering, her nostrils flared with the thrill of the hunt. We covered every house on four blocks. The group's energy was flagging, but Chloe still held the lead. Louis and I smelled the end coming soon. Thank God, it would soon be over.

And then we heard The Scream. A cry so anguished it cut through our hearts. We looked around quickly and saw Chloe collapsing on the sidewalk in a heap. It seems she had stopped to check the amount of candy she had amassed when she discovered that her huge shopping bag was empty. Zippo. Zilch. Nada. She'd taken a shortcut through a rosebush and the thorns had torn the bag and the candy was spilling out faster than she could stuff it in. She was sobbing. She was bereft.

Louis, so close to being in the car and on the way home, went slack-jawed. The impact of having to do it all again was beginning to hit him. And me. By now, it was dark and there were hundreds of kids, most of them older now, aggressive, past the cute stage, clogging the sidewalks. Our path was clear, however. We had to begin again. Which is what we did, scavenging an extra smaller bag from one of our group and giving it to Chloe, who had not yet recovered from defeat. Louis looked like he had been clubbed as we trooped from house to house behind Chloe. Of course, they had to be new houses since etiquette precluded repeat shoppers.

After a couple of blocks and a few ounces of candy, we called it a night and drove home in silence. There was very little conversation and certainly no lectures on greed. Any lessons to be learned were self-evident.

Christmas was far and away our favorite holiday. We would take Chloe to Mr. Greentrees and pick out an eight- or nine-foot fir, plus a tiny tree for Chloe's room and a smaller one for Lois, which was strung with dog biscuits and went beside her basket in the kitchen. Lois wore a red collar with large brass jingle bells; in December, you could track her by following the sound of the sleigh. Of course Lois had her own monogrammed Christmas stocking and presents. The dog industry was created for people like me.

We got Dr. Christmas—"Tree Stylist to the Stars!"—to put up the outside lights and my brother and Louis helped with the lights on the living room tree. We had swags of evergreen and holly over the fireplace and doorways; I tied candy canes on the chandeliers with red French ribbon. Every Christmas in LA, we hosted a sing-along full of friends and food and spiced wine. After dinner, we all gathered around the piano to sing carols. It was swell.

On Christmas Eve, which was usually in Sun Valley, I would help Chloe write a note to Santa. She was always polite and modest in her requests. Then we would leave a glass of milk and a plate of chocolate chip cookies for Santa, with a side of carrots for the reindeer, on the coffee table in front of the fireplace. Around one in the morning, Louis and I would eat the cookies, pour out the milk, and put the carrots back in the fridge. Sometimes we would leave boot prints around the hearth and pieces of coal as Santa tracks. Then I would write a grateful thank-you from Santa in my Santa script and by 6:00 a.m., the day would begin.

The Yuletide ritual persists to this day, minus the bootprints. And Chloe is in her late twenties.

❧ 15 ❧

In LA, from the month of September on, it's one awards show after another. Emmys, Golden Globes, SAG Awards, Independent Spirit, Oscars. You start getting ready at 11:00 a.m., leave at 2:00 p.m. in full makeup, borrowed jewels, and a gown. You're finished in time for dinner. It takes a village: hair people, manicurists, makeup and tanning people, and stylists, obviously. They are called your "team." The studio pays for it. Thank God.

The red carpet is a grotesque marketplace. A celebrity souk filled with publicists, press, police, and fans. Most people of a certain age try to do it with as much grace as possible, to be as genuine as possible under the most artificial construct. Most fail.

The press line over time has gotten longer and deeper, stretching for blocks. I always had Pat Kingsley or Heidi Schaeffer, her lieutenant, taking me through, playing bad cop, keeping me moving through the line. They knew who was important for your particular medium, whom you should stop in front of and for how long. They understood it was an ordeal, and part of the deal. You'd go from one lame-brained interview to the next. "What's the difference between you and the character in this film?" "How much does this mean to you?" "How long have you been together, you two?" I'd hand my bag to Heidi, then pose for the photo. These days the bags get credit, so they don't get handed off; the women know how to display the bags gracefully, since they are usually gifts from designers. Today, everything is a gift. You don't have to spend a shekel; as long as you're photographed in it, or with it, or on it, it's yours. Today, the game is totally different and everyone plays to win.

When I started *Murphy*, stylists didn't exist. I knew Ralph Lauren when he was still making ties. I knew Donna Karan and Oscar de la Renta and Bill Blass. I'd call their PR people and they were always lovely. They would offer to let me keep gowns. I would be thrilled, send a note, flowers, or an engraved something. I had a beautiful Oscar de la Renta I wore for an Emmys show, a pale ice pistachio green halter-neck with a lightly beaded top.

When stylists came on the scene, I started working with Jane Ross. Once she found me a Bill Blass to wear to the Emmys, a strapless gown that was a dark gold and russet cut-velvet jacquard and with it, canary diamond earrings, emerald cut. Chic as hell. Years ago, it was fun wearing the jewelry. Jane would pull pieces worth a hundred thousand out of her pocket. If it was worth even more, the jewelry was brought by security guards to your door with a form to be signed.

These days you see a lot of women who can really work the red carpet. They are pros, giving photographers twelve positions, the coy over-the-shoulder-with-the-backless-dress shot. The hip-forward-cocked-thigh-in-the-slinky-slit-dress shot. The shoulders-back-so-you-don't-see-my-nipples-or-the-double-faced-tape-holding-up-the-halter-top-of-my-dress-which-is-no-wider-than-a-sock look. The look that says you can't believe they let you into the game and the one that says you can't wait to get out.

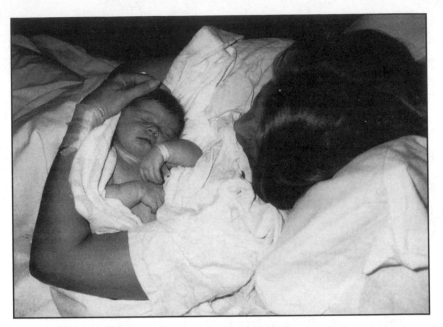

Chloe, shortly after her arrival.

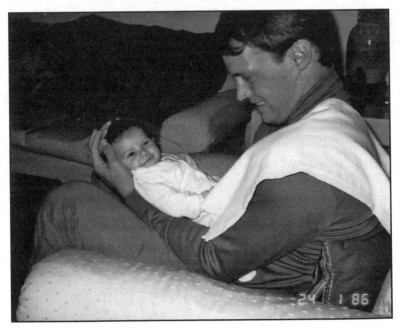

Chloe meeting her uncle, my brother, Kris.

Chloe with Nourson, the dog of Le Coual.

Chloe during her fourth summer
at Le Coual.

Searching for a bedtime story.

Chloe and Lois, partners in crime.

LEFT: Chloe, Louis, and I during the first year of *Murphy Brown*.

RIGHT: Justine, Chloe, and Cuote.

BELOW: A tea party at home with Chloe and Mom.

On the way to an Oscar party.

Kris, Mom, and Chloe.

BELOW AND LEFT: My wedding to Marshall in New York, June 2000.

BELOW: Diane and Andy Rose, Mom, Marsh, me, Chloe, Kris, and Wendi Rose.

With my costars on
Boston Legal,
James Spader and
William Shatner.

Chloe attending
events at Vogue.

Chloe with
her fiancé,
Graham Albert.

Chloe and
Graham
entering their
party.

Chloe, me, and Graham celebrating their engagement.

Marshall and Kris (ABOVE) and Chloe and Connie Freiberg (LEFT) at the engagement party.

Marshall and Jerry at six months, before
he grew to the size of a small buffalo.

Marsh and me, at the beginning

LEFT:
Chloe,
age five,
on the beach
at Malibu.

BELOW:
Chloe, age
twenty-eight,
on the beach
at East
Hampton.

❖{ 16 }❖

Louis had been told he wouldn't live a long life; I think that's why he always galloped through it. Some part of him knew the clock was ticking. His modus operandi was always to be moving. If you were talking to him on the phone, he'd be pacing and smoking his pipe.

In 1993, when Louis was sixty-two, he was told he'd need to have open-heart surgery, a valve replacement where they'd swap out his failing machinery with a porcine version. I could see he was afraid; he would get spiky, irritable. He did not want to talk about it. When he did, he intellectualized it: "One prevents death: modern medicine. One exploits you your whole life: capitalism." He was French. In this case, we decided to use the modern medicine available at Cedars-Sinai in LA, where they excelled at this procedure, and the capitalism served us extremely well as my SAG card covered the very expensive surgery. The week before the operation, he was testy and frightened. Justine flew in from Paris and Cuote from Boston to keep him company and be with Chloe. Shortly before the operation, he wrote them a letter that was essentially a good-bye note:

My dear children,

I want very simply to tell you how much I love you. I have not been an ideal father, not what I should have been, but you give me so much joy and feeling that I hope that I have given you a little back that was true/responded in kind. What gives me the most joy is that in spite of all the constraints—the separations of your lives—you are so tenderly united. One brother and two sisters who are friends, accomplices, who find that again each time. My biggest wish is that nothing separates you ever, that your love for each other will only grow stronger over the years. I hug you very very very tightly. L

Louis got through it. We rehabbed together. He'd walk but it was very labored, minutely measured. He could take only a few steps at a time. A few steps on the patio. A few stairs. Then I would drive him to the park where the ground was flat for a two-minute walk, and then three. Each day, a minute more. Very slow, very meticulous rehab, timed to within minutes. It's frightening when you have someone who's been through that kind of major surgery; they are suddenly so fragile. And you're in charge.

Having survived open-heart surgery and a quiet recovery at our house, evidently Louis was finding these timed walks too routine. It must have felt very confining. And yet two weeks after the surgery, my brother suggested Louis jump off the roof of the pool house into the pool. Who was stupider: Kris for suggesting such an insane idea, or Louis for doing it?

Of course, I was out of the house when it happened and didn't find out until later. But it is a perfect picture of each man. Kris had become very close to Louis and made him laugh harder than anyone else with his sweeping bouts of reckless abandon.

Perhaps this is best illustrated by Kris's signature stunt: driving while mooning. I still don't understand how he managed to physically manage this maneuver, but he would stick his bare ass out of the driver's window *while driving the car.* Once he did it with my mother in the passenger seat and Louis and me following in the car behind. Louis laughed so hard I thought he was going to black out. My mom's face was a mélange of horror and fury. I was simply slack-jawed.

The Pool House Jump was right up Louis's alley. He was a physical guy, like my brother, fairly fearless, and enjoyed a certain element of risk. But let me point out he had just had his chest cut open and a valve replaced two weeks before. If the jump hadn't killed him, his chest could have opened like a melon. Any way you look at it, death was in the picture. It was a miracle Louis wasn't killed, and it was a miracle I didn't kill my brother. As it turned out, Louis only had a little time left.

They warn you about depression after surgery. I think Louis was relieved instead to have come through it. He felt like a conqueror, I suppose, invincible for a moment. Three weeks after the operation, he flew off to Nice to be president of the jury at the annual Cannes Film Festival. He wanted to return to the festival he and others shook up in 1968, when the festival was ended prematurely in solidarity with the student protests that had spread across France. He'd regained some of his strength, looked lean, mean, and handsome. It was a way to say, "I am back from the brink of death. *Je suis revenue.*" I didn't try to stop him.

Murphy Brown had wrapped, so I flew out the second week of the festival to be with him. He was thrilled to see me. He loved the Cannes Festival. He'd always had a complicated relationship with his home country; in turn, they'd always felt he'd betrayed and abandoned them for the States. Now he was glad to be back in their embrace.

The first time I was at Cannes, I was twenty-one. It changes very little. It is a movie market-place, packed and noisy, with people jostling and yelling. Starlets ripe and luscious pose for photo ops in a garish display of merchandising. LA awards shows with better wine. The sleaze quotient is offset by the ageless glamour of the French Riviera: the palm trees swaying along La Croisette, the old Hotel Carlton, the beauty and the $65 burgers of the Hotel du Cap, the world-class restaurants, the stunning shorelines, swanky and romantic as Fitzgerald.

Being at Cannes with Louis was wonderful. He loved being there, and they were very happy to have him. Cannes is all about being out and about. When you're the president of the jury, seeing three films a day for two weeks, it's all about being in throngs of people, going from event to event with the press following, one dinner to another cocktail to another screening. One day we went for a lovely lunch at Cap d'Antibes with Michael Barker, head of Sony Classics. Louis was completely engaged, relaxed, very alive, his eyes bright. Dressed for dinner, he looked incredibly elegant in his *smoking*. He had dodged a bullet; he was back.

Louis's whole mood at Cannes was a revival in every sense. *Paris Match* did a big feature on him, with a double-page spread of him doing an extreme yoga pose on the roof of the Carlton while wearing a little Speedo, his surgical scar running the length of his chest.

The festival schedule was so tightly packed that we saw the last screening on the final afternoon, they held the vote, then dashed to a room upstairs to change into black tie. As Louis's designated arm candy, I slipped into a Donna Karan pantsuit, acid green raw silk with a long matching green chiffon scarf embroidered with sequins, along with strappy gold heels. We hopped into the presidential limo and whizzed to the Palais des Festivals with pennants fluttering as we sped through the streets to make it in time, accompanied by a motorcycle escort, with full bells and whistles, which he loved. We were preceded on the red carpet by the elegant Isabelle Adjani, among others. Under Louis's direction, the jury was split for the first time in its history, awarding the Palme d'Or to both Jane Campion's *The Piano* and Chen Kaige's *Farewell, My Concubine*. The announcement of the tie caused commotion in the crowd, which made Louis, a born provocateur, happy. He felt both films were of superior talent and was confident in his choice.

As we left Cannes, Louis was exhausted but radiant.

❧ 17 ❧

Christmas, 1994: We were going skiing in Sun Valley, which was something of a family tradition. I had been given the Warner Bros. plane and Louis; Chloe; Lois; my mom; her beau, Craig

Stevens; my brother, Kris; my stepson, Cuote; our friend Ingrid, once Chloe's nanny but now part of our family; and I were happily aboard.

Traveling by private jet is a very nice way to fly; it's a perk negotiated in your contract and I started using it the second year of *Murphy*. The trip wasn't guaranteed, but you could put in for where and when you wanted to travel and they assigned you a priority with the booking agent. *Murphy* was supporting Warner Bros. during a slow time, so my priority rose over a few years. We used the jet mostly to go to Sun Valley and New York.

The Warner Bros. Gulfstream G4 was hangared at Burbank Airport. You'd show up and the plane would be waiting just outside. No security checks, rifling of bags, or restrictions on what you carried on board. Your bags were loaded and you walked up the stairs with your dogs; the pets' names were right on the manifest.

Every time I got on the jet, I all but wept with gratitude. It took me years to get over feeling I'd have a heart attack; I couldn't believe I was responsible in some way for getting this plane. Warner Bros. had a number of perks. When Steve Ross was president, they'd loan out the house in Acapulco. When you arrived, they'd have sneakers for everyone in their size, along with bathing suits and trunks and tennis clothes. The Warner Bros. house in Aspen was available for skiers. I never set foot in any of those houses, which were probably restricted to movie people. Television was still low on the totem pole. The plane was plenty.

The seats inside the G4 were beige leather clouds with gold seat buckles. A flight attendant fed you beautifully on board: breakfasts of bagels, cream cheese, salmon, omelets, granola, yogurt.

The flights were effortless. For me, there was no greater luxury. The dogs would go into suspended animation, just waiting for it to be over. When we landed, we simply walked right off the plane into waiting cars, our luggage loaded for us.

This Christmas, the luxuriousness of the flight was lost on Louis. He was unusually cranky throughout the entire trip. Almost unbearably so. None of us knew what was wrong with him. He'd arrived in LA for three weeks in December in a mood that was blacker than pitch. I attributed it to the untenable situation of his commuting from Los Angeles to New York to France. The trip and constant travel were exhausting and it was beginning to take a toll physically. He was now sixty-two. It was asking too much. We all gave him a wide berth because his anger was palpable.

He'd also begun to act erratically. Once while on the chairlift, he dropped his ski pole and actually leapt off the chair to get it. He was, unbelievably, okay after the jump, which was only about ten feet off the ground. I was not. He seemed miserable. As days that should have been idyllic passed in Sun Valley and Louis's black mood continued, I wondered if the marriage was coming to an end.

Thank heavens for Cuote and Kris. They were always trying to roughen the edges of Chloe's virtual Only-Childness. In Sun Valley they put her mattress outside in the snow on the roof. She had asked for deodorant for Christmas and they dumped a shopping bag of Ban and Arrid Extra Dry on top of her while she was reading on her bed. We had snowball fights where she and I stockpiled neat pyramids of snowballs in preparation for the great battle. We could taste the victory and it was sweet. And then Cuote, with a cigarette in one hand and a snowball in the other, came from behind and slaughtered us as we hunkered behind our cache of weapons, waiting for the match to begin. I was so grateful for their hijinks, which lightened the otherwise bleak mood Louis had cast over all of us.

Louis returned to Paris in January 1995. It was a relief to get a break from his darkness.

He returned in February with pneumonia. I think he wanted to be home while he was ill and as much as he mistrusted LA, home was with Chloe and me, where he knew he'd be taken care of.

Louis was still not right even after the pneumonia was cured. Alain Bernheim, an old friend from Paris, came by to visit; we had lunch on our patio. Later he took me aside; he'd noticed a profound change in Louis's behavior and a slight slurring of his speech—something those of us who'd been close to him had missed because it had snuck up on him so gradually. Had Louis had a CT scan recently? He called his internist, Rick Gold, and it was arranged.

Of course, that was just the beginning. Louis's hematologist at Cedars-Sinai, Barry Rosenbloom, was brought in. There were, apparently, anomalies. Of course. Three or four years earlier, Barry had diagnosed Louis with lymphoma, which we discovered when Louis had taken an Alka-Seltzer to calm his stomach after a big holiday meal. We hadn't realized he had a medical condition that made him overly sensitive to aspirin; he began bleeding and couldn't control it. I'd taken him to the hospital for transfusions. After extensive blood workups, Barry determined that he had myelofibrosis, which had then morphed into lymphoma. Louis's blood didn't have enough platelets; he had a clotting deficiency. "Generally the course of the illness is five years," Barry told us. "Any way you can reduce stress or eliminate unnecessary activity would help your prognosis."

What was more stressful than Louis's usual stations of the cross, traveling constantly between Paris, New York, and LA? Or his breakneck pace on his film projects? Couldn't he stay with us for a few months? He would have none of it. He'd already had to have open-heart surgery in 1992; we'd blamed that on the strain of our bicontinental relationship. And still it continued.

Because he didn't accept the diagnosis, Louis lost confidence in the medical expertise of his LA doctors—among the best in the world—so he'd flown back to New York to begin an endless round of doctors' visits and tests to get a second opinion. A better opinion. I was just leaving the house to give a speech to the senior class of Westlake School for Girls, my alma mater, when the phone rang. It was Louis's doctor in New York.

"Candy, I was going to fly out to tell you this, but I'm swamped here," he said. "I think that with the symptoms Louis has and exhaustive blood workups, I'm ninety-nine percent sure he has AIDS. I gave him an AIDS test, but the results won't be back for a week. I want you to get a blood test immediately." Louis had apparently contracted an opportunistic infection that struck many patients with AIDS. It was possible that he'd contracted the AIDS virus from his many transfusions.

It was a half-hour before I was due at Westlake—too late for me to cancel the speech. My head was spinning. I delivered my remarks on autopilot, then went straight to get a blood test and waited for the week to pass.

As soon as *Murphy* went on hiatus, I went to New York to be with Louis. Cuote, then at graduate school at New York University, was exhausted after three weeks of taking Louis around for a series of gruesome tests, including spinal taps, and to see a parade of neurologists. Now it was my turn.

Louis's results came back; he didn't have AIDS. And so neither did I. He had other letters instead: PML—progressive multifocal leuko-encephalopathy, an inflammation of the brain. It attacked the neocortex and the symptoms were slight and early. But they were manifest in his speech, his coordination, and his handwriting, which had begun to deteriorate. And, of course, his strikingly black moods. PML normally attacked people with immune deficiencies, such as people with AIDS. It was rare. And it was fatal; there was no treatment.

Louis was small but tough. He refused to hear it. He blocked it out. He was going to work harder than ever; maybe he thought he could outrun it. I thought it was possible that his denial of his diagnosis would be in some way therapeutic, in the way of placebos or a concrete mind-set. Maybe his normal helter-skelter work schedule would help him. He was working on a film about Marlene Dietrich that John Guare was writing and they planned to continue working on the script. He went to meet with Uma Thurman about it; I bought him some Casablanca lilies to bring her.

Two days later Louis flew to South Korea to try

to get a release for a movie that he had no hope of getting. I tried to talk him out of it. It was not only medically unwise and risky; it was pointless. Barry Rosenbloom, his LA doctor, had been clear with Louis that he should not exhaust himself and try to avoid unnecessary stress. Louis was adamant; he was fine. His way of fighting his illness, I believe, was to not simply ignore it but to deny it.

My darling, I am leaving this enchanted house with lead feet. It has been so good to be here with you and the little shrimp, I have already forgotten my medical miseries and shall remember most the wonderful time we had the 3 of us, and how generous and loving you have been through this ordeal. I love you always more because you keep getting better and better—it's amazing, you know! A big hug for the 2 of you.

L.

Perhaps Louis was so resolute because he'd always known he would die early. He'd had scarlet fever when he was twelve and been bedridden for a year during the war; he kept a heart murmur for the rest of his life as a souvenir. He'd made *Murmur of the Heart* partly based on that experience.

In any case, it was clear that Louis had made a

conscious choice to reject whatever information the doctor communicated. Louis and I had our own don't ask, don't tell policy: if he didn't ask, I didn't bring it up. If he'd brought it up, I would have told him anything I knew. But he never did.

After South Korea, Louis decided he wanted to go to Le Coual and he asked Cuote to go with him. I couldn't go because Chloe was in school. I sensed that he knew that it might be his last trip to his legendary home, which meant so much to him. That house had such a strong personality. Le Coual had always been his talisman. It had almost magical properties. That was his spot where he'd do his writing and where he'd worked so hard to create a place where his three children from three separate mothers would always feel welcome. I sent him off with my blessing. Perhaps he thought that if he was there, everything would resolve itself. His younger brother Vincent went with Louis and Cuote for the visit.

They were there two weeks. It was terrible, exhausting. By that time Louis was having real trouble walking and difficulty speaking. He was weakening very quickly. When he returned home to LA, it felt like our lives had been hijacked. Quite simply, we had been invaded by this force field of catastrophic illness and we could not escape. A nightmare had begun.

And we were the lucky ones; we had money. We could afford care, we had the best doctors, we had family and loving friends. But it was difficult to breathe swallowed up as we were in the belly of the whale.

The horror of Louis's illness was that it completely took him captive. It seemed designed to provoke him and challenge who he wasn't. How quickly it moved around his brain and incapacitated different centers of it. I couldn't get over how rapidly he'd deteriorated in those few short weeks abroad. "My body is betraying me," he tried to tell me.

A few months into his illness, we now needed full-time nursing. Louis could no longer walk unsupported. He was sometimes delusional. We never had a conversation about it as he got sicker and sicker. He was completely stoic about it all. One day as I was helping him walk to the kitchen, he said, "It's very sad to not be able to walk." That was the closest to a complaint I ever heard from him during the year of his illness. He showed constant courage.

The enormity of what was happening began to hit me. Sleeping was impossible. I started a regimen of two Tylenol PM and one Ativan before bed. Ativan. A miracle drug. It made it all bearable for a few hours.

We retreated into our tiny house in Los Angeles. It was a lovely, cozy cottage in a stand of eucalyptus trees, patrolled by owls, coyotes, raccoons, and rats. Also the odd snake, though not the rattling kind. Birds nested on our patio as our cats waited smugly beneath the nest, an expectant strike force. I kept the house filled with flowers, inside and out. Before I left for work every day, I would put CDs on the stereo that Louis loved: jazz, Mahler, Fats Waller, Astor Piazzolla's Argentine tangos.

Some people found it impressive that I continued to work. First of all, I had no choice. A series contract is binding. And the series was called *Murphy Brown*, and I played Murphy, present in every scene. The show was still a big hit. But the truth is, going to work kept me sane. As sane as was possible during that time. It was my support system.

I loved everyone on the cast and crew and I had seen them get married, have children, sometimes get divorced; I'd seen their kids graduate from high school. We were a family that stuck together. Going to the *Murphy* set was a huge comfort, and the familiarity of the set was something I looked forward to every morning.

When Louis came to LA sick, I was almost at the end of Season 7 of *Murphy Brown*. The daily grind of a series was wearing on the other members of the cast by now. But not me. They'd come back after our one week off a month, grumbling about being back at work. I'd arrive relieved, thrilled, soothed to see them after a solid week of Louis's doctor's appointments, hoisting the wheelchair out of the trunk of the car as we wheeled from neurologists to hematologists to ophthalmologists to physical rehabilitation. Pretending to help Louis prepare for his next movie—it was obvious that we were merely going through the motions. Interacting with nurses and cooks. Looking after Chloe.

When Louis got sick, the cast and crew were all there for me. That was the first instance when they wrote Murphy out of a few scenes. Sometimes Louis would come to the set just to have a different venue. I'd watch people's reactions to his wheelchair. This dynamic, vibrant man could now scarcely speak. They knew what was happening.

Louis hated to be seen in his wheelchair; he felt it was very demeaning. As soon as he was brought onto the stage, he would try to get out of it. I knew that would be trouble, but everyone was wonderful to him. Bob Daly, head of the studio, got him courtside seats to some all-star basketball exhibit at Warner Bros. Kobe Bryant practically fell into his lap after a three-point shot; Louis loved it.

Work was a place where laughter, often bawdy laughter, was usually heard. That year our director was witty, beloved Peter Bonerz. Faith and I would browse through catalogs at the rehearsal table until they had to be confiscated; the newly introduced Victoria's Secret catalogs were popular with the guys as well. But work for me was a place of solace, especially then.

Everyone on the *Murphy* set was considerate and sensitive, almost to a fault. Since I'd had to fly back to New York early on when we were still trying to figure out Louis's diagnosis, I'd let people on the show know what was going on. Louis's guest appearance on *Murphy* was the year before, so the crew all knew him. Grant Shaud let me work out my frustration on him, never flinching if the pretend shove the script called for turned into more of a roundhouse punch. Grant became my punching bag that year. Literally. I'd hit him with scripts. I was trying to process so much that I didn't know how to begin, so I'd whack him.

Learning the dialogue was difficult during the best of times; now my memory was useless. I would hide my lines all over the sets—on the banister of the staircase, in the bottom of a coffee mug. Thursday nights before the Friday tapings found me with Beverly Dixon, our dialogue coach, tears streaming down my face at the effort of trying to memorize fifty pages of lines. The scripts were always well-written, always smart, well-informed, usually very witty, often moving —but I could no longer learn them the way I had been able to in the past.

• • •

During our three-month summer hiatus from *Murphy*, all I did was care for Louis. When you do a television series, you hope your life conforms to the series schedule. You get sick only during hiatus. And then it usually hits with a trifecta. Every flu bug, every lurking bacteria, every vagrant virus that has been patiently waiting to pounce attacks with precision force. But I couldn't allow myself to succumb. All attention had to be focused on Louis.

We tried to find things that would distract him. I'd bought an air hockey table for Chloe and her friends. Louis, while he could still stand, loved playing it and would challenge all of us to games. He'd support himself with his left hand while whacking the puck with his right. It was the only physical thing he could do, and he was ferocious. "I can do this! I'll cream you!"

I rented a house on the beach at Malibu so he could have a change of scene. He'd been house-bound for months. We had close friends over for luncheons at the beach house. Jodie Foster, who was perfectly bilingual in French, came to visit us there. She'd been interested in a part in *Damage*, the story of a doomed love affair, which Juliette Binoche ended up doing. Louis had liked her very much and thought she was extremely talented but didn't know if she was right for the part. Jodie, being who she was, stayed friends with him anyway.

My mom's housekeeper, Ubol, adored Louis and would make lemongrass soup for him, which he loved. As his illness progressed and chewing was difficult, she would puree the soup. Faith Ford made gumbo for Louis, which was one of his favorites; I'd meet her husband at the top of Mulholland Drive to make the drop.

Trying to keep Louis entertained or engaged was exhausting. Once, while I was reading him an article from the Science section of the *New York Times*, droning on about neurons, Ubol brought him a platter of guacamole and chips. His eyes lit up and he exclaimed, *"Now* you're talking!" and dove in. I hired a wonderful Brazilian woman named Edna Grover as chef. She was a welcome presence in the house—very calming, with a wonderful lightness and a wicked sense of humor. Our old calico cat Pearl stayed with Louis in bed. *"Elle m'adore,"* he said proudly, patting her with his one good hand. Lois kept constant watch over Louis, always with him; she never left his side.

I took Chloe to Aspen for a week to stay with our friend Martha Luttrell, just to get away from it all. When we returned and walked in through the gate to the patio, Louis was standing there in his pajamas, supported by Danette, the nurse. His arms were open. "Oh, my darling, my darling," he told me and we held each other tight. In that moment, for all that we'd lost, I felt that our relationship went back to the beginning.

Soon the effort to speak became exhausting and humiliating for Louis. It would take minutes to make himself understood; he finally voluntarily stopped trying. He'd make sounds but finally gave up even that because it was too much trouble for him. He would nod his head and shake it to indicate yes or no, pleasure or displeasure, or gesture with his good hand. He understood everything that was said but had no ability to respond. He couldn't communicate well, but his mental acuity remained mostly intact. Our friend Herbert Allen brought us to his ranch and we were sitting at the dinner table. Guests were engaged in a political discussion, and Herbert asked Louis a question about dates and truces in Bosnia, a complicated but a yes or no question. Louis nodded a vigorous yes. He was absolutely tracking, but he had become trapped in his body. A body he could now barely move.

The tension was affecting everyone in the house. Caring for a critically ill person dredged up long-suppressed memories of the deaths of other family members and sharpened the sense of loss in all of us. There was no escape.

And into this came Larry. He arrived in the well-manicured hands of a woman in a small Mercedes as I was walking Lois.

"Is this your puppy? I found him on the street."

She held out a ten-week-old Cavalier King Charles-ish black-and-white puppy. I explained that he wasn't mine but offered to take him, which I did, carrying him snuggled in my shoulder as we walked home. He had no collar or trace of ID, and I put up no flyers or made any effort whatsoever to find the owner. I named him Larry, went straight to the pet store and ordered a tag that said so, and his arrival immediately lifted the gloom that lay over the house.

There is nothing like a puppy. Everyone fell in love with him except Louis and Lois. To Louis, he was an interloper, and when Larry would trot past Louis in his favorite armchair in the kitchen, he would try to kick him with his good leg. After a few close calls, Larry just looped around him, out of range.

Lois was not happy with Larry from hello. He, however, worshipped her. He would sleep on the carpet below her chair. It took a few months, but Lois finally came around. In fact, we used to call him her personal trainer because Larry got an increasingly sedentary Lois moving again. At her next birthday party, Larry wore his new Superman costume.

It really costs you to take care of someone who's critically ill day after day. You just want to escape. I was in a black anger. I think I felt that my life, which had always been blessed, had suddenly been hijacked by this completely other force. We were all trapped in it.

Chloe, who had never been that close to her father, knew that she should take care of him out of duty. I never asked her to. This little nine-year-old would read to him, feed him, and bring him funny things that he'd love, like a pair of huge padded Goofy slippers from Disneyland that he loved and never took off. They'd always had a slightly fractious relationship characterized by long absences; for him to come back into her life under such catastrophic conditions was so difficult for her. The sadness was huge. One night I came into her bedroom to tuck her in and she and I ended up lying on her bed with tears streaming down both our faces. I felt like my heart was breaking. I'd drop her off at school and watch her screwing herself up to walk into her classroom with a bright, cheery greeting: "Good morning, peepsters!" But every day was a struggle. In photographs from that time, she has dark circles under her eyes and looks drained. We didn't really discuss Louis's prognosis. If there was any dialogue, it was "When will it be like before? When can we have our life back?"

In April, I took Chloe to Hawaii for a week. It was spring vacation and we needed a break; we were all on top of each other in our tiny, charming house. We went to Kona Village, where we had our own cottage on the beach. Chloe immediately joined the kids' program and they disappeared all day, consumed by activities. It was just what she needed. I learned to scuba dive and when she went with the kids to the luau at night, which was intended to give the parents quiet nights together, I had dinner alone in the dining room and retreated to our cottage early and read. One night a gynecologist and his wife from Boston asked me to join them and I gratefully did.

There were no phones at Kona Village and no television. There was one phone booth in the lobby we all shared. There were no cell phones then. This was a good and a bad thing. The good was that this meant that the yahoos would go to the other glossy resorts that replicated their home away from home. The bad was that when your child was busy, you were on your own. But the nature of the hotel was self-selecting. It drew a certain low-key crowd. Despite the fact that *Murphy* was at its height at that time, during the entire week we spent at Kona Village, not one person came up to me to ask about the show or for an autograph. That was striking. The only other celebrity was Andy Garcia, who was there with his family; they were lovely. It wasn't until we boarded the plane to return to the mainland that I realized how singular the Kona ambiance was. The plane was filled with The Others: the guys with open shirts and gold chains, the women with towers of hair. Loud voices. Oblivious.

•••

Friends responded differently to Louis's dramatically diminished condition. Visitors would arrive through the patio gate; Louis and I would be sitting under the trees. Those who hadn't seen him in this state would visibly register shock even though they had been gently warned. Some had a gift for communicating with him and engaged him in conversations in which they knew he was interested and asked questions where he could respond yes or no. Louis was highly informed and driven by curiosity. "Where do you want them to sit?" I'd ask, and Louis would point to the appropriate chair. He felt he wouldn't look as compromised from certain angles. Donald Sutherland, who'd starred in Louis's *Crackers*, brought a book of poetry and read to him. Julianne Moore had done *Vanya on 42nd Street* with Louis and sat with Louis on the porch while I waited outside. Andre Gregory, whom Louis had directed in *My Dinner with Andre*, brought wonderful, eclectic CDs wrapped in different colors of paper. Andre had lost his wife Chiquita a couple years before; he got it.

Mike Nichols and Diane Sawyer came, as did Buck Henry and Lorne Michaels. Lorne and Louis had always gone to Yankees games together; Lorne had season tickets. Bette Midler and Martin von Haselberg visited. Bette and Martin lived just down the hill from us in Coldwater

Canyon. They sent flowers from time to time, adding grace notes to our lives, as did Alice and Michael Arlen. Others, including Wallace Shawn, David Hare, Julianne Moore, Peter Davis, Jacques Cousteau, Andre Gregory, Nora Ephron, and Jodie Foster, sent thoughtful, entertaining letters to try to lift Louis's spirits.

From Wally Shawn, June 19, 1995:

Dear Candice,

I've just written Louis a letter, but I didn't mention that of course I would still LOVE to pay a visit if you and he ever thought it would cheer him up, divert, or amuse him in any way. I have no idea what state he's in or what state you're in—I mean, I can guess certain things about your probable mood a little more easily, I suppose, maybe. I wish I could do something for you, but I know I can't. I'm thinking of you, though—and personally I've always been half-inclined to believe that those medieval monks who stayed in their monasteries and prayed for people actually had some effect.

From Alice Arlen, August 27, 1995:

This summer I went way way out on the Badlands near us, which are red and deserty and mysterious and look like fairy castles. I went to what locally are known as teepee rings, though no one knows how they got there. Circles, absolutely perfect, about the circumference of a small circus tent, made of flat stones sunk way into the red dirt. . . . Lots of wind, flat, like the top of the world. You can just see the tip of the Grand Teton eighty miles to the west. You can see what's known as Crowheart Butte on the Reservation to the east, in the Owl Creek mountains. You can see the biggest concentration of glaciers in North America to the south, in the Wind Rivers. You can see the Absarokas to the north, stretching all the way to Montana.

I made a little fire, which was almost impossible in that wind, but I used charcoal starter. I stood in the middle of the teepee ring. And I said your names.

Oh, and I heard a joke this summer, which probably you've heard, but anyhow, here it is: A man called Joe comes into a bar carrying a suitcase. He asks for a free drink in exchange for showing the bartender something great. From the suitcase, Joe takes out a miniature grand piano. And then he takes out a twelve-inch man called Bill. And Bill sits down at the piano and starts to play Cole Porter songs. The bartender is impressed and says he sure would like to have something great like Bill and the piano. Joe explains that the bartender can have anything he wishes for if he'll just give Joe another bottle. The bartender brings out a bottle; then Joe tells him to rub the magic suitcase and wish for anything he wants. The bartender wishes hard. Pretty soon there is a great noise and thumping and squawking on the roof, and soon after that, the roof falls in from the weight of a million ducks. "But I wished for a million *bucks!*" screams the bartender. "Well, do you think," asks Joe, "that I wished for a twelve-inch pianist?"

Fax machines were fairly new. We got one to distract Louis. John Guare, the playwright and Louis's screenwriter for *Atlantic City*, would fax incredibly witty and intelligent and gossipy bulletins from New York:

22 Aug 95

. . . Albee's *Three Tall Women* is just terrific and get to it when it comes to the Taper. You just can't go out only to rock and roll concerts, smoking joints and waving your hands in the air. You got to get some culture.

24 Aug 95

Sam [Cohn] has moved into his new quarter on CPW with Jane; all of ICM is leaning forward wondering about CAA. His office screwed up last week. Sharon Stone showed up at Stoppard's *Arcadia* with 5 friends, dressed to the movie star 9s for a night at the theater. Sam's office had never made the call to the box office. No tickets available. She said Hey no problem. Can't see Stoppard? I'm off to *Babe*. Tom was there that night and said Well, at least she didn't come to *Arcadia* because she couldn't get into *Babe*.

29 Aug 95

I trust you're watching the tennis Open. Monica Seles is great. In the duel they're setting up, I vote Sampras over Agassi. Do you think Brooke Shields puts on the *Pretty Baby* video when she wants to turn Andre on? A grotesque thought.

20 Sept 95

I got four messages yesterday from the set [of *Marvin's Room*] saying that Meryl wants to hang up the phone. Meryl wants to hang up the phone. There's a scene where she's on the phone and it cuts away before the call ends. But 4 people called me yesterday to say Meryl wants to hang up the phone. So I brilliantly just faxed off something that went to the effect of "Goodbye." She hangs up the phone.

You've heard the story about Fellini going to heaven. St Peter says God wants you to make a movie. Shakespeare has written it. Michelangelo is the art director. Mozart's doing the score. Laurence Olivier is the male lead. Fellini: And who's opposite? St. Peter: Well, God has this girl . . .

27 July 95

Went to see the bill of 3 one acts by Mamet, Elaine May, and Woody Allen. Linda Lavin is sublime. Elaine's piece about a hooker calling a suicide hotline is about to be brilliant and then it ends. It's a play building to a scene à faire and the moment it gets there, it's like they didn't pay the electric bill and shut off the lights. It stops at the very moment it gets blazingly interesting. The centerpiece of the evening, Woody's play, is so bitter without being dark that you wonder about his impulse to write it. It too goes so far and then pulls back, pulls back, pulls back. Dealing with that impulse to open doors with daring bravado and then spend all your energy not to go down the new corridors—I saw Joe Orton's play *What the Butler Saw* at the National in June in a not great production, but still the dizzying fact is Orton goes too far. The play is still thrilling.

I guess it's why I like to work with you. No, I guess it's why I wanted to work with you— to see *Feu Follet*, a picture that went too far, Zazie—the key story you tell is the one with the punch line, "Too much for Paris?" Does Candy know that? How much is too much for Paris? I think that's what makes Woody's films so popular—besides the fact that some of them like *Crimes and Misdemeanors* are just good—that he boldly flings open doors; the audience's relief is that he chooses then NOT to go down the newly opened corridors. It's amazing the money audiences will pay not to go do those corridors and, I guess, more amazing, that fact of acknowledging a closed door even exists can be taken for courage. Somewhere TS Eliot says Life is a struggle to think well of oneself.

20 July 95

Everybody sends you their love. But then I hope you know the amount of love you generate here in hard-hearted New York. Remember that evening Lee RazzleDazzle [Radziwill] said to you, "What's wrong with America is all these foreigners they let in. America should just close its doors and stop letting all these foreigners in." You looked at her: "But, Lee, I am a foreigner." She said, "Oh, Louis, I don't mean fabulous foreigners."

21 July 95

Does Chloe know the song "Abba Dabba Honeymoon" as sung by Debbie Reynolds in the MGM musical *Two Weeks with Love*? It made her a star and might well be a new cut on your answering machine announcement. [Chloe used to leave lively, witty welcomes on our answering machine. Once I encouraged her to sing "Diamonds Are a Girl's Best Friend" and sign off with, "Leave *your* diamonds after the beep."] Look, Lana Turner was discovered at a soda fountain. It seems very cyberspace to be discovered on an answering machine. I want to be part of Chloe's career!

10 Aug 95

To get another call when I came home yesterday—hurrah! All I could think about was phrases like: Did my old heart good / keep those phone calls coming / your call put a bounce in my step / he's my friend / my bosom buddy. I looked up "friendship" in the quote book: Montaigne: friendship, the highest degree of perfection in society. Dumas: Friendship is forgetting what one gives remembering what one receives. Disraeli: The gift of the gods and the most precious boon to man. La Rochefoucauld: Nothing but a system of traffic in which self-love always proposes itself to some advantage. Thoreau: Only a little more honor among roués. Mark Twain: A holy passion, so sweet and steady and loyal and enduring in its nature that it will last through a lifetime, if not asked to lend money.

So it's all clichés but then I learned yesterday that the word *cliché* comes from the French for stick—a printer's stick. In the 18th/19th century, printers liked writers who used phrases like unbridled lust, a stitch in time, birds of a feather because they didn't have to set those phrases in type. The printer would just reach for the stick that had the phrase all ready set. In fact, writers of clichés were paid more because it made life so much easier for the printer.

Well, you've never done anything on any stick.

Marie-Christine Breton, Louis's wonderful assistant, flew to Los Angeles to say good-bye to Louis. Armande Gonçalves, the caretaker at Le Coual who had been with us for twenty years, called. She couldn't understand anything Louis was saying but simply responded, "*Oui, monsieur*, rest assured we will take care of it. Everything will be done as you want." She knew that what Louis needed was reassurance that Le Coual would continue to be maintained—which it has been, and beautifully.

One of the most moving visits came from Jacques Cousteau, the legendary oceanographer, marine conservationist, and filmmaker. Louis had started his career at twenty-one as cameraman for Cousteau's first movie, *The Silent World*. Cousteau had been looking for a cameraman who was also an excellent swimmer, and Louis got the job. He spent a couple of years on Cousteau's boat, the *Calypso*, exploring underground river caves and the wreck of the *Andrea Doria* off the coast of Massachusetts. They became very close, like father and son. The first night Louis took me to meet Jacques over dinner, he and Louis dove right in. The conversation started on substance and ended on substance—no chitchat. Jacques opened with, "This is what's left of the oceans," and for the next two hours over a wonderful seafood meal, they spoke in French about the state of the planet. I was dazzled.

Jacques was going to be in Los Angeles for a few days and wanted to visit Louis. My brother, Kris, picked Cousteau up at his hotel and drove him up to our house in the hills. Cousteau was very distant and reserved on the way to the house. This aloofness was a bit of a disappointment for my brother, who'd idolized him as a kid. Kris brought him onto the patio, where Cousteau saw his able-bodied lieutenant now in a wheelchair.

When Cousteau finished his visit, he got back into Kris's car and broke down into sobs. He was undone by what he had found.

During Louis's illness, we reconnected at the depth we'd had in the first five years of our marriage. But getting through every day was like climbing a mountain. I was on call from early morning to late at night, getting Louis up, getting Chloe off to school, heading off to work, going back on duty the second I got home from work. Close friends would ask if I was talking to anyone during the period of Louis being ill. I was not. I was handling it. But just barely. Our house was in a permanent state of high alert. The constant and urgent priority was always Louis.

At night tears would spill from my eyes, waterworks with no control. I would sit in bed at night, hiding in the housekeeper's room behind the kitchen. I slept on the sofa bed there, since Louis was now in a hospital bed—just washing my face with tears. I got it out in any way I could and I remember thinking, "I hope I don't get cancer from this" because I felt so clobbered in such an unyielding way. I read the Bible in that room, and I'm not a Bible reader. I prayed. I was looking for support, something to soothe me, to buck me up. I was just treading water.

Even though I was fairly certain Louis wasn't going to survive, I made totally irrational choices.

Some odd, aggressive woman had somehow gotten my number; she worked for a half-baked doctor in Tijuana who could, she assured me, cure Louis with some vials of serum for $75,000. I actually stumbled along with the scheme until something or someone helped me come to my senses. That's the danger of magical thinking; you'll do anything to save the one you love. You're at your most unguarded and vulnerable.

After a couple of months of Louis's illness, I was testy. Worse, I was livid. I never expressed any anguish or sorrow. I never cried or complained: I just seethed. It was not pretty. The situation was so huge that I had to deal with it somehow. It wasn't going away. My friend Connie said, "There's this man who has had good results with a specific kind of therapy that brings up grief in people skilled in repressing it." Perhaps I should give his primal scream therapy a try. So I went to visit the Warlock.

I drove to the little ranch house where the Warlock worked out of his garage, which he'd converted into an office. He was a tall, very powerful-looking man. We talked for a few minutes, then he told me to lie down on the couch tucked into the corner of the office. He covered me with a blanket and said, "Start breathing. I want you to take deep, deep breaths." I don't remember whether he said to scream, but somehow that simple action reduced me to a state of hysterics. I started taking deep, gulping breaths and then some mechanism released the grief. I started to sob and sob and sob at the top of my lungs. Then I found myself screaming. This went on for about fifteen minutes. The Warlock returned, we spoke a few minutes more, then my time was up and I left. I felt like a raw wound, but at least it unblocked stuff, got it moving. Some of the repressed feelings had been given voice and been expressed. I felt better.

I began seeing the Warlock once a week. I would lie down on that couch and instantly think of Louis, of the anger at my life being taken away from me. I was angry at Louis for coming home to be taken care of, for throwing our tranquil household into this all-consuming, whirling vortex.

One afternoon, after my shrieking session, I drove to meet Louis and his brother Vincent and Vincent's then-wife Dorothy at a Japanese restaurant called Matsuhisa on La Cienega. It was owned and run by a man named Nobu Matsuhisa who went on to create the tony, haute cuisine restaurant chain Nobu now known around the world. It was a very popular restaurant but we went early, at six o'clock, and got the tiny private room where we sat at the counter. Louis loved Japanese food. We hadn't taken him out for dinner often since his illness, but he was understandably suffering from cabin fever. Dinner went well. Louis was able to still swallow, so that was good.

After dinner, I pushed Louis's wheelchair into the parking lot to collect our car. At that time in LA, shows like *E* and *Extra* were just starting up, and teenagers with video cameras would circle Beverly Hills and Hollywood, scanning the hot spots for compromised celebs. These hit-and-run paparazzi commandos would drive two to a car, cruising the fertile ground. Suddenly two kids with backward caps in a VW Passat pulled in front of us and started shooting video of Louis in his chair. We were still keeping his illness quiet then; nothing had been announced. I freaked out. I jumped in front of Louis and started yelling, "You cocksuckers! You motherfuckers! Get the hell out of here!" I started beating on the roof of their car with my fist. I was enraged; I'm surprised I didn't punch anyone. The kids were so terrified that they jumped back into their Passat and screeched away.

I was literally shaking after my psychotic break. Louis was staring at me. Vincent looked stunned. Dorothy said, "We hadn't realized how much this was taking out of you, Candy."

I called my old friend and publicist, Pat Kingsley. She did whatever she had to do to suppress the footage.

From then on, whenever I saw the Warlock, I was careful to go home after and collect myself.

Louis's relationship with Chloe, usually fraught with absences, long ones, began to redefine itself during his illness. She became his caretaker, and in doing so, they found a connection with each other that was very powerful and moving.

Chloe was my caretaker too:

August 10, 1995

Dear Mama,

I know Poppy being sick is really hard for you. So I just want you to know I'm right beside you. And I'll all ways love you more than anyone or anybody. And if there is anything I can do to help you just ask.

Peach Pit

I didn't tell Chloe about her father's prognosis until I felt we'd arrived close to the time. I weighed it very carefully. "You know, I don't think Poppy is going to get well from this." She was very emotional. A week after that, we went to church, which we didn't do regularly, with our friends Dey and David Ladd, whose daughter Shane was Chloe's best friend. They were having a fund-raiser to reroof the church's terra-cotta tiles. Everybody could donate and write a message on a tile for the roof. Chloe immediately wrote down on hers, "Louis Malle is a man who will soon leave us, but he will be in our hearts forever." The Ladds and I just looked at each other.

When the illness went on and on, Chloe and I were taking it hour by hour, day by day. At night I would just lie in her bed with her as tears came down our faces. You just want it to be over. While you have a hope of curing them against all odds of recovery, you also just want it to be over, because it's such a huge weight and anguish to deal with all the time.

Chloe came to truly love Louis during the last few months of his life. When he could still speak, his first words of the day were always, "Where's Chloe?" A month before he died, when speech had fled, he gestured for the nurse to wheel him into Chloe's room while she was at school. He sat there for half an hour, just looking.

On Halloween, Chloe had a small party at our house with friends. Louis came out in his wheelchair. By then he could use only one hand to make signals and point. He didn't want to use an alphabet board: it was too undignified. Chloe walked her friends over to him and said proudly, "Guys, this is my dad." They were very alike.

I came upon Louis and my brother sitting together in the kitchen. Louis was in his wheelchair, struggling unsuccessfully to speak. Kris took his hand and said to him, "I know what you're trying to say: I'm the funniest guy you know." Louis smiled and nodded his head vigorously. My brother continued: "And you love me very much." Louis locked eyes with him and slowly nodded.

When it looked like Louis was close to the end, I arranged for Chloe to be with Ingrid in New York, then spend Thanksgiving with our friends the Kennedys in East Hampton.

After Louis had gone to sleep, Danette, his wonderful nurse from Belize, would sit with me in the kitchen and try to prepare me. "When they do die, you want to not be there when they take the body out, because that's very traumatic to see. Whoever is there," she explained, "it activates whatever losses they've suffered—spouses, mothers. That death could trigger difficult memories of other deaths. Nurses are professionally equipped to not have it penetrate them past a certain point; the rest of you would be more deeply affected."

Louis could barely swallow or breathe in his last days; he was struggling, fighting for his life. Cuote, Kris, Vincent, and I were by his side. He died on November 23, 1995. It was Thanksgiving Day. He was sixty-three.

The day after Louis died, Kris, Vincent, Connie, and I went to Forest Lawn to choose a casket: a simple, elegant one, because the service was going to be in Paris. We were in that period between death and acceptance, a kind of limbo. It was useful to have things to do. We arranged with the consulate in LA to have the body flown to France for the funeral. We gave the funeral directors what we wanted Louis to wear: his favorite T-shirt that read "I Survived Catholic School," blue jeans, and the beloved Goofy slippers from Chloe for his feet. Cuote, Vincent, Kris, and I wrote letters to be tucked into the casket. We also included a few of his books: a memoir by François-René de Chateaubriand in French, essays by Rousseau, and a book about Le Pétomane, the famous farter who was all the rage in Paris in the 1920s.

A week later we flew from Los Angeles to New York to pick up Chloe and Ingrid. Ingrid had been Chloe's nanny since she was six months old. She was my close friend, like a sister to Chloe, and worked as Louis's assistant. She lived in our extra apartment downstairs. We left for Paris.

Louis's funeral was held at the Church of Saint-Sulpice in Saint-Germain on the Left Bank. The cathedral was filled with family, colleagues, and friends. Louis's youngest sister, Catherine, had organized it impeccably. She approached me as we entered the church. "*Il faut tenir ses émotions, Candice*," she cautioned me. Keep it under control. Get a grip. Be discreet.

The nave was filled with sunflowers, the flowers that grew around Le Coual. A beautiful jazz score was playing. Louis was the first person to have a jazz artist record a film score, in this case his second feature, *Elevator to the Gallows*, a murder thriller starring Jeanne Moreau in her breakout role. This was Louis's first feature with a tracking shot; he'd done it by placing the camera in a baby carriage to follow Jeanne down the Champs-Elysées. He had asked Miles Davis, hugely popular in France at that time, to record a trumpet score for the film. Miles did this in one night in Paris in a recording studio while watching the film on a screen in the sound stage. His haunting score was replayed in the cathedral.

There must have been a thousand people at the funeral. Jeanne Moreau was there. Playwright David Hare, who'd written the screenplay for Louis's *Damage*, flew in from London. John Guare came in from New York. Louis's old friend, writer-director Nicholas Meyer, flew with his daughter Rachel from London. Rachel, who'd lost her own mother the year before, was a great help to Chloe, who was in bad shape. By the time we arrived in Paris, she'd come down with a 103-degree fever, chills, and a flaming sore throat, as if all the suffering of the previous year had caught up with her at once. She lasted for half the service, then Ingrid took the two girls and Nick out a side entrance.

Cuote, who had been in New York for Louis's illness and back and forth to see him in LA, sat in the front pew looking battered and exhausted by the long siege we had all passed through. Cuote's mother, Gila, and her husband came from Munich. Justine had wanted to wear jeans to the service. She was in the flush of her Marxist phase and eschewed any form of adornment or materialism. Someone had convinced her to wear a dress; she paired it with Doc Marten combat boots, yet she still looked lovely. Louis, who was moved by *l'esprit de '68*, would have appreciated her fervor. Alexandra, Justine's mother and family to us all, was sitting in a pew toward the back; I took her to sit with us in the front. I knew very few people in the church, but in any case I was focused on the front, looking at Louis's casket.

I don't remember much, except suddenly being given a crucifix to bless the casket and cross myself, which, being a rogue Episcopalian, I had never done. Now I was winging it in front of a thousand French. Forehead (Father), then . . . *right* breast or *left* breast for the Son and the Holy Ghost? I fudged it. No one mentioned it. But at the end of the service, we remained in our seats while people filed out and paid their respects to the family. One of the first was Jacques Cousteau, who looked broken. He leaned in to kiss my cheeks and said, *"C'était mon fils"*—"He was my son." This was especially moving because Jacques had lost one of his own sons a few years earlier in a plane crash.

Cuote, Justine, and I filed out with Vincent and Catherine and walked down the stone steps. We watched as the four pallbearers loaded the casket into the hearse. The casket was sent to be cremated; we would scatter the ashes later. We gathered for a reception after the funeral.

We were none of us behaving entirely normally in this situation. My mother, I realized, had come to Paris for the funeral primarily because it would give her an opportunity to see Louis's brother, Jean-François. In one of the weirder chapters in our marriage, Louis and I had introduced Mom to Jean-François, thinking he would be someone she would enjoy having lunch with once in a while in New York City. But we forgot that Jean-François was a notorious ladies' man, a handsome, smooth, rakish devil. A Harvard graduate, a racehorse owner, and head of Lehman's in Europe, he'd left a trail of broken hearts in his path. My mother's was now at the end of the list.

During their affair Mom had lost twenty years. She wore a ponytail for the first time. She had a spring in her step; she was girlish. She went to Paris to visit him, frequenting a famous club, Les Bains, ate at his favorite haunts. Jean-François had taunted Louis at the time: "I'm going to have an affair with your mother-in-law. I'm going to marry her and then I'll become your father-in-law and then I'm going to cut you off!" This was, unfortunately for my hard-hit mother, a joke.

Jean-François, characteristically, moved on. My mother was devastated. "He was the one," she announced. Frankly, it was, as moments go, slightly awkward, somewhat too close to a Louis Malle film. Too close for Louis Malle, in fact, who never mentioned it once during the entire few months of their affair.

But now we were at the reception and my mother, looking elegant and demure in a dress and a chapeau, was sitting down next to Jean-François, who had just lost his little brother and who looked wrecked. He now proceeded to get more wrecked, and now his brother's mother-in-law was confronting him about who the hell knows what, and frankly, Mom, it was not the time.

I came back to Los Angeles and had one more week off before I had to report back to work. I was completely out of body for weeks afterward; just putting one foot in front of the other was a challenge. I decided to get a leg wax; it just seemed like something to do. Eve, who always did it, looked at the robot standing before her. "Come," she told me, took me into a back room, and gave me a massage, the most soothing treatment she could think of.

My mission was to restore Chloe's life as soon as possible. The first thing Chloe and I did was have our Christmas party. Everybody showed up because they knew that was what was needed.

That was my way to try to kick-start life again. Chloe and I went to Michael and Eleanora Kennedy's home on Long Island for Christmas and then returned to LA.

Louis's things were in Los Angeles, New York, Paris. I didn't do anything with them for quite a while. I eventually flew to Paris to go through the apartment with Louis's lovely assistant, Marie-Christine Breton. I gave Louis's ties and some sweaters to his friends. I kept a lot of his clothes for Chloe, who wanted them. She always thought she would have them cut down for her. She kept his monogrammed shirts that he'd worn to death—cuffs and collars frayed. She also kept his sweater vests, which she still wears. She'd started wearing a locket with a tiny picture of Louis around her neck. One day she had a track meet and shortly before her race, she took the locket off, opened it, and propped it up against her track bag so Louis could see her run.

On March 4, 1996, we had a memorial service for Louis at the New Victory Theater in New York. The theater was where Louis had workshopped his final film, *Vanya on 42nd Street*, about New York actors rehearsing Chekhov's *Uncle Vanya*. John Guare, Mike Nichols, Alice Arlen (dear friend and screenwriter for *Alamo Bay*), Chloe,

Andre Gregory, and Wallace Shawn from *My Dinner with Andre* all spoke.

Wally described Louis as "a hedonist who got pleasure from looking at reality. I was always concerned about how little he lived up to the stereotype of the Frenchman, particularly the food. . . . it was the people who made him hungry. No one had a more acute appreciation of how difficult it was to convey the world to a stranger in a dark room."

Mike said:

Directing a movie is like sex. You never see anyone else doing it, so you're not sure you're doing it right. We'd compare notes about this fierce and wonderful job. He was the only filmmaker I talked to at any length about this. He was always so modest and tentative. . . . Louis's genius in his films was that he reminded us how ordinary cataclysmic things look as they happen. . . . Even a young boy sleeping with his mother: ordinary in Louis's hands and amazingly okay. After the press screening of *Murmurs of the Heart*, Louis's mom said, "Louis, it brings back such memories!" . . .

Bit by bit, it comes over us that we shall never hear this laughter again, and that this one garden is forever locked against us, and at that moment begins our true mourning. For nothing in truth can replace that true companion. Old friends cannot be created out of hand. Nothing can match the treasure of common memories. . . . It is idle having planted an acorn in the morning to expect that afternoon to sit by an oak, so life goes on. For years we plant the seed, we feel ourselves rich, and then comes other years when time does its work and our plantation is sparse. One by one, our comrades depart, deprive us of their shade.

People went out of their way to show up. Herbert Allen had arrived that afternoon from Africa; he didn't know if he could make it, but he came right from the airport. Susan Sarandon, with whom Louis had had an affair for a few years during the filming of *Pretty Baby* and *Atlantic City*, was in the audience, as were Diane Sawyer, Joan Didion and John Gregory Dunne, Brooke Hayward, Peter Duchin, Diane von Furstenberg, and Bill and Rose Styron. Film-makers who loved and respected him, like Sidney Lumet, turned out to pay their respects. Bette Midler also attended.

I'd asked all three kids if they'd wanted to speak. Cuote and Justine chose not to. Chloe was nervous about speaking, but she definitely wanted to. Her remarks were very personal, really powerful. She'd just turned ten. She was so like

Louis: a small person with a force and a strong will who wants to work and make her mark. Mike Nichols introduced her.

I love my Poppy. I always will. There were times, though, I was ready to kill him. I remember once at Le Coual, our house in France, I told my mom I didn't like him. I was five at the time. Now I think about that time again. Who would ever say they didn't like their father? Though at that time, I was convinced he never loved me. Of course he loved me; he just didn't know how to show it sometimes. We were always competing against each other. He had so much energy. I remember once, two weeks after he had open heart surgery, he jumped off the pool house roof into the pool, which my mom was not pleased about. For his sixty-second birthday, all he wanted was a pair of Rollerblades. His last ten months were a difficult time. He couldn't speak, he couldn't walk, he was in a wheelchair, which he despised. Before he'd been such a character, so speedy, so good at things. He hated being ill. He tried so hard to fight the illness, but it clung to him with so much power, even his spirit couldn't fight it. One night, during his last few months, I went into his room and squeezed into his uncomfortable hospital bed. I put my hand on his. I stayed there like that for a long time. That was the first time in ten years I'd told him I loved him. I had to get used to this new Poppy. Slowly, as time went by, I did. In November I left to spend Thanksgiving in New York. It was a simple good-bye, and it was the last.

People were stunned. She walked offstage and burst into tears.

John Guare was the final speaker.

The Vatican just released a list to celebrate the hundredth anniversary of filmmaking: the top forty-five films of all time that best demonstrate human values. Louis is on the list. Becky [John and Louis's assistant] wrote, "Louis just got a better seat in heaven." I'm guessing he's asking to see the manager. . . .

Louis seemed so inexportably French. . . . What fascinated me was in this age of the auteur, no Malle film was ever like any other Malle film. A Malle film seemed to have only one constant: to go too far into undiscovered territory and make you respond in a way you never could have presumed. You felt the Malle films were literally being discovered as they went along, and that the role for the director was to set a world in motion and to allow the results, no matter what. . . .

One day in 1979 out of the blue, he called to say if he could come see me. A rabbi in Winnipeg had given him $7.5 million to make a thriller, but Louis had nothing to film. He was making one last stab before he headed back to France, because he hated to lose the opportunity. Did I have any ideas? I did. Atlantic City was heavily in the news. . . . Because of tax consequences, filming must come to a stop December 31 or the rabbi would lose the tax break. It was at the end of July, so the film would have to be written, filmed, and completed in six months, almost to the day. This was Louis Malle. No, no, it didn't seem to be a problem. In ten days' time, I would be delivering the first draft of the script. . . . We typed and talked and typed and fought and typed . . . and weeks later, we were back in Atlantic City, shooting the movie.

"Who will be the cameraman?" I asked. "It doesn't matter," Louis said. "The film will always be the history of a combat between the director and the cameraman. . . . As long as it's beautiful, the mind accepts it. But I always have to have the same soundman. The eye sees beauty, but the ear hears the truth."

One day I was shocked to see Louis facing the camera, but with his eyes shut tight, his face bunched up, his hands bunched into fists, not even breathing. "For Christ's sake, Louis, watch the scene!" I said. "I don't have to watch the scene. When it goes well, I know. I become the camera. . . ."

It was New Year's Eve; Louis called cut and wrap. We'd made the deadline. I thought we would lose Louis to France. Adele and I went to New York with him for dinner at an Indian restaurant. Candice was there. Adele told me in the cab, "It's serious. He's going to marry her." And he did marry her. And everything changed in Louis's life. He settled down, or his version of settling down. Louis was free in New York, even invisible. "I'm only home in two places: New York City and Le Coual." I believe New York, Candice, Justine, Cuote, and Chloe gave him the courage and the objectivity to go back to his past and the past of his own country. He'd come back with *Au Revoir Les Enfants* or *May Fools*. . . .

We're not just here to remember Louis, not just to celebrate our friend, but to thank Candice for the incredible support she gave to us, Louis's friends, and to tell Candice that we're all friends and we don't go away.

In 1954 when Louis was on the *Calypso* with Cousteau, they were all talking about the fact that the *Andrea Doria* had just sunk. I believe the *Calypso* was the first boat on the scene. Louis went down as far as he had ever gone to see the sunken hulk of this vessel. His oxygen was giving out, and he was coming back up to the surface. He looked up and saw the sunlight that was streaming through the water. Around him, green ribbons suddenly appeared, making circles in the water, green ribbons appearing out of nowhere, like a strange ticker tape parade. He felt so light-headed and happy. He hated leaving the sea, because he belonged here alone, with all this light and beauty and the green ribbons, away from the world up there. Louis's oxygen was giving out. He came to the surface and instantly experienced an overwhelmingly brutal pain. His eardrums had burst. Those ribbons were not ribbons, but his own blood, which shows up green underwater. His eardrums would heal once, but not twice. His diving days were over. He would become a director, but stay in part a deep sea diver. . . .

That's what most truly defines Louis, a man who was most at home alone under the sea, going as deep as he could, getting as close as he could to the wreckage. Surrounded by sunlight and beautiful green ribbons that very soon as the price of living on this beautiful earth would turn into unbearable pain. But that never made him afraid to seek out new oceans, to go deeper, to say, "Be calm," and to make those of us lucky enough to be his friends go deeper too.

Lorne Michaels had the memorial filmed for us without being asked; he just set it up and did it, which was typical of him.

There was a reception afterward at a club. It all just passed in a blur.

There was a sense of tedious busyness after all that. Endless bankers came from France to settle various affairs. I'd drag myself home from the *Murphy Brown* set and a tall, elegant man with a finely waxed moustache would try to explain to me Louis's financial estate plans in French. For six months, almost all I did on weekends and in my free time was respond to condolence letters; there were four hundred in all. They mean a lot, these notes, and it's not for nothing that we keep them.

Jacques Cousteau wrote, "I keep a painful memory of my visit to him last month. He knew what he was going to endure. But in a mixture of joy and tears, I was very happy to have kissed him with all my heart." Nancy Sinatra enclosed a "little poem that . . . has a little magic in it" to help me through my "year of firsts." Director and dear friend Richard Attenborough wrote, "His reputation as both a man and a filmmaker scarcely knew of an equal. He was a true poet of the cinema: an original, an auteur: someone whose work will stand for all time as a record of his time on earth and a testament to that which he thought of value." "It isn't that Louis died," Art Buchwald noted, "but that he lived which is so important." Louis's wonderful assistant, Becky Browder, sent a card that read, "I send you all my love and have found comfort in knowing that Louis has certainly, by now, taken charge up in Heaven and has called more than one Angel an idiot. He was wonderful to me and I will miss him every minute of my life."

There were so many extraordinarily kind letters.

Dear Candice,

I was fortunate enough to be in Paris for Louis's service. I was in the back of the church (in costume) with Anthony Hopkins and Jim Ivory and was wearing a wig that made me look like Olive Oyl. I thought that would've made Louis laugh. And I hope he would have liked the fact that a movie was shooting right next door to Saint-Sulpice.

I am so sorry for you and Chloe. I know how great your loss is. I feel so lucky to have worked with Louis and known him a little— he was one of the most empathetic people and directors I have ever met. He also had the amazing quality of being really emotional in his work without being sentimental. As an actor, it was such a privilege to be seen through his eyes—he treated us all so carefully and with so much love and compassion. The way he shot you, you felt really seen and understood. In life he was equally compassionate to me.

I will miss him so much. I had hoped to know Louis for a long time. But I feel so fortunate to have been a part of his life and his work for the time that I did have. All my sympathy is with you and your family.

Love,
Julianne Moore

From Nora Ephron:

I dreamed about Louis last night and how much everyone loved him. You were in the dream, and Mike, and all of you were talking about him, and I cried as I listened to you. He was such a wonderful man with such a wonderful spirit, and I can't stand that he's gone. I know how strong you've been all these months and how hard this was for both of you. I wish you much love.

Chloe began to protest the endless note writing to acknowledge the condolence cards: "I don't understand. Something horrible happens to you, then you have to do something horrible again."

She wanted to go back to life as it was, which we couldn't. I had to read many condolence letters in French, some of them official. Louis's brother Vincent had to help me respond to ones from the minister of culture, for example, because I had no idea of the proper format in French.

Bob Daly published a full-page photo of Louis in *Variety* from Warner Bros. that said simply, "Farewell to a Friend." Louis had never worked for the studio, but I had, and I was always very touched by that.

After the initial period of shock ended and there was an exhalation, it took several weeks before the reality set in, which was that I had become Louis Malle's widow. *Widow.* The word was Dickensian. I don't know what I would have done if I hadn't had Chloe—she and I got each other through it.

Certainly the grieving wasn't traditional—whatever that was. Part of me was relieved to have it all over even as I missed Louis terribly. I thought I was better than I was. I began to become depressed late at night—the time he would usually call for our long catch-up conversations. I noticed that the weeping of mourning operated with a different mechanism than other kinds of crying. Your eyes don't mist or tear up; there's no sudden welling. It's like water over a tiny dam, so powerful it lowered the water table.

I felt adrift. I heard Chloe tell someone on the phone, "You think you are prepared, but you never really are."

That summer Chloe and I went to Venice for the first time, then Le Coual. It wasn't something I was looking forward to, because that house was always so much about him. We scattered Louis's ashes there, everyone choosing a spot that had the greatest personal significance. Vincent, who loved a good bottle as much as Louis, sprinkled his share down in the wine cellar. Built in the fifteenth century, chilly even on the hottest summer day, this spot, with its endless racks of wine, had been sacred for Louis. Chloe scattered her share on the carpet in his study. I spread mine in the field in front of Le Coual, which for me has always had one of the prettiest views of the house.

How could I replace what influence Louis would have had on Chloe? He had been so superior intellectually and culturally. In LA, Chloe and I went to endless concerts and museums, even a production of *Zulu Macbeth* in Zulu. We took her cousin, Jackson. I took her on trips to Morocco and Moscow with our friends the Kennedys, visiting every museum and cultural highlight just as Louis would have done. Other kids came back to school tanned and peppy after two weeks in Hawaii or Mexico. Chloe staggered in pale and jet-lagged from St. Petersburg. I was trying to replace Louis, fill in the holes as much as possible, take up as much of the slack. It was a fool's errand.

I don't believe in an afterlife. I wish I did, but I'm willing to be convinced. A tiny part of me thinks Louis might exist someplace on some level, but I don't think anyone's had any visitations.

Well, perhaps. At Le Coual, the bathrooms were up in the tower, one of the original parts of the building. The night after we scattered the ashes, I was upstairs in the bathroom when a huge white barn owl alit on the deep stone sill outside the window. It stayed there for perhaps half a minute, peering at me two feet away, then flew off. Back in California, my brother, Kris, a very rational guy, was staying in our house, where Louis had died, when suddenly both electric gates to the home and the private walkway swung wide open. "Fuck that," Kris declared, and ran straight to his car and drove away, leaving the doors unlocked. My stepdaughter, Justine, wrote a screenplay about Louis's death. In the play, he appears to her on a train, silent but very much there as a presence. I read the screenplay and was very moved and impressed.

When Louis was ill, Chloe had written a note, a declaration, really, and signed it with her name: "I do and always will love life. Chloe Malle." I realized that I had existed for two reasons: to see Chloe into this world and to see Louis out of it.

Louis could be a troublemaker; he liked to stir the pot. He was a Scorpio who often told me, "I have my little Scorpio tail." But our connection was very strong, very deep. We loved each other completely, then were pulled apart by distance. By work.

I survived it. Chloe survived it. I think about Louis all the time and how he would be such a great father to Chloe now because they have a similar intellect and appetite for life, a go-for-broke dynamism and metabolism. I miss his dry, wicked wit, the brilliance of his brain. He was knowledgeable and fascinating to listen to on any given subject.

Louis and I had fifteen years together—more like ten, really, if you count the absences because of our work. They were the richest years of my life.

❦ 18 ❦

After Louis's death, one of my missions was to give Chloe some of the intellectual and cultural exposure that he would have provided. For her first vacation after Louis died, we met our friends, Eleanora and Michael Kennedy, in Washington, DC, during spring break. We toured the monuments, the National Mint, the Vietnam Memorial, the Library of Congress, the Smithsonian, and Arlington National Cemetery; we saw the Cherry Blossom Festival at the Tidal Basin and visited Dumbarton Oaks. To cap it off, we had a family dinner with the Clintons and spent the night in the Lincoln Bedroom.

Louis and I had been invited to the White House on three occasions when Ronald Reagan was in office. Twice we'd had to decline: an intimate dinner with President Mitterrand, which we couldn't attend because Louis was off filming; and the state dinner for Prince Charles and Princess Diana, which Chloe's late arrival forestalled. The third time was a state dinner for the prime minister of India. I borrowed a Chanel dress, a navy chiffon strapless gown with a satin Chanel bow and a camellia at the breast and I slicked my hair back in a ponytail with another Chanel camellia and a big navy bow. I added large Chanel pearl earrings and an antique diamond and sapphire bracelet that Louis had given me; I felt I could have taken on anyone.

The Clintons were the ones who made our overnight in the Lincoln Bedroom possible. I'd first met them at a fundraiser in Beverly Hills before President Clinton was elected for his first term. It was during all the Dan Quayle/Murphy brouhaha. When we were introduced, Clinton exclaimed, "Whoa, you're really in the center of the storm here." He was followed by Hillary, who was warm, enthusiastic, with a laser-like focus. Both were engulfed in a swirling cloud of energy. It was an electric force field. Never had I met two more dynamic people.

The Clintons, now in the White House, had sent a very kind condolence letter after Louis died. Two months later, in February 1996, they invited me to a state dinner for Jacques Chirac, then the president of France. I was in the middle of shooting *Murphy Brown*, so I borrowed a chocolate satin Valentino strapless gown and jumped a plane to Washington for one night. Our friend John Guare sweetly came down to DC from New York to accompany me.

When John and I arrived at the North Portico of the White House, a Marine in full dress uniform offered me his arm and escorted me down Cross Hall. We were led down a press line, then announced by someone with a microphone: "Candice Bergen and John Guare." Attendance at a state dinner, for a few hours, confers the status of Master of the Universe; there was definitely the sense that one had arrived. Then John and I were escorted to the receiving line and introduced to Al and Tipper Gore, Jacques and Bernadette Chirac, and President and Mrs. Clinton. Greg and Veronique Peck, Michael Douglas, and Oscar and

Françoise de la Renta were also in attendance. Afterward we were directed to a salon for drinks and mingling.

At dinner I was seated at President Chirac's right hand. He was a tall, elegant man, unexpectedly charming; his appeal didn't register on TV. He'd followed the very austere Mitterrand into office, and the French delegations were known to be somewhat reserved, but Chirac was very personable. We chatted about Louis and he expressed his condolences. He told me how he'd worked in the American Northwest as a young man and toured all the national parks.

"*Je suis un grand fan de vous*," he said. "Please, next time you come to Paris, visit us at the Élysée Palace." Then he confessed that he was still working on the toast he'd make at the dinner. "Jefferson was the third president, yes?" He wanted to verify it before he spoke.

Hillary sat on Chirac's other side. I loved her immediacy and intelligence, how present she was. Her warmth and ability to connect with people are striking.

After dinner, there was dancing in the East Room to musical accompaniment by the Marine Band. When the evening was over, I got a few hours' sleep, then caught the first plane back to LA; I had to be on set for *Murphy* in the morning.

At some point during the evening, Mrs. Clinton had said, "We would love to have you and your daughter stay here in the White House one night if that would interest you."

I took her at her word; I'm the last person to insert myself in social situations, but I didn't think she'd have offered if she hadn't meant it. It was a gesture of pure kindness; I never played a part in the campaign. The Clintons were paying back nothing. Later they were accused of abusing rights to that bedroom, but that wasn't my experience. I knew they'd invited actor Paul Glaser and his son after the death of Paul's wife, Elizabeth Glaser, who did so much to raise AIDS awareness; it was a solicitous gesture on their part to offer this experience to people in distress.

So a week before Chloe and I found ourselves in Washington, I called Mrs. Clinton's social secretary. Might we stop by? "Yes, please come by, and they'd love to have you stay the night in the Lincoln Bedroom."

Two days before we were supposed to stay, on April 3, 1996, the Clintons' friend Ron Brown, then secretary of commerce, died tragically in a plane crash while on a trade mission to Croatia. I called the social secretary, assuming our visit would be canceled. "No, it's all right," she told me, "but could you come the following night instead?"

On the appointed day Chloe and I were given a VIP tour. We were shown where they arrange flowers, ushered past a warren of staff offices and past a gallery of presidential portraits. I thought

I'd remembered reading that Socks the cat had died, so I felt a jolt of joy when I saw him on a scratching post topped with a feline penthouse. "My God, he's alive!" Then Chloe and I were shown into the Oval Office, where Clinton was waiting, seated behind the Resolute Desk. He showed us the Remington bronzes, Saint-Gaudens's bust of Lincoln, Rembrandt Peale's portrait of Washington, a mallet from a Supreme Court justice. He couldn't have been more gracious, explaining each article of historical interest, sometimes remarking, "I was a great admirer of his work."

When Chloe and I returned for our sleepover that evening, we were shown in through a back entrance and escorted to the Lincoln Bedroom by an aide. The bed itself was extremely long and skinny—like Lincoln himself—with a huge carved headboard. There was a little menu for breakfast, which would be served in the sitting room opposite the First Family's sitting room.

Mrs. Clinton took us into the living room of the First Residence, pointing out a multicolored blown glass sculpture by artist Dale Chihuly on a central round table on the way. We followed her into the breakfast room, where we had an early, slightly awkward dinner with the Clintons, who did their best to put Chloe and me at ease despite the stress of their friend's death. After we finished dinner, the president left the table to attend fundraisers, and Hillary excused herself soon after.

I'd brought a disposable camera and snapped a photo of Chloe watching *I Love Lucy* on the Lincoln bed. It was 10:00 p.m. and we were both in our bathrobes when there was a knock on our door. It was the president, back from his round of fundraisers. He proceeded to give us a personal tour of some of the room's more interesting artifacts. "This is the desk where Lincoln signed the Emancipation Proclamation," he told us.

My mind was fixated on my bra, which I'd left at a rakish angle on the back of a chair—why, of all nights, hadn't I put it away? As the president was explaining yet another piece of historical interest, I tried to inch over to it as it glowed radioactively in the corner. President Clinton continued to point out more historical gewgaws. The man had energy to burn. Did he never sleep? Finally he excused himself to go into the bedroom across the hall to make calls.

The next day we walked to the South Lawn and joined a small crowd, including then Press Secretary George Stephanopoulos, and saw the Clintons off in Marine One.

19

Before *Murphy Brown*, my movie and television income was unreliable, so I picked up endorsements here and there. Cie Perfume—"for all the women you are"—paid me very well. I'm sorry to say that I wasn't a fan of the scent. They had to put a rider into my contract that I was no longer allowed to refer to the perfume as "Lysol."

Murphy Brown was such an instant hit that more endorsement opportunities came to me very quickly. In 1990, Sprint made me their corporate spokeswoman, a position I held for eight years. Sprint's scripts, created by J. Walter Thompson San Francisco, were very witty and fun to play. It started great and just got better; the people at Sprint were very decent and very generous. I'd work only five days a year, shooting the spots on a Saturday during the season when we were shooting the show.

Meanwhile, our salaries on *Murphy Brown* increased quickly. The show made us rich, by any definition. TV money: there's nothing like it. It was the first major money that I'd earned for years. I remember when John Ratzenberger, my old friend from *Gandhi*, did an episode of *Murphy*. He came onto the set and we were comparing notes on working in television. "The first year of

Cheers," he told me, "we were all consoling each other about not having a place to live. Two years in, we were complaining about not finding a good live-in chef." Charlie had moved up to Santa Monica, where he had a lovely new home with a pool. One day he found ducks had landed there and stayed for several days, turning the water green with duck poop. He bought them an inflatable kiddie pool so he could reclaim his own, but the ducks weren't having it. Charlie used the kiddie pool instead. Joe Regalbuto was the first to invest in land, buying a property at the base of the mountain in Deer Valley, Utah. I immediately began calling him our Land Baron. Grant Shaud bought a house and a prized vintage Mustang. Faith Ford bought a house as well, which she decorated with great taste and savvy.

The more I made and the more successful I got, the bigger my head swelled. I started taking Sprint for granted. (I was very discreet about what they paid me, but numbers were widely reported.) The lovely Sprint people would offer me an additional fortune to shoot a few spots in a new territory, and my response would be to whine, "Now I have to do Sprint *Canada?*" It got out of hand. I was in my forties; I knew better. God knows if I'd been younger, I might have spun out of orbit. As it was, I would do what was asked of me, but be long-suffering about it. Was the commercial script less than sparkling? I have to say *that?* After the fact, when that easy money went away, I'd think, "Where's Sprint Canada when I need them?"

When you're famous, things come to you. It starts with free sneakers and goes uphill from there. Vendors started walking the stages of the show bearing trays of high-end sunglasses. You just picked out whatever you liked and they'd make you whatever prescription and color lens you needed. The hope was that you'd wear it out in public and be photographed in it. The next week it'd be designer handbags, then clothing, then luggage.

The networks gave us presents as well. One year when Howard Stringer was president, he gave every one of our producers, cast, and crew a portable stereo radio CD player, a big deal at the time. The ambassador to talent at CBS was a lovely woman who would give the leads of shows exclusive gifts. One year, I received a luxurious Loro Piana cashmere blanket. Another year two breakfast trays with a tea set in bone china.

Bob Daly, chairman of the board for Warner Bros., which produced *Murphy Brown*, outdid them all; you'd wait panting by the door for his gifts. Bob was immensely generous. He never told anybody who made these unique presents, and he only gave them out to thirty stars. One year it was a life-size Santa Claus in a red velvet suit trimmed with fur and a lifelike face and beard, a bag of toys slung over his shoulder. Next year, he sent a stuffed full-size reindeer with bells on his harness to accompany Santa, and the year after that, we got hand-painted wooden sleighs piled high with presents. It became a complete life-size Christmas tableau. The jewel in the crown, however, was the magnificent three-foot-tall Victorian dollhouse made out of dark chocolate with the names of your pets and children written on the sides with frosting and smoke made of spun sugar curling out of the chimney. Later I took mine to Children's Hospital, where Tom Selleck also donated his. Among studio execs, Bob Daly stands alone. He was by far the classiest, and he has remained a friend.

There's a whole industry that contracts out to studio lots and film sets. Every season, a couple of months before Christmas, I would meet with a "corporate gifter" to decide what to give as a gift to the entire cast and crew of about 120 people. The first year, it was a tasteful polo shirt with *FYI*, the name of Murphy's fictional news show, embroidered on the pocket. The second year, I got everyone white terry robes with *Murphy Brown* on the back. The next year, ten-speed bikes.

Free stuff has never lost its thrill. Every year, they up the ante on swag. When I did the Emmys in 1984, I got a sweatshirt for their thirty-fifth anniversary. I was ecstatic. Now they give you iPads and smartphones and trips to Bali and designer watches. I did some Emmy show a few years ago and went to my first gifting salon. I nabbed an espresso machine, a pair of aviator sunglasses, a man's watch in rose gold that everyone thinks is real, boots for Chloe. Celebrities are escorted to the "gift suite," usually accompanied by publicists and personal assistants. It's like a souk. Products are stacked cheek by jowl: luggage next to GoPros next to cameras next to pearls. Select the color and press "send." People get feverish loading up on goodies as assistants follow, hoping to catch the spillover. And the best part is you don't have to thank anyone; just pick it out and open it at home.

The flip side to the perks of celebrity is celebrity itself. Jack Nicholson is one of the few stars I've known who is a great celebrity. He's everything you want as a fan, engaging and having fun with autograph seekers. I was always furtive, hunched over; my whole posture said, "Go away!" Because Murphy was such an icon and became so impor-tant for women as a role model, whenever I was in New York during the series, the attention could be uncomfortable. I'd be walking down the street, and women would pass me and grab each other, then circle back for a second look. People think New Yorkers are blasé. I beg to disagree. What was fun was doormen in front of buildings calling out, "Hey, Murph!"

With a child, the attention became more intrusive.

"Is my celebrity a pain for you?" I asked Chloe.

"A big one," Clovis replied. She was eight. It was the first time she'd mentioned it.

The upside: No ticket is too tough. No seat impossible to book. You are welcome, wanted, everywhere.

I was never a big celebrity, but TV notoriety comes on very fast. It also disappears quickly. You can feel it the day after you appear on a TV show. The first time I guest-hosted *Saturday Night Live*, I felt a difference in the atmosphere around me on the street the next day. There was a stir in the air; the molecules shifted.

20

When the press starts referring to your show as "the veteran series *Murphy Brown*," you have stayed too long at the party. We probably should have stopped after our fifth or sixth year, optimum for half-hour story lines, but we just kept things going.

Yet our final season carried a powerful message, which left a deep imprint on me. In it, Murphy Brown battled breast cancer. It was an emotional year, not only because it would be our last, but because we deliberately cast actors who were actual breast cancer survivors on the show. We'd have scenes of Murphy in encounter groups with breast cancer survivors and wives, mothers, sisters, and girlfriends—and there was nobody on that stage who hadn't in some way been affected.

The show was informative about the physiological effects of breast cancer. We even had a special wig made that showed Murphy's patchy hair regrowth after undergoing chemo. By this time, her son, Avery—played by an excellent Haley Joel Osment—was a little boy, old enough to interact with Murphy Brown, and there were some very tender scenes of him being solidly there for his mother. Strikingly professional and prepared, completely mature, Haley was later nominated for an Oscar for seeing dead people in *The Sixth Sense*. Once after he paused a little too long before saying his line, the director asked, "Haley, can you pick up your cue?" He replied, "I was just waiting for the laughs that would come."

Young girls would come up to me all the time to tell me how much it meant to them to watch that last season of Murphy with their mothers who were fighting the disease. In Bergdorf's, a young woman close to tears tentatively approached and said, "My mom and I used to watch you on *Murphy* during the last year of her life." We hugged. It was extremely moving. Surveys showed that because of our season on breast cancer, the rate of women having mammograms went up 30 percent. It was a very intense year, wonderfully written and sensitively handled by our key producers, Janice Hirsch and Jhoni Marchinko, Diane English, and our writers—a real mix of humor and heart.

Diane English returned to write the finale, the 246th and 247th episodes, which ran as an hour-long show, "Never Can Say Goodbye." In the show, Murphy Brown underwent exploratory breast surgery. Barnet Kellman returned to direct. George Clooney, then a breakout star in *ER*, which was shooting on the stage across the street, did a tiny cameo as a doctor. Between scenes, he came over to say hello and asked, "How are you doing?" I burst into tears. Murphy interviewed God (played by Alan King) and Edward R. Murrow (we found archival footage and inserted it into the scene). Diane herself appeared as another doctor.

Afterward, we took curtain calls. The audience was packed with family and friends. It was a long, standing ovation. The full impact of the series ending would take weeks and months to sink in. It was more of a marriage for us than most marriages. As in some marriages, when they end, they end amicably. We were always hovering at the edges of each other's lives. Years after the series ended, Bobby Pastorelli was found dead of a heroin overdose in his bathroom. Grant and I were the only ones from the show who could attend his funeral at a church in New Jersey. Glenn Close, who was a close friend of Bobby's, spoke beautifully. At the end of the mass, the pallbearers were beefy guys with open shirts, wearing gold chains and black leather jackets. Authentic. A young girl, dark-haired, lovely, followed the casket; we never knew he had a daughter.

Murphy gave me something solid I could be proud of. I'd done many indifferent movies, a few good ones, but most not. I'd somehow squeezed an Academy Award nomination out of my movie career, but it was a wispy, erratic, undistinguished one. *Murphy* changed that for me. From the beginning of the show, I was recognized for my work, not my looks—*and* I got to play comedy. I got to learn *how* to play comedy; I definitely put in my ten thousand hours. That was worth a lot. And I got a lot of very heavy, shiny gold statuettes. I liked that part too.

Once I was considered too "patrician" to succeed on TV; now it was my home. It has been very good to me. I have always been grateful for that, grateful that I was let out of my restrictive, confining little vitrine. Playing Murphy was pure pleasure and sheer luck.

Things are sudden in television. When you have a success, it's literally overnight. And when it's over, it's immediately over. After the last episode of *Murphy Brown* aired, people moved on to *Mad About You*. The attention had tapered off in the last few years anyway, but when *Murphy* ended, it was like turning off a spigot. I was standing outside of Mr. Chow, waiting for my car after dinner with a group that included Warren Beatty and Annette Bening. The paparazzi were waiting outside en masse. I braced myself. They pounced on Warren and Annette, yelling, "Hey, Warren! Annette—over here!" with cameras flashing. They ignored me completely. After Annette and Warren left, it was just me standing there like a schmuck with the paparazzi, waiting for my car.

I'm in my late sixties now. I've been through a few cycles. People can be jolted awake when you're in something new: "Oh, where have you been?" Increasingly, though, I'm around people who are so young that they have no frame of reference for you whatsoever. It always startles me. There's never a dawning: "Oh, yes, *Murphy Brown*." Instead, it's "How do you spell that?"

"B-E-R-G-E-N."

"And can you spell the first name too?"

Seriously?

I have no idea what the lasting impact of *Murphy Brown* has been. I was so busy getting through the doing of it. Why has the series lasted so long in the public imagination? Maybe because Murphy herself was such a gold standard for smart, strong, independent, individual women. I always wished I'd grown up with her when I was a young girl. I think if I had had a character like Murphy to identify with when I was younger, I would have gotten to where I wanted to be in a quarter of the time. I am always struck by the number of women who come up to me and say they watched Murphy with their mothers growing up.

Chloe called from San Francisco, where she was covering an event for *Vogue*. She said a young woman at a party approached her and politely said that if she hadn't watched *Murphy* growing up, she would never have become a CEO. It was Marissa Mayer, head of Yahoo!.

Diane English had everything to do with that legacy. Interviewed for the twenty-fifth anniversary of the show's premiere, she told a reporter that if we made a reunion show of *Murphy* today, she envisioned the crew of *FYI* going strong, just like *60 Minutes*, "only a little older and a little creakier." One of the show writers imagined an episode with Murphy Brown having a fling with Jon Stewart. "If Sarah Palin runs for president, I'm going to ask CBS to put us back on the air," Diane told the *San Francisco Chronicle*. "Six episodes, that's all I need."

When the series ended, Chloe was twelve. We moved to a new house; Louis had died in our old house. That wasn't a reason to move, but it was a tiny house and Chloe was getting bigger and there was no room for friends to visit. We found a fantastic property. It was Roger Moore's house. He had bought it with the money he made playing James Bond. The headline in the real estate column in the *Los Angeles Times* said, "Murphy Buys 007's House." The property had a guest house, pool, tennis court, fruit trees, avocado trees, and three and a half acres at the top of Coldwater Canyon in Beverly Hills. I made it as kid-friendly and family-friendly as I could. We had a media room in the basement. If anyone was downstairs, you couldn't hear a word they said or screamed, so that's where Chloe would have her sleepovers. We entertained a lot. Sunday brunches, lots of dog costume parties, small dinners.

In the months after the show wrapped, I was at loose ends. One day Chloe came home from school and I reported: "You know, I measured the hair on Larry's tail today and it's sixteen inches long!" All Chloe said was, "You need to get back to work."

Doing what? I wasn't interested in doing another television series at the time. I went on a few half-hearted meetings for movies of the week, but the endless string of meetings got old very quickly.

Then I was invited to do an interview show for the fledgling Oxygen channel. The Oxygen cable network was aimed primarily at women, and they were looking for original programming. I would do five hour-long interview shows a week, which was a *lot*.

The show was run by Scott Carter, who now produces Bill Maher. We flew to Washington, DC, to interview Madeline Albright at the State Department. We did a week in New York where I interviewed Hillary Clinton, late playwright Wendy Wasserstein, Sigourney Weaver, and architect Maya Lin. I wanted it to feel like the end of a dinner party, where everyone is comfortable, relaxing after a meal, sipping after-dinner drinks and chatting.

Exhale with Candice Bergen was an unbelievable challenge. I fell asleep every night on my piles of research. It forced me to do homework on fascinating people: writer Malcolm Gladwell, food critic and writer Ruth Reichl, Dr. Irene Pepperberg, who studied African Grey parrots, Tori Murden McClure, the first woman to row solo across the Atlantic, marine biologist Sylvia Earle, Julia Butterfly Hill, who camped in the top of a giant redwood for more than two years to prevent it from being cut down, Temple Grandin, animal behaviorist and autism activist. Exceptional actors Jodie Foster, Diane Keaton, Sally Field, Anne Bancroft, and Michael Douglas. Singers k.d. lang and Patti Smith. Architects Frank Gehry and Michael Graves. Fashion icon Diane von Furstenberg.

Exhale went for two seasons before sputtering out. Then Chloe turned fifteen, we had a party on the tennis court, and a new chapter began.

5

Time Marshes On

❦ 21 ❧

It was clear that I missed having a man in my life the day I visited the rheumatologist. After working on the concrete floor of a sound stage for ten years, I was having some back and knee issues, and when the doctor touched my back, I found myself thinking, "I wonder if he's married." I'd been so bonded to my daughter that I hadn't noticed how lonely I'd become.

My friends saw that I wasn't interested in dating, so they didn't try to convince me. I started playing Carly Simon's CD *Film Noir,* a collection of tragic love songs, while I was in the bathtub, thinking of the kind of man I wanted to be with. I missed the everyday male details—him shaving in the mirror in the morning, socks carelessly scattered around the bedroom. Some women seem to hate males. *"Men,"* they spit. Not me. I had always enjoyed the company of men. I missed having one in my life. Louis's sister, Catherine, said, *"Il n'est pas bon d'être seule, Candice,"* It's not good to be alone. Maybe it was time to get out there again.

That meant dating and I dreaded going through it again. It was awkward twenty years ago; what would it be like now? I'd had exactly three dates with three guys in the three years since Louis had died. A dinner, a lunch, and a drink. One was someone I knew slightly for a long time; he had dropped off a card: "Want to have lunch?" He was a decent, smart guy, just not right for me. Then there was dinner with a senator, a fix-up through friends of mine. I was home very early. He was very polite, he sent flowers, but it was clear that that was it. Then drinks with a journalist—another fix-up through mutual friends. There was no sense of excitement. The men that did interest me would always be polite at parties, but then they'd turn around and introduce me to their twenty-five-year-old girlfriends named Cloud. At fifty-two and single, I saw that I was way past the age range of most men. It felt like I had disappeared, as though someone went "poof" and I became invisible.

Yet something was shifting. As I listened to Carly in the bathtub, I began to declare my intentions to no one in particular: *I want to be with a man who is utterly decent and kind, who is also playful and has depth. I would love to have the kind of physical connection where we just grasp each other's hands without knowing it. I want someone who loves life. An enthusiast.* No cynics need apply.

One day in the fall of 1998 I got a call from Don Hewitt. "Marilyn and I are having a dinner. We'd love you to come."

Years earlier, when I was twenty-five, Don, the producer for *60 Minutes*, had asked me to join the team of reporters. I'd turned it down, knowing I wasn't up to journalistic snuff. The experience would have deepened me, made me someone more, and I thought I had some tiny ability but that it needed to be nurtured and coaxed out. I don't know that I could have done it. Most of all, I couldn't see being locked into one job for a period of time. I regretted my decision right up until I started doing *Murphy Brown*, when I realized, hey, I could *play* a journalist and have a great time doing it.

After Mike Wallace did a piece on me for *60 Minutes*, Don began talking about my appearing on the show again. After ten years of *Murphy Brown*, I was ready to make a change. I knew I'd get a lot of flak, but I thought it'd be worth hunkering down and passing through it. In fact, the person who started getting the flak was Don. The bona fide journalists were not happy. What were we thinking? Both of us just looked at each other and pulled back from the idea. "Let's just forget it; it's not going to work." I figured this get-together was a consolation prize.

Don was very shrewd. He knew better than to announce a fix-up. He called me three days before the dinner. "A man's coming to pick you up," he said casually. "His name is Marshall Rose."

"Who's Marshall Rose?"

"His wife died three years ago," Don told me. "They were married for thirty years; he was very much in love with her. He has a beautiful house in East Hampton. He's rich, he's successful, but most of all, he's a fine man, very old school."

I figured Don was doing this as a courtesy, having someone pick me up, just letting me know. Well, fine, how nice of him to do that.

I found out that Marshall had been the chairman of the New York Public Library. He was a real estate developer and philanthropist. He'd turned Bryant Park from Needle Park into a beautiful jewel of a park behind the library. I learned that he'd nursed his wife through two bouts of breast cancer. I figured he'd be this decent, short, round, older guy.

He was not. When Marsh showed up at my apartment, I was surprised, a bit taken aback actually, to find a handsome, elegantly dressed man waiting for me downstairs. We had a quick drink in the living room, then he took me to the Hewitts' in his car. He looked down at my feet as we pulled up to the apartment; I was wearing my usual flats. "Are you wearing shoes you can walk in, because I thought I could just walk you home after the dinner and I could let my driver go." I didn't know it then, but Marshall had planned ahead—as usual.

I was seated next to him at dinner. Conversation was effortless and relaxed. The waiters came with dessert—lemon meringue tart. "Would you like to share this?" he asked me.

"No, thanks, I'd like my own." That didn't scare him off. (In fact, he told me later that was when he knew.) He was charming, lovely, with incredibly kind brown eyes; I was instantly attracted to him. Even with his slight Brooklyn accent, which I later told him was a "considerable part of his charm," there was something very refined about him; he was innately elegant. I found him completely fun and unpretentious. My reaction surprised me; parts of me woke up. *Huh. I'm not dead.*

After a lively dinner with Don, his wife, *New York Times* journalist Marilyn Berger, Mike Wallace, Morley Safer, and Alan and Hannah Pakula, we talked nonstop the twenty blocks back to my apartment, walking in the crisp October air. He talked about his love of travel; it seemed he'd been everywhere. And his love of books; he was a voracious reader. Marsh also had a passion for architecture; he pointed out his favorite features on buildings as we strolled by them. (Ten years later, he got Frank Gehry to build his first building in New York City, the dramatic IAC tower for Barry Diller's media empire, which looks like a ship under sail.)

For such an accomplished man, he was strikingly humble. "Marshall, how is it that someone as successful as you is so modest?"

Marsh grinned. "Like Churchill said, I have much to be modest about."

He was leaving the next day to go to Austria for a hunting trip. *Jews with guns?* I wondered.

"I'd like to call you when I get back," Marsh told me. "Could I have your number?" He took out a pad and wrote down about fifteen of them—the number in my car, my dressing room, my home in New York, my home in LA . . . we started laughing.

A week later, I called him.

"Marshall, it's Candice Bergen."

"Oh, I just got home and was watching television and eating a pizza."

That struck me as poignant. "Gosh, don't you have someone there to take care of you?" It turns out that he just happened to have sent out for pizza; I didn't know then that he had a fabulous, formidable house manager named Marina Borges.

"I would have called you from Austria," Marsh told me, "but there was no phone in the hunting lodge." Said the Jew from Brooklyn.

Two weeks later, I returned to New York. We made a date to meet at the Metropolitan Museum of Art. It was a beautiful fall afternoon on a Monday. I walked briskly to the Met, wearing an Armani jacket and pants. Marshall stood in front of the museum in a navy blazer and gray flannels, again looking very sharp.

"The Met's closed, but we have special access," he told me. Marshall had called his friend, Bill Luers, then chairman of the museum, who got us in after hours. Marshall was proud of himself; we were the only visitors. It was a slick trick, no question.

We walked through a few galleries, passing the odd guard. We stopped in front of the few Vermeers, but I barely noticed the art.

"Our dinner reservation isn't until eight o'clock," Marsh told me. "I live just across the street. Would you like to have a drink at my apartment first?" His apartment was done in impeccable taste, in one of the more distinguished buildings along Fifth Avenue. There were French doors and a terrace overlooking Fifth Avenue, Central Park, the Metropolitan Museum of Art, and the reservoir, and beyond that, the George Washington Bridge. Here I thought this guy was in some kind of studio apartment sending out for pizza, but he had an entire floor of an elegant building, with four bedrooms. It was the floor above Jacqueline Onassis's former apartment.

I was as impressed by the culture it reflected as with the hominess and warmth. There was a beautiful Degas pastel over the fireplace. The walls were hung with a museum-quality photography collection from first-rate photographers like Tina Modotti, Edward Steichen, and Atget, which I later learned his wife had assembled. We sat in the library and had a drink, talking easily for an hour and a half, until it was time to go to dinner.

"Do you need to use the facilities?" he asked me, ever courtly. "The *WHAT?*" I responded, ever not. We walked to dinner, while Marsh stopped to greet about a dozen people he knew on Madison along the way. Of course, he turned out to know the owner of the restaurant, so we were shown to a lovely banquette. The dormant half of me came back to life again at that dinner. Everything was all sparkly. It shimmered, gave electricity to life. Marsh was a shockingly nice man, fun to be with. As he walked me home, we found ourselves standing at a corner and I realized that I had reached out and taken Marsh's hand—my fantasy from the bathtub. Oops. I quickly undid it. But it signaled what I felt first from Marsh: absolute trust.

I set out to trap him. I had to get in line.

By now I'd learned that he was quite the hot item on the market. He was, after all, a straight and successful man. Women were calling him day and night. "I felt like a piece of meat in Lobel's," he told me later, naming the high-end butcher shop. When they were sitting shiva after the death of his wife, Jill, women with no connection to him or his family had actually followed mourners from the funeral up to his apartment to slip him their numbers. "If you ever want to see a movie or have dinner . . ." One woman left her CV on a DVD.

I found it terrifying. These women were hard-core, take-no-prisoners types. They were playing for keeps. It was business. One day I went to a manicurist around the corner, a place where his wife used to go, and where Marsh sometimes slipped in early so that women wouldn't buzz about him while he got his nails buffed. All the women there stopped talking the second I walked in. Then the whispering started up. "That's the one he's seeing now."

Marshall didn't want to go out with any of the women who'd had anything to do with Jill's immediate social circle. A friend who ran the Victoria's Secret fashion show invited him to the annual event. As the heavenly creatures strutted the runway, the friend nudged Marsh. "Which one of them would you like to go out with?"

"How about their mothers?" Marsh replied. He had no interest in going out with women of an inappropriate age. He knew exactly what he wanted: me. Although he didn't seem to think dating *me* was any big deal, which frankly I found surprising.

We spent hours upon hours walking through the park and the city. It was such fun to enjoy it with him, a born and bred boy from Brooklyn turned ardent fan of Manhattan.

It was also fun to get to know a man again. His family lived in Brooklyn; he'd grown up not poverty-stricken but middle-class poor. His father was a furrier; he always had dye under his finger-nails. Marsh used to help him make the coats.

He was very low-key about his philanthropy. He's built three high schools pro bono in the Bronx in conjunction with the Robin Hood Foundation; he's very involved in education. He doesn't like to be in the press. When Liz Smith referred to him in her column as "tycoon philanthropist Marshall Rose, who's dating everyone alive," he made fun of himself. "Tycoon? Try 'typhoon.'"

We quickly fell into a routine of walking everywhere, walking and talking. I was smitten; it was thrilling—it was like being reborn. I loved the attention he paid me, how present he was. Marsh was clearly born to have a wife. He was brilliant at relationships. He'd seen his wife through two bouts of breast cancer. I'd been married for fifteen years, all of it faithfully but a third of it absentee.

We were like two really old teenagers, with all the fizz.

One night I told him, "You know, Marsh, what I'd really love is to read the Sunday papers with you." The next morning I watched him shave for the first time; we read the papers in bed.

I started leaving notes in his sock drawer, or inside the medicine cabinet with his toothbrush, so he could find them after I left for LA. I set little rubber ducks bobbing in his Water Pik basin. I learned later that he kept all those notes in a leather file.

Chloe and I were in Sun Valley over Christmas, skiing without Marsh. I'd write him a fax every night, as well as talk to him on the phone. Marshall wasn't as comfortable writing, but he was always extremely demonstrative, holding my hand, stroking my face. The first time we saw a movie together, he looped his hand around my thigh; I loved it.

I caught myself drifting off all the time, trying to recapture a moment, being dreamy. In the car pool, I was always in a great mood—singing, playing Motown, Elton John. We'd be doo-wopping in the car. Diana Krall was just happening then, and she became our Johnny Mathis.

I was staying with Eleanora and Michael Kennedy in East Hampton, where I knew Marsh had a home. I'd seen a piece of stationery in his apartment with the house address on it. "Let's go find the house," I told Eleanora and we drove around until we did. We couldn't really see it through the hedge, but it looked lovely. "This is good, Bergen," Eleanora decided. Marsh was in.

I told my friend Carol Ryan in London, who gave her approval, sight unseen.

Marsh and I would have these toddler conversations where you babble on the phone for forty-five minutes because you don't want to be apart. It's the first blush of a relationship, so there is a strong current between you, this physical connection where you want to be always near each other.

We were chatting on the phone in November. I was in my bedroom in LA when Marsh from New York said that he had to talk to me in person.

"Tell me, Marsh," I noodged.

"Well," he said, tentatively, "I think I'm falling in love with you."

"THINK?!" I blurted. "Whadda ya mean, *think?!*" It seemed so obvious that was the direction we were heading. Afterward, he said he'd felt like a gopher that finally got the courage to stick its head outside the hole and felt a cannonball whizzing past. It was a relief when I'd told him I loved him back. It had been three years for both of us since our spouses died and life was looking up.

Our first Christmas together, we walked up and down Fifth Avenue, looking at the holiday windows, sipping hot chocolate at Rockefeller Center. For Christmas, I'd gotten him an anthology of Frank Sinatra CDs, which struck me as an appropriate new relationship gift. Marshall pulled out a beautifully wrapped shoebox. Inside was a pair of navy blue suede JP Tod loafers. I was especially touched because it meant that he'd noticed what I wore. They were perfect. The perfect size. The perfect color. The perfect style. That's the thing about Marsh: he pays remarkable attention. He pointed out that inside the toe of one of the loafers was another box, which held a bracelet from Fred Leighton of pale blue baguette aquamarine stones. It too was perfect for me, simple and elegant and gorgeous, as if I had designed it myself. I was truly staggered, as surprised and stunned as I have ever been. I later learned it was the first time he'd been back to a jeweler since his wife had died. I panicked and ran out and got him something more than Sinatra CDs, finding an antique pair of cufflinks, tasteful but boring. Under the time constraints, I did what I could. But his present took time and thought and playfulness and some courage. It said I meant something to him. I was knocked off my loafers.

Two weeks later we had a fantastic New Year's Eve together at my house in LA; Chloe was out. New Year's morning we took a two-hour hike where I lived on the Santa Monica Mountain Preserve. When we returned and I made scrambled eggs and smoked salmon for breakfast, Marsh sat back and said, "Isn't it great just to do nothing?"

Later, on the terrace, Marsh was very quiet for several minutes, thinking with his eyes closed, hands behind his head. Then, "Can, I want you to move back to New York."

"I know, I know." We had spoken about it a few times.

"No, I mean as my wife."

I was sitting on a ledge and dropped to the ground. "Oh!" I moaned. "This is . . . *soon!*" Here was a man who'd been deeply in love with his late wife, then dated many women, and after only three months with me, he *knew*. He's really capable of surprise attacks; once he knows what he wants, he moves in to close the deal.

I didn't know what to say; he caught me completely off guard. "Oh, but Marsh . . . I . . . Chloe . . . and our house . . . and I don't know how it would work," I sputtered.

"Candy, people move all the time," he said calmly.

"Yeah, but they haven't just lost their father and they're not only thirteen." But I didn't say no. Unlike most of the women who were trailing him in New York, I wasn't looking to get married. My nonanswer was my answer for the moment, and Marshall discreetly dropped the subject.

A couple of weeks later, Marsh came back to LA and took me to Cabo San Lucas in Baja California. It was fairly remote and undiscovered—which means that George Clooney and Jennifer Aniston didn't go there yet. A new hotel, Las Ventanas, had just been finished and Marsh had gotten a gorgeous casita for the week—the nicest in the whole place, our own house and our own little pool. The golf course on one side, the beach on the other. He had faxed me a day-by-day schedule. The itinerary should have been the tip-off. It began:

Monday, January 6

8:00 a.m.: desert hiking
1:00 p.m.: picnic lunch Playa Pulmos
3:00 p.m.: scuba lesson
4:00 p.m.: ocean kayaking
6:00 p.m.: massage
8:00 p.m.: dinner

Tuesday, January 7

8:00 a.m.: deep sea fishing . . .

The man was nothing if not organized. And energetic. Cabo is a place to sunbathe and golf, but Marsh had managed to fill our week there and I was never bored for a second. I never had time. When some Americans recognized me at an outdoor restaurant and the band asked me to sign their guitars, he thought it was hysterical; he wasn't put off by it at all.

His goony side was on full display at Cabo. During the ocean kayaking portion of the schedule, I was paddling along when I heard a little splash behind me. I turned around to find Marsh tipping the kayak back up and climbing onto it. "I was coming over to kiss you," he explained, dripping wet, "and I flipped over."

Marsh travels well and is well traveled. It was hard to mention a place he hadn't been. He was good at it and loved the planning, the research, the exploring. There was nothing indifferent or blasé about this man. He was an enthusiast, up for any adventure—I liked that. He was also interested in almost everything: art, architecture, ruins (but not too many), theater, music. He'd tell me, "I'm the last of the great romantics." And it's true; he loves to celebrate romance.

The first time Mom met Marshall was at a dinner I'd arranged on the patio at Spago in LA, where he joined me, Mom, Chloe, and Kris. Mom gave Marshall her warmest smile. "Marshall, do you speak Yiddish in the home?" Kris almost left the table; my mouth hung open. Marsh barely noticed.

Mom was in some ways ill at ease with Marsh because she was intimidated by his fancy New York social circle. She knew he'd been head of the library and was friendly with Brooke Astor. It was, in fact, a swanky crowd.

Eventually she accepted the relationship. I don't know how much of her reluctance was because Marsh was Jewish; I don't know if she was happy for me. But Marshall put in the time to win her over, especially after she became bedridden. We'd sit in her bedroom, Connie, Kris, Chloe, Marsh, and I, and Mom would dutifully ask him how the Knicks were playing.

Chloe was a harder sell, understandably so.

For the previous few years, every spring break, Chloe and I would travel with our friends Eleanora and Michael Kennedy and their daughter Anna, who was then Chloe's best friend. The first year, when the girls were ten, we went to DC for a week. The next, Paris, Moscow, and St. Petersburg. The year after, we rented a house in Marrakech. The spring after Marsh and I met, we were planning a trip to Jordan and Israel; Marsh and I had known each other six months and now he was taken into the fold. I made Chloe lug around a copy of *Exodus* for background; I always encouraged her to read something relevant to wherever we were traveling. The six of us met in London and flew to Amman, Jordan, saw the world's first shopping center (Roman), then drove to Petra, the Eighth Wonder of the World.

The approach to Petra is on foot or horseback. The horses did not look up to the task so we walked through the sand along a narrowing riverbed flanked by tall, steep, rocky cliffs called the Siq. After walking twenty minutes, you come round a bend and the Siq suddenly widens, fanning out dramatically to reveal an immense valley and the hand-carved façade of the

Treasury, built around the third century BC, its two stories of ornate columns emerging out of a huge wall of red stone.

Petra is a necropolis discovered accidentally by a British painter; it covers some sixty square kilometers. It is spectacular and was featured in Spielberg's *Indiana Jones and the Last Crusade*.

We were all having a lemonade in Petra when Chloe announced, "Mama, I think it's time for you and Marshall to start having sex." Hel-lo.

I almost did a spit take. Marsh and I had been going through a charade where he would book in a hotel when he came to LA and I would visit, but I'd leave at five thirty in the morning to be home before Chloe woke up. When we traveled, we'd take separate rooms and Marshall would come padding down the hall in his bathrobe after Chloe had fallen asleep in the room she shared with Anna.

"Well, we'll certainly consider it, sweetie," I replied casually. Perhaps it was the only way she thought she could have any control over her life.

Of course, Chloe and I had long ago had the inevitable sex conversation you're advised to have driving in the car while the child is in the backseat so she doesn't feel overwhelmed. She was eight when I told her, "Then the man puts his *zizi* in the woman's *zizi*" (which is what we called it in France). I watched her in the rearview mirror as she looked out the window with a grimace. "Ew, that's disgusting."

Mom had responsibly seen to my own sex education without a lot of fuss. I was twelve or thirteen when she sat me down in the living room. "The man's sex organ is called a penis," she told me. "You probably call it a hot dog." She had a book in her lap that she gave me. It was like Sex Ed 101. Instructive, with sex reduced to the most scientific medical terms. There were illustrations.

As my relationship with Marsh developed, Chloe was less than enthusiastic. I worried that I was preempting her adolescence; her project was to establish her own turf. Just as she would have been breaking away from me, I betrayed her first by falling in love with Marshall; he was her competition:

Dearest Mamoushka,

I love you sooo much! Especially on days like Easter! I want good things in your life, always, and I am so glad that you and Marshall have found each other. I don't ever want you to feel awkward about it with me. You tell me whatever you want to. Thank you infinetly [sic] for our trip. It has meant the world to me. Jordan was so amazing. I learned and experienced so much. And Petra, the 8th wonder of the world, was extraordinary. And Israel, as you know, was one of the best things I've ever done in my life! I love Israel so very much all due to the trip and a little reading here and there.

Mommy, I love you with such a passion. If you can believe it, Marshall loves you only fraction as much as I do. I know it doesn't always seem that way but remember I do at those times.

Joyeux Paques,
la Pit de la Pêche! [Peach Pit]

I stole Chloe's thunder; she was supposed to be the one running around with her head in the clouds. Instead, she had to be the grown-up. She wanted me in LA. She needed to have a mom. She knew that if she didn't accept Marshall in the most distant, formal, polite way that she wasn't going to see enough of me. As it was, I was in New York one week a month. Kris, who lived in the guesthouse on our property, Connie, and Mom all watched over Chloe while I was away.

There were painful moments. Once we were in Deer Valley on a ski holiday, having a fondue dinner, and she brought up Marshall. "Do you think the two of you are going to get married?" she asked.

"Maybe." I answered honestly.

She burst into tears. I hated myself.

• • •

Chloe went to Harvard Westlake in Los Angeles on the academic fast track; the kids there ran in packs. I was known as one of the stricter moms. Chloe had an earlier curfew than her friends. I'd call the house where the next party was going to be to make sure there would be a supervising adult on the premises. When Chloe was in seventh grade at her elementary school, John Thomas Dye, they'd held a parent-teacher assembly and told us, "We just want you to know that when they're eleven, twelve, and thirteen, you have to be even more proactive as a parent than when they were younger. Kids are bringing guns to parties now; you have to be much more vigilant. As the children get older, there are many more risks, many more traps to fall into; they're going to be driving soon." One of Chloe's school friends had been killed in a car accident with a sixteen-year-old behind the wheel. We had been warned.

I was lucky. Chloe was an antismoking fiend, and she was pretty tolerant of my strictness. "You know, Mom, it's always the parents who were wild as kids that are really strict as grown-ups," she told me. What could I say? When Chloe was in ninth grade, I could see that things were starting to spiral out of an age-appropriate zone. Sometimes Chloe and her friends would have a sleepover in the TV room downstairs, which was almost soundproof. However, if you walked by, you could overhear them. One day they were all watching *Sex and the City*, and I overheard them talking about sex in a shockingly coarse, vulgar way. They had learned some choice phrases and were trying to sound more experienced than I hoped they were; it was very sobering.

When Chloe was thirteen, she passed through a slightly physically awkward period. She always had such a huge personality, I thought, maybe it's better if she's not beautiful; it'll be easier for her because she has so much to give and beauty complicates things. Then a year later she became utterly exquisite, like a young lady from another century. What exactly was Chloe learning from the *Sex and the City* ethos everybody seemed to be living and breathing? We would rarely talk about sex; we talked about birth control and safe sex. I wanted to head her off from meaningless sexual hooking up.

I represented a different end of the *Sex and the City* spectrum—one closer to my own real-life situation—when I played Enid Frick, the fictional top dog at *Vogue*, on the show. Michael Patrick King, a friend who'd been on the writing staff on *Murphy Brown* and become the executive producer of *Sex and the City*, taking over from Darren Star, offered me a cameo, which I figured would score points with Chloe, since the series was insanely popular.

It was wonderful to be on the set at its height.

My character, Enid, might have been the queen of the magazine world, but she was also a desperate single woman, raging at Carrie Bradshaw because Carrie had snapped up one of the few age-appropriate eligible men in Enid's orbit—Aleksandr Petrovsky (played by the dashing Mikhail Baryshnikov.)

> **Enid:** He's my age and you've got him and I am in no-man's land. Literally. No man anywhere. Men can date anyone any age, but let's be frank. Most of them prefer the bimbos, so . . . if you're a successful fifty-something woman, there's a very small pool. It's very small. It's a wading pool, really. So why are you swimming in my wading pool?

Enid was much too small a part for anyone else, but for me, I loved getting a glimpse of the girls and seeing what the set was like. Sarah Jessica Parker was the most adorable girl, infallibly nice to everyone; she helped to set a great tone on the set. She was extremely professional and hard-working, always prepared. Their schedule was exhausting; it was especially hard if you have a family. Hats off to Sarah for making it work. And brava to Patricia Field for making such an event out of every costume.

In any case, I was learning that as a single woman in her fifties, sex was very much in the air. I'd assumed that part of my life was long over, but a new part of me had sprung to life.

I started to wear skirts, which I never did, because Marshall said, "You have lovely legs. Why don't you show them?" I started to feel feminine again, which I hadn't felt in a long time. I loved that Marsh, a true metrosexual, appreciated women who are beautifully dressed. He notices the cut of a dress or jacket, how women put themselves together. I began paying more attention to how I looked, dressing in a less comfortable manner than with my tomboyish moccasins and jeans. I didn't have many dressy clothes, but I did have my wardrobe left over from *Murphy Brown* and I splurged on new underwear, which is, after all, the whole point of having a relationship.

Any effort I made—a new outfit, a change in hairstyle—was noticed and appreciated. Suddenly I had date nights to look forward to. Every meal was celebratory.

"You look very beautiful tonight," he'd tell me. It hit me how long it had been since someone had said that. I'd been focused on being a mom for thirteen years and used to taking care of people around me. Now I was being taken care of, it was as if I'd drunk a potion.

Yet we were both at vulnerable points in our lives. I had to keep talking to myself. "Pay attention here. Be responsible. You do not want to hurt this man; he's just starting to heal."

● ● ●

I introduced Marsh to people at our annual Christmas party in LA. Every year we'd have a party with a traditional Christmas buffet and carols around the piano. Diane Keaton, Sally Field, Steve Martin, Bette Midler and Martin von Haselberg, Diane English, Pat Kingsley, John Calley, and Bob Daly were frequent guests. What people liked was how much Marsh seemed to love me; he had warmth, intelligence, and elegance. Chloe stood in the background, keeping her distance as much as possible.

Kris and Connie liked Marsh too, although they thought he was too adult and reserved for me. When he's not comfortable with people, Marsh tends to go into his mature mode. Connie reminded me of how much I loved to decorate our LA home for Halloween. I strung a leg and hand over the gate, as if some ghoul were escaping. "Pal," Connie asked me, "will he get your gate?" Marsh got more than you would have expected. Everyone close to me over time saw that he wanted the best for me.

I was now seriously considering the move back to New York, which had always felt so much more like my real home. If I hadn't been seeing Marshall, I don't know that I would have had the courage to think about it, but I felt so guilty at the idea of taking Chloe out of her school, away from her friends. I started buying her lots of things—a lavender Kate Spade bag at age fourteen. Some girls had Fendi baguettes. This was way out of character; like my parents, I was very restrained about shopping. Mom warned me, "Candy, you're trying to buy her approval of Marshall." Bingo.

As much as I loved Marsh, I was still reluctant to remarry. We came from two totally different tribes. I wasn't yet comfortable in his, or he in mine. On the other hand, Chloe needed a grown-up. Also, Chloe wanted to be Jewish; all those bar and bat mitzvahs had left their mark. By her count, she'd been to fifty-eight and could recite the service in Hebrew. She missed having a traditional family, one where the father lived at home with the mother and child. One of the reasons I'd wanted to move to LA was so that I could give her as close to a traditional family structure as possible, with my mother's house within walking distance and Sunday dinners on the patio at Orso.

A brush with illness prompted me to think about marriage. When Louis was sick, I'd had sharp pains in my feet, but I couldn't be bothered to deal with them—there was too much else to do with *Murphy Brown* and taking care of Louis. Months after Louis's death, I finally went to a podiatrist, who said it was systemic, then sent me to a hematologist, who diagnosed a blood disorder. There was a small possibility that the problem could morph into something more serious. What about my child then? Maybe some of that concern had factored into my thinking about Marsh. If something happened to me, Marsh and his daughter, Wendi, would be there. I'd have a mature adult in the wheelhouse just in case.

Part of what so attracted me to Marsh was that he was instinctively paternal, an innate caretaker. At first, he wasn't relaxed and tried too hard. His sense of fun and humor didn't come out and he'd be too serious. When he loosened up, it all came together.

Marsh is especially gifted at relationships, me not so much. A half-Swedish only child till I was fifteen and Kris was born, I was an introvert except when I was forced to be an extrovert, the classic profile of an actor; I was never warm and fuzzy. Marsh is.

His house manager, Marina, did her part, making an extra effort to cook us romantic dinners, which she served in Marsh's library in front of the fire in chilly weather or out on the terrace when it was warm.

At a party the following summer, Sally Quinn told the group, "So Marshall and Candice are together. You know, I remember when Marshall was first single and people were saying, 'Marshall Rose is on the loose.' This was when he'd just lost his beloved wife. And now . . . Candy's got him!"

I was flying from LA to New York every two or three weeks for four days at a time. Little by little, Marsh had been making me feel more at home in his home. He built me my own space in the dressing room, complete with bookshelves and a desk. The coziest, prettiest nook. When would the rest of me follow?

❧ 22 ❧

"Do it." Sue Mengers sat there curled in her bed like the caterpillar in *Alice in Wonderland* and expelled a plume of smoke from the joint in her hand. She was wearing a caftan. She was always wearing a caftan, usually mine. This was a blue one I had made in Morocco, which I'd given to her. All of her friends contributed to Sue's caftan fund. Ali MacGraw would have caftans made for her. Joanna Poitier, while decorating Sue's house, would find antique ones.

Sue's house was a kind of Show Biz Command Central. Situated on the corner of Lexington and Beverly Drive, a block from the Beverly Hills Hotel, it was a French Regency designed by famed Hollywood architect John Woolf, who'd designed homes for Cary Grant, Bob Hope, Judy Garland, Barbara Stanwyck, and others. You faced a see-through fireplace as you entered, beyond which lay the living room, whose tall French doors gave onto an oval pool. There were two sofas upholstered in peach velvet; Sue always sat in the corner of the sofa facing the front door. The house had been decorated by her husband, Jean-Claude Tramont, an extremely tall, extremely handsome, highly educated, and charming Belgian. Jean-Claude had a dry, caustic wit that, toward the later years of their marriage, he turned on Sue. He once flung her way, "If Steven Spielberg had been married to you, he'd be running a deli now." She never recovered from his death from prostate cancer in 1996.

The house was elegant and gracious, surprisingly refined—all of the things Sue was not. Yet Sue always looked like she belonged there—to the point that she never left the house. Her travel consisted of walking the short, book-lined hall from her bedroom to the living room to the dining room a few yards away, or from the bedroom to the study and back to the bedroom, with periodic trips to the bathroom. Toward the end of her life, our visits were almost always in the bedroom, which was piled with books, all of them read. There was an Aubusson tapestry hung on the wall behind her bed, and antique French fauteuils on each side of it. The paintings were nineteenth-century landscapes and portraits. Virginia, her faithful housekeeper, would serve us dinner on trays, which we'd eat sitting next to the bed, or often on it, side by side, while watching *Access Hollywood*.

Virginia, born in Mexico, was Sue's chef, caretaker, and keeper of the stash. When Sue would say in her baby voice, "Virginia, can I have one of my funny cigarettes, please?" Virginia, a very proper Catholic woman, would smile shyly and return with a couple of joints on a Sèvres porcelain plate. She was rewarded for her loyalty and devotion with meeting Hollywood Royalty, who routinely came for lunch, drinks, or dinner. Jack Nicholson, for example, was a regular, but the closest Virginia ever came to losing consciousness was meeting J-Lo.

After her death in 2011, Sue Mengers became more famous than any of her clients, who had included Ali MacGraw, Michael Caine, Barbra Streisand, Farrah Fawcett, Ryan O'Neal, and myself, among others. Shortly after her death, her friends began getting emails and phone calls from writers wanting interviews for forthcoming books and plays about this uncensored, rapier-witted woman. She became a cottage industry overnight. Graydon Carter, editor of *Vanity Fair* and a close friend of Sue's, wrote an appreciation of her in the magazine and commissioned screenwriter John Logan to write a one-woman play about her. *I'll Eat You Last* opened on Broadway in 2013, starring Bette Midler as Sue. She was brilliant and it was a huge success. Bette did deep research on

Sue and talked to all of her friends to flesh out details about how she laughed, walked, sat, and ate. Anything that made her who she was. Shortly before Bette started rehearsals, Sherry Lansing, former head of Paramount Studios, philanthropist, and icon of working women, gave a small dinner for Bette with a few of Sue's closest friends, including Joanna and Sidney Poitier, agent Toni Howard and David Yarnell, myself and Marsh, and of course Sherry and her husband Billy Friedkin. The entire dinner was spent reminiscing about Sue. One of the many delicious flourishes Bette brought to the play was to capture a moment when Sue had a joint in one hand and a cigarette in the other and was smoking both simultaneously.

When I brought Marsh to meet Sue, we had tea in the living room. It was the first time he'd heard a woman say the word "cocksuckers" and her stock phrases, "When I was alive" and "Life is shit." He was reeling. Nevertheless, Sue was a supporter; she had sound reasoning. "Chloe is grown up, Candy, she's not going to need you the way she has. You're going to be alone and life is long. Marsh is successful, attractive, and you're clearly physically attracted to each other."

"But, Sue, we're from completely different tribes."

That was putting it mildly. I was second-generation show folk through and through; Marsh knew nothing of that world. He'd come home from the office with his briefcase and a striped power tie; it couldn't have looked any stranger if he'd been in a wetsuit. To me, it was the most exotic work wear that I could imagine. Once he was seated next to Mary Tyler Moore at a dinner party. She introduced herself by her married name, Mary Levine, saying, "I'm in television." Marshall smiled. "Oh, what do you do?" I set about bringing him up to speed on popular culture. He'd never seen *Seinfeld*, for example, and had barely heard of *Murphy Brown*. We had our work cut out for us.

Marshall's first Hollywood party was at Sue's house, a dinner in honor of Lorne Michaels. Lorne's close friends Evelyn and Mo Ostin arrived. Mo is a legend in the music industry who'd signed everyone from the Beach Boys and Neil Young to Prince and the Red Hot Chili Peppers. Jack Nicholson, Warren Beatty and Annette Bening, Anjelica Huston, and Joan Collins were also there.

A starlet in attendance sat down next to Marsh and pulled out a hash pipe. His eyes bulged. Ever the gentleman, he lit the pipe for her but passed it on, as did I, because those days were over.

Robert Downey Jr., recently released from prison on drug-related charges, arrived with his handler, a hot-looking blond, buff guy whom he introduced as a Sober Coach.

Joan Collins was curious about his experiences in the Big House. "What do you do about sex in prison? I mean, don't you get horny?" Downey smiled and shrugged.

When Bill Maher arrived after dinner, the subject inevitably turned to politics, where Marsh held his own. For me, it was an ordinary dinner at Sue's; for him it was like falling down the rabbit hole. Marsh was just trying to put one foot in front of the other.

I thought he did beautifully. Warren took me aside afterward and said, "I'm in love with Marshall."

"Well, you'll have to get in line."

Marsh's next Hollywood event was an Easter egg hunt at Elizabeth Taylor's house. I'd known Elizabeth socially all my life. She'd been to my parents' house several times when I was a child; she'd guest-starred on *Murphy Brown*. She'd always been lovely to me. This would be Chloe's second time at the egg hunt; I thought it would be interesting for Marshall. We picked up my old pal Rupert Everett along the way; I knew he was writing a book and it would be fun for him to include the occasion.

Referred to in the press as an "estate," Elizabeth's house was surprisingly modest, with very little land and a small pool. A few kids with Easter baskets roamed listlessly around as someone dressed like a big rabbit hopped by.

Carrie Fisher, a good friend of Elizabeth's and, for a minute, when Liz married Carrie's father, Eddie Fisher, her stepdaughter, was there, as were Barbra Streisand and James Brolin, and Veronique and Greg Peck. A group of gay guys sat by the pool, all wearing tight black T-shirts and necklaces that said "Fuck." One was a legendary Beverly Hills hairdresser; another was a very famous dermatologist who in LA was treated like a head of state.

The hunt had been called for one o'clock. We got there at two, knowing that Elizabeth never showed before three. She appeared at the appointed hour, having been coiffed and sprayed, made up and eyelashed, making an entrance on her walker. Obeisance was paid. Everyone gathered around to say hello. Elizabeth gave Marshall a lingering once-over, a slow head to toe, sizing him up. She liked what she saw.

Early on, when my friend Mike Nichols met Marsh, he had his own opinion: "He's perfect for Candy now."

Marsh was taken aback when I told him. *"Now? What about later?"*

Most women thought I was incredibly lucky because they knew how few men were attracted to women of an appropriate age. My great friend Carol Ryan fell in love with Marsh from the first moment she met him in London. Later at a dinner she gave for us at her house in Bridgehampton, she raised her glass: "And I want to toast to Marshall and Candy, because Candy, who's taken care of so many other people for so long, now has someone to take care of her."

I in turn had to pass muster with *the* woman in Marsh's life: Marina, the true chatelaine of the apartment. She was Marsh's chief of staff, the chef and house manager, who'd been with his family for thirty years. Marina is Brazilian; she's highly intelligent and commands the home in a way that brooks no interference. Once Marina, intensely allergic to mold, answered the door to Marshall's apartment wearing a gas mask. This was never referred to by her or the three slack-jawed guests she was admitting and never mentioned since.

It was the advent of 2000. Everyone was a tad apprehensive about Y2K; we thought all the computers were going to crash. Marsh and I decided to have a New Year's Eve party together. Marina had been used to Marshall and his wife organizing elaborate, elegant dinners. I wanted to do something more fun and festive. Marina was on one side of the dining room and I was on the other: our first face-off across the table. Marina was talking about the menu. "I thought we could have fish."

"Fish? On New Year's *Eve?"* In my mind, "festive" did not include fish.

"Ms. Bergen, you with your California ways!" she scolded me.

"What?" I said, "No, we're not having fish for New Year's Eve dinner. Let's have classic comfort food. Something like chicken pot pie." Which is what we had, all baked by Marina with the year 2000 added to the top in pastry cutouts. All delicious. We had eyeglasses emblazoned with 2000, gold and silver balloons all over the ceiling in the living room and dining room.

Marsh invited Stanley and Melinda Jaffe—Stanley, the producer and former head of Paramount, was his best friend—architect Charles Gwathmey and his wife Bette-Ann, his oldest friends, Elihu and Susan Rose, and my old pals Eleanora and Michael Kennedy. It was the first time that Marsh's friends had seen us together in this apartment; they had been very close to Marsh and his late wife. They enthusiastically welcomed me into the fold. It was a lovely dinner, fun and festive, as requested. Everyone sang Cole Porter songs around the piano after and the world didn't end, not because of Y2K or anything else.

Despite our Y2K showdown, Marina and I became friends. Marshall once happened to meet someone she was dating after her first husband had died and told her, "Watch out. This relation-ship's better for him than for you." So when

Marshall started dating me, she told him, "Watch out, this relationship's better for you than for her." She would feed me details about the previous women Marsh had dated. Marsh is a guy's guy, but he's incredibly discreet. You couldn't pry any information out of him on his private life.

Marina had a nickname for every girlfriend. It was fodder I could use to tease him for years. When he started dating an elegant French gallerist, Marina began ending every exchange with an exaggerated, "*Oui*, Mar-shall." Once a close friend of Marsh's asked Marina, "So, what's this one's nickname?"

"This one's Boss Lady," Marina said. "This one's staying."

Marina knew before I knew. I kept waffling back and forth, back and forth. I'd sit at the desk that Marsh had built for me in the dressing room and think, "Well, I can't *not* marry him now, he's built me a desk!"

One day I was in the men's department at Bergdorf's, looking for a gift for Marsh, when I saw a small nineteenth-century tortoiseshell and silver mantel clock about six inches high. It was exquisite; I knew it would be his taste. I examined it and saw that the back was completely plain—solid silver—born to be engraved. I knew exactly what it had to say.

Almost a year and a half after Marsh first proposed marriage, I gave him the gorgeous antique clock hand-engraved in script, "Time Marshes On. I want to spend the rest of it with you."

Marsh took the engraved message as the acceptance it was meant to be.

We finally got married on June 15, 2000, in Marsh's apartment. It was a very small ceremony, only about twenty people. Don Hewitt and Marilyn Berger, who'd initiated it all and whom we thought of as our godparents. Mike Nichols and Diane Sawyer. Eleanora and Michael Kennedy and their daughter Anna. Mom and Kris. It was easier than having to deal with which of our many collective friends to invite. Marsh's group is particularly vast; I worried that they would be intensely offended if they weren't invited, and some were. I went to personally apologize to them afterward, but we were determined to keep it intimate. Marsh decided he'd have his two oldest, best friends, Stanley Jaffe and Elihu Rose. Of course we had Marsh's two children. Wendi, his very beautiful, stellar daughter, came with her husband, Joe, and two-year-old son, Alexander, who started singing "Itsy Bitsy Spider" during the ceremony. Andrew, Marsh's son, a composer and music producer with great charm and humor, came with his singer/musician wife, Diane.

I decided not to invite Justine and Cuote, preferring to discuss the upcoming wedding with them by phone. I didn't want them to feel obligated to make long, expensive flights to New York, but the truth was I felt uncomfortably guilty marrying someone else after Louis's death, especially in front of his children. I handled it very badly and insensitively and it was awkward but now happily has worked itself out. They are two exceptional kids whom I care a great deal about and I would hate not to have them in my life.

I had my dress made by Richard Tyler, who charged me a fortune: an ice blue satin sheath, which I wore with matching Manolos and an ice blue satin wrap. My wedding necklace, which Marshall had given me that day, was an exquisite nineteenth-century chain of diamonds and filigreed gold. I held a bouquet of sweet peas and narcissus, the stems bound with ribbon and streamers, made by the ever-amazing Marina, who'd also made one for Chloe and Anna. Mom wore a designer suit in her favorite color, lavender, embroidered and lacy.

We stood beneath a chuppah that Marina had decorated to look like a magnolia forest with leaves; she called it a "hoopla." Marshall's rabbi, Peter Rubenstein, officiated with Chloe acting as co-officiant, kind of a rabbi pro tem, at my urging. Wearing a pale blue Tocca sheath and a yarmulke, she recited the kaddish. In Hebrew. Peter handed

Kris the silver kiddush cup filled with ceremonial wine. Kris, known to be a big drinker back in the day, asked, "Do I kill it?" Peter nodded and he drained the cup. Marshall stepped on a glass wrapped in a napkin. It was done.

We began with drinks out on the terrace overlooking Central Park, but the women were getting nervous because of the hair humidity issue, so we moved it to the living room. We repaired to the three tables in the dining room for the dinner afterward. Everything was beautiful; Marina had arranged exquisite flowers and made a delicious dinner. Kris and Mom gave toasts. When it was my turn, I raised my glass and made a shiksa's Yiddish rookie mistake. "I have *bashert*," I said. *I have destiny*. Yeah, right here, in my pocket. I'd meant to say that I'd felt overcome with joy.

Andy said he had known something was brewing when he went into Marshall's sock drawer to borrow some socks and found a love note from me. Andy told us that Marsh had kept every note and memento.

I was stunned by how unique Marshall's kids were—sophisticated, intelligent, and kind. Wendi wrote me a note telling me how grateful she was that I had brought joy back to her father's life, that he'd found his sense of humor again. She wrote that he'd come alive for the first time since her mother had died; how lovely it was to see that. I felt completely accepted by them.

It wasn't until the wedding reception that I found out that the dinner party had been a setup all along. I had no idea. Marsh hadn't been friends with the Hewitts for that long, but he'd been having dinner with them when my name came up. Marsh looked interested. "Would you like to meet her?" Don asked. "Absolutely!" So they'd set up a dinner where Marsh would pick me up; the fix was in.

During his toast, Marshall said, "Usually lightning doesn't strike twice, but in our case it has."

I felt out of body during the entire wedding and reception. After the guests left, I lay down on the bed still dressed in my wedding drag. Marshall lay down in his suit next to me. He seemed agitated about something. In fact, he was having a tiny panic attack. Suddenly he seemed frightened that he was taking me out of my life and into his. Was it going to work? Had he done the right thing by bringing us to New York? Was he going to be able to make me happy here? I tried to reassure and calm him as we lay together. "Marsh, this was exactly the right decision. I've never been happier. I'm so thankful that you're in my life."

We postponed the honeymoon while I went to Austin for two weeks to do *Miss Congeniality* with Sandra Bullock. It was the first time I'd worked since *Murphy Brown*, and I was fairly nervous about it. Luckily my old friend Michael Caine, with whom I'd worked on *The Magus* in 1968, was on board. He played the role of the pageant coach tasked with making Sandy's undercover FBI agent a credible beauty pageant contestant, with advice like, "Eyebrows, there should be two." I played the role of a scheming beauty pageant director.

Afterward, Marsh and I flew off to Switzerland to go hiking for our honeymoon. Marsh is very athletic, a gung ho hiker. We went to visit two of Marsh's closest friends in Gstaad, an elite alpine resort in Switzerland where, as it happens, I'd gone to boarding school. On our first day there, we were walking around the village when we were stopped by an attractive older man who owned a nearby ski shop. "My God, is it Candice Bergen? Are you the one who set the Olden on fire and it had to be shut down?" Yep, that would be me.

The Olden was a wooden chalet with hearty alpine cuisine that had been there forever. It was Gstaad's oldest and best restaurant. As a fourteen-year-old in a Swiss finishing school, I wasn't allowed out at night unchaperoned. Nevertheless, one evening I snuck out with some older girls to get fondue at the Olden. There must have been eight or ten of us around the banquette when I had a brainstorm: Wouldn't it be swell to flavor the fondue oil with a little wine? I tipped my glass of wine into the pot of hot oil and there was an explosion. The low ceiling caught fire and they had to evacuate the whole restaurant in the middle of February; everyone was standing outside shivering in the snow. I had not only caused the fire, but I was out against restrictions. I was grounded for a month, allowed out only for ski afternoons, the winter sport. Which is why I was remembered in Gstaad.

Back in New York, Marsh's panic attack seemed more like a premonition. I was finding married life claustrophobic. When you married Marshall, you were really married. "Aren't you going to have breakfast with me?" he'd ask. But I wasn't hungry at eight o'clock and liked reading the papers in bed. He'd say good-bye five times if he was leaving the kitchen for the library. "Marsh, ease up!" I told him. "Well, you know what they say," he said, "The English leave and never say good-bye, and the Jews say good-bye and never leave." I often felt like I was going to implode. Marsh wanted us to have a traditional marriage, where we'd actually spend time together.

"This is what marriage is, Candy," he told me. "The whole point is to be with a person as much as possible." *Really?* Because it seems like *a lot*.

I was in shock. Marsh was needy for a kind of

closeness I thought was excessive. He and his kids were incredibly close; they'd have dinner together, then go home and call each other to discuss it on the phone. When he hung up, I asked him, "Didn't you just spend an entire dinner with them? What do you have to talk about?" "A lot of this is because their mother died," he explained. To me, it was overcommunication.

In the beginning, while I loved him very much, I resented Marsh for marrying me. I very much wanted to be married to him; I just couldn't face the reality of it. I'd lie on the bed and think, "He tricked me! He closed the deal when I wasn't looking, and now I'm stuck in this marriage, and what's worse, I've trapped my daughter too, so I can't retreat! I'll have to stick it out until she graduates. How will I do it?" I'd do slow burns. I would scowl and smolder for hours, have tiny tantrums where I spread stuff all over the bed. I spent a lot of time hiding out in Chloe's room, watching *Law & Order*. I turned to stone. There was a long period where I would have to do deep breathing. Once, after being especially cranky, I said to Marsh, "I know I'm a shrew." He put his arm around me and said, "Yeah, but you're my shrew."

I felt such a pull. I couldn't bring myself to sell my old apartment on Central Park South, which many thought was the best apartment in the city. I missed it. I'd kept it for thirteen years and would loan it to my theater friends, but it was mostly empty. It was exactly how I wanted my place to be, *objets* and mementos honed over years. After that first New Year's Eve, I never spent another night there; I'd go there mostly to pick up clothes. Marsh and I had never spent a night there. When things felt too claustrophobic, I'd go and just hang out in my house. Get a little distance. At Marsh's apartment, I wasn't encouraged to bring much of my stuff. Marsh didn't want the Tiffany lamp? And what about all my art? What about some humor? When my friend Ali MacGraw came to visit, she asked me, "Where are *you* in here?"

But wasn't this exactly what I wanted? Wasn't he the guy I fantasized about before we met? Was I not thinking about moving back to New York after I finished *Murphy Brown*? Was this not my plan? And did I not trust this man implicitly? Was I not attracted to him and still am? What was my problem?

The tribes were dramatically different. I barely knew any business people beyond brushing by them in various dealings. To me, it was totally foreign to carry a briefcase and leave for work every day at 9:15 and return at 5:30. I couldn't understand anyone who could submit themselves to such a life. I'd always been with show folk; they're a weird and wacky bunch. When I was on a show, we'd work well past midnight on Friday and get up Monday at four thirty in the morning;

Marsh couldn't process it. He couldn't understand that we didn't have a set schedule; it made him crazy. He didn't understand that things came up where you had to change your shooting schedule. He's hyperpunctual and so is his family; it's like a drill team. I remember we were going somewhere with his kids and were scheduled to leave at noon, and I found them waiting on the bench by the front door at 11:45.

I felt suffocated. Marsh was anxious, fussing around me constantly, telegraphing every move as a bulletin from the front. "Okay, I'm going to be in the living room reading."

So what? I'd think.

"What time do you want to have dinner?" he'd ask, sometimes first thing in the day. "I don't know! It's nine thirty in the morning!" I was cranky all the time.

I was finally able to confess to him, "I'm suffocating. You're asking for too much. I don't know how to be a traditional Jewish wife. I'm a Scandinavian Gentile. I don't fit the job description."

Marsh learned to pull back. Now I rarely have breakfast with him. For me, it's lights out at 1:30 or 2:00 a.m., up at 7:30 or 8:00. We're on different clocks. It's official.

Of course I loved how decent and fine Marshall was. He was innately elegant in the way he behaved, always attentive, respectful of people, regardless of wealth or status. He saw you into and out of a car. I loved that Marshall's first greeting is a big hug. I always loved men who hugged other men, the most attractive thing to see. Louis would shrink from the hug of another man; it was beyond the realm of his French family's experience.

Marsh was generous with his career advice, and good at it too; he was a lawyer who knew a little about show biz because of his friend Stanley Jaffe's tenure at Paramount. He gave back constantly to the city.

Marsh would rather have nails hammered into his eyeballs than say anything negative about someone. He loves to laugh, is modest and self-effacing. I knew so many men who were hard-core cynics; Marsh is an optimist. As a real estate developer, he told me, you have to be an optimist, because you're betting huge amounts of money on projects that will take years to complete. He'd lost his money in the 1970s when the market bottomed out and had had to make it back again.

He only believes the best of everyone. He views everything very positively. He'd take me to Knicks games at Madison Square Garden. The Knicks City Dancers would perform at halftime, these incredibly hot dancers who wear very little, switch their asses, do gymnastics. Everyone else sits there with their tongues out. "They just work so hard," he'd say. "Think how often they have to practice. They have jobs, and they go to school!" In no way would it have occurred to him to label the dancers as bimbos.

Marsh has come to expect that all of my friends are going to be, if not crazy in his eyes, at least eccentric and weird. I would never have it any other way. One morning I was in the breakfast room supervising a play date between Jerry, our enormous white goldendoodle, and Jerry's big brother, Clemenza, who lived two blocks away. Natalie, my then hair colorist, was doing my highlights. My friend and assistant, BB, was helping me out. She'd brought her two-year-old daughter, Cate, who was sucking on a pacifier that looked like buck teeth. Marsh stuck his head into the room and took in the scene: Jerry and Clemenza growling and gnawing on each other, Cate on the floor with her *Deliverance* pacifier, Natalie affixing silver antennae all over my head. Marsh sighed and turned and left. It was just going to take time.

For the first year we were married, I commuted between New York and LA. Chloe had one more year of school, because Harvard Westlake changed campuses for tenth grade, and it was more logical to move to a school in New York at that point. Chloe hated the idea; she didn't want to leave her friends or her school. I figured we'd do things in half measures, with me commuting back and forth while she finished up ninth grade. Marina shrewdly started courting Chloe. She'd send me back to LA with lovely containers of Chloe's favorite cookies. When Chloe came to New York to visit, Marina made it a point to find out her favorite dishes and keep the fridge full of her favorite treats. She knew that Chloe was the priority.

By the time Chloe finished her freshman year at Harvard lower campus, I was ready to leave LA. Our home there was the home I made for Chloe and me. I'd put a lot of care into that, into creating a house that we loved to be in together, that worked as a house for teenagers, a beautiful, gracious home to entertain in. We'd served lunches out on long tables on the terrace every weekend. It was a running buffet. I'd added a fantastic kitchen and family room to hang out in, with big comfy sofas and armchairs, a long breakfast table and banquette. It was an easy way to entertain that she and I would both miss.

It was emotional leaving Casa Costa Mucho; we were very attached to it. But it was hard to be in LA when I wasn't working, and as Chloe grew up, she was out more and more, becoming more independent. Also, I missed the seasons. I missed the energy and smarts of New York City. God knows there are legions of smart people in LA and I knew many of them. They were great company, but I didn't have as many friends there as in New York.

We decided not to take Lois, who was twelve and hated travel. She wouldn't have adjusted to the city. Kris moved into my house from the guest house and he and Otilia Orellana, our house manager, took care of Lois.

Marsh, being the optimist and naïf that he is, would say, "Moving here will be hard, sure. There'll be some bumps along the road."

Bumps along the road? Hello? Chloe was moving at fifteen, the worst time to be separated from her peer group, leaving her friends, her dog, her uncle, her school. We'd done it as sensitively as possible, but there was no getting around it—it was traumatic. On the one hand, I'd felt reborn, but I was anguished because I was putting my daughter through such a wrenching time. I was convinced getting her out of LA would be the best thing—especially during the perilous teen years. I'd always thought, "When I finish *Murphy*, we'll come back and we'll get a normal apartment, and she'll go to school in the city. She'll become culturally adroit and engaged with the East Coast." Now the moment was upon us and it was anguishing.

We finally moved to New York in the fall of 2001. Marsh had a welcome packet for Chloe: a MetroCard so she could take the subway or the bus, membership cards to the Metropolitan Museum of Art and MoMA, the number of a taxi service she could call, and a cell phone—her first. "You can go anywhere with these cards," he told her. "New York for a kid is a candy store. There are endless ways to learn and engage."

Chloe's first day of school was September 10, 2001. The next day, the World Trade Center was attacked. She was taken to the home of one of her classmates in Riverdale, in the Bronx; she couldn't get back into Manhattan. The bridges were closed. Finally, at nine thirty that night, they went to the subway without their MetroCards. The woman in the booth waved them ahead and said, "Go on, honey, get on home." When she did get home, the three of us walked up Fifth Avenue. There were memorials outside every building. Candles and photos and flowers. Everyone was doing whatever they could. The next day we went to Lenox Hill Hospital to give blood. They had to turn away donors.

Two weeks after the attack, my old friend hair wizard Maury Hopson called and asked if we wanted to volunteer downtown, preparing and serving food at Ground Zero. Marshall drove Chloe and me downtown to serve dinners with David Bouley of the Bouley Bakery. With other volunteers, we peeled carrots, shelled peas, prepared meals, drove the food down in a van, and served it to first responders at the pop-up cafeteria, the Green Tarp. When we stepped out-side, we could still see the fires burning. The first responders arrived, hollow-eyed, shell-shocked; they were the walking wounded. Chloe was moving more dinners than anyone because she was so welcoming and cheerful. Then Marshall drove the van with David Bouley to different restaurants around the city to pick up surplus food. It was a profound experience to have shared.

Marsh tried hard—sometimes too hard—but it was still very tough for Chloe at first. A few years earlier I'd taken her to a therapist in LA, a wonderful woman, to help her get over Louis's death. Chloe had been keeping a journal, which was helping, but she was still clearly distressed. When I fell in love with Marsh, the therapist had a phone session with Chloe and suggested ways to embrace her new life.

"He's driving me crazy," Chloe told her.

"Chloe, just breathe deeply and focus on your breathing."

I caught Chloe breathing deeply a lot. In through the nostrils and out through the mouth. Very discreet, but clear to me. Marsh never noticed. She never said anything rude or impolite to him even once during the transition; she never complained.

"Decorate your room. Make it absolutely your own." More good advice from the therapist that I would have done well to follow. Chloe set very specific tasks for herself to claim her own space. She took over the room that once belonged to Wendi, Marsh's daughter. It had a beautiful view of the park. I got her a big bulletin board, which she made into a giant collage with artifacts she'd brought from LA: an Elton John pennant, an Audrey Hepburn photograph, weird glasses, a movie poster from *Almost Famous*. The collage was a bold statement: "This is who I am."

She'd bring home found objects from the trash, which drove Marsh and Marina nuts. Once she brought home an entire door she'd found discarded and proceeded to paint a portrait of Jesus on it and propped it up against a wall. She went through a Virgin Mary period, making a collage captioned "Mary has a bright idea" with an actual lightbulb above her head. The whole hallway was dedicated to her work. Marsh forced himself not to say anything. She put up a gold-fish shower curtain in her bathroom and added a toilet seat decorated with a tropical seascape, complete with flamingoes and seashells in bright turquoise and pink. Over her bed she attached these huge five-foot-long plastic cherry tree branches that she'd carried on the plane back from Japan when we'd gone there with the Kennedys on one of our spring break vacations. They cascaded over the soffit above her bed like the most gorgeous pink canopy. As a final touch, she taped colored paper lanterns all over the ceiling.

She'd taken the therapist's advice to heart. The room was now hers.

Chloe's sixteenth birthday was her first in New York. Like any teenager dreaming of a driver's license, she had a fantasy of the perfect wheels. "My ideal car is an old Volvo station wagon in a kind of blue-gray color and I'm going to have Indian curtains inside. It's going to say 'the Chlo-mobile' in red lettering on the side." For her birthday, with my friend BB's help, I got her a plastic model of a Volvo station wagon, painted it gray-blue, put tiny Indian paisley curtains inside, and lettered THE CHLO-MOBILE on the side in red. Marshall got her a real Volvo station wagon. Again with BB's help, I also decoupaged a bedside table, cutting out photos from magazines with tiny manicure scissors for weeks, adding in copies of family photos. A love letter cum apology for all the disruption in her life. I asked Justine if she would come from Paris and hid her in Chloe's closet. Chloe opened the door to find her there.

Chloe told me, "You have to promise me you won't stay home to be with me at night. I want you to live your life as you're living it. I don't want you to accommodate me." Then I'd hear Chloe crying inside her closet and it would break my heart. I knew she needed to be left alone. There were moments that felt right when the three of us were having dinner and we were comfy and laughing a lot, and then there were moments when Marsh would be talking about something she found insanely boring and she'd breathe in through her nostrils and out through her mouth.

I tried taking Marsh with Chloe and me to Sun Valley for skiing. I barely paid any attention to Marsh; I was so focused on how Chloe would be. Since Louis died, it had always been me and Chloe, just the two of us skiing. How would it be going to the same place we'd been to with Louis? It was . . . all right. Chloe was . . . polite. She put up with it, she never complained, but it was hard. Marsh and I then took Chloe to Aspen for spring break, which was more fun because we had no history there.

Marshall would knock on Chloe's door every morning to wake her up for school—*wham wham wham!* It was like the Gestapo; it gave her a heart attack. "Marshall, just take it down a notch." I thought it would be great for Chloe to have more of a traditional father. After all, Louis used to call Chloe "Dumbbell" as a nickname; they had an antagonistic relationship. And I thought Wendi, Marsh's daughter, would be a wonderful older friend.

Marshall would often try too hard and work too hard; he was unctuous. But he scored in the gift department. When Chloe was little, I got her frog galoshes—she loved them, and when she outgrew them, she went into mourning. She said, "I wish they made them for grown-ups." Marshall somehow found frog galoshes in her size; it was such a coup. It killed her. She hated giving him the credit for it.

It took a couple of years for Marsh to win Chloe over, but it wasn't until he relaxed that it happened. She started getting him Father's Day gifts, even though he's always been clear that he doesn't for a second pretend to take that place, although he loves her and is very proud of her. When she got him a Father's Day cake, I was stunned.

Chloe and I have an exclusive language we use to communicate. We call it Bunnyspeak because we call each other "Bunny." When we do Bunnyspeak, we lose *l*'s and *r*'s, substitute *w*'s, like Elmer Fudd crossed with baby talk: "We'll be decowaiting the Chwistmas twee." "Dey awe coming earwy." "Who's a good bunny?" It's vewy annoying. Proliferating nicknames are integral to Bunnyspeak. Chloe's my Birdterd, French Fry, Muffin Top, Whizpopper, Clovis. I'm her Mamoushka, her Mooter-Scooter. Chloe and I call Marsh, Marsharoony; the man had never had a nickname in his life.

Chloe and I email and leave notes to each other in French Bunnyspeak. "Buh-nee: J'aime toi plus que tout les whizpoppers dans les mondes. (Je suis just kidding) Grand Bisou, Le Pit de la

Pêche." I'll get an email from Chloe confirming travel plans: "Bunnnnnnnyyyy! I am on da twain wight now. I will cawrll da bunny when I awive in East Hampton. Who ruvs da bunny!"

Chloe and I find Bunnyspeak adorable; we are alone in that. To Marshall, it is unbearable: exclusive and annoying. He just walks away. "I'll be in my office."

From the beginning, Marshall and I had an unspoken bond. We had both lost our first spouses within months of each other. His wife died in March, Louis in November. It was a very subterranean, powerful connection. Once early on he talked about going out with a woman who'd told him, "Divorce is like a death." And he thought, "No, it is not." On one of our first walks in Central Park, he took me to a flower garden he'd endowed for Jill at the end of Literary Walk. There were tears in his eyes. That visit was the first time that the memory of her didn't over-whelm him, which was how he knew, he later told me, that I was it for him.

There were many Rose family photos all over the apartment. The mantel in the bedroom featured a family portrait. I wanted to be sensitive, but it felt a little crowded. Beautifully framed family montages lined the halls; I felt like I needed to make a patch of my own. After two years, I mustered the courage to say, "You know,

I'm living in this apartment now. Could there be one place where the family photos are kept but not all over the apartment?"

Marsh understood. "Are you happy in the apartment? Do you want to sell it and get another one? Do you want to sell the house in East Hampton?" He wanted to make me comfortable. Marina took the photos down.

"Do we really need two libraries?" I asked him. "And do they really need names?" They were called the Brown Library and the Green Library. We turned the second library into a TV room—really, the Dog Room, since I filled it with funny portraits of dogs—and that's where we have our dinners on trays in front of the TV.

We redid East Hampton a few years later. Even though both he and Jill had exquisite, precise taste, I wanted a little touch of my own. We ended up taking down walls, turning a back porch into a breakfast area, redoing the house completely. It meant my accommodating joint decisions on how to decorate a house. I couldn't believe Marsh wasn't gay. He talked incessantly about Pelham Gray and the Viennese Secession. He's a builder, so he knows about proportions and fabrics and scale. He has a well-developed sense of design but I found it a tad austere. To me, a house should be inviting and comfy, a little eccentric and cozy. I'm comfortable and happy there now, and Marsh agreed to soften the landscaping. We added a secret garden, flower borders, a fountain, and seated nooks. Years ago, after my saying how much I love apple trees, we arrived at the house in May to find six apple trees planted in the garden. "Happy birthday," he said, grinning.

When you start a relationship at an advanced age, time warps in different ways. You can skip the awkward dating phases—because life is now too short—and you either jump right in or move on. On the other hand, you've both built up such a backlog of relationships and friendships; you can be crushed by the combined weight of them all. When I felt overwhelmed, I would go into my inert pose.

And luckily, Marsh noticed; he notices everything. If it had been under my care, our relationship would have withered in the first year of marriage. But Marsh is a born nurturer. Maybe it's a Jewish thing. In my experience, Jewish men are protectors and providers; they take care of those they love; it's encoded in their DNA. They also take care of those they like. And those they've just met. And total strangers. It's automatic. They don't even ask; they just assume it's their responsibility, like taking out the trash (which Marsh does not do).

Marsh is very gifted at relationships and talking things out. He does not fight, but you know not to push him too far because he's very definite about what is and isn't acceptable. He would sit down next to me in the middle of one of my Scowl-a-thons. He'd take my hand and say, "We're in this for the long haul. This is a marathon, not a sprint." *That's* original, I sulked to myself, but, of course, he was right.

Sometimes if I was cranky, Marsh would gently suggest, "Let's go for a walk." I'd think, *Oy.* And we'd talk it through as we circled the Central Park Reservoir. Or he'd sit me down on the bed. "Let's talk through this." He'd make me, in the most grounded and connected way, deal with what was bothering me. He sent me to a brilliant analyst for sporadic sessions. It wasn't how I'd ever dealt with anyone before; it really got my attention.

If I did something unkind—make snide remarks —he'd call me on it later. He never raised his voice. By then I learned I had to apologize, sort of—"What I said was out of line." He'd say, "That's okay, everyone has bad days. Thank you for acknowledging it." He had a way of getting to the heart of the matter with no drama. It was very impressive. I tend to burrow in and shut down and he refuses to let that happen. It hasn't been a problem for a long time, since I've been so good. With Louis, I was more the caretaker. With Marsh, I'm taken care of.

I'm seeing many women find romance after the age when we're supposed to. Often they've found it under extreme conditions; they've lost children, husbands. I've seen women find love after great loves, and love after never having found love. I see it over and over. Marshall was a miracle. And it was not a walk in the park. You just have to be open to that possibility and hope.

Marsh uncovered romantic dreams that were long buried in dust. There is pure luxury in that. But no one understands that better than the two of us. And of the two of us, he is the greater romantic. By a long shot. We talk on the phone often during the day and he says, "I love you" at the end of every conversation. To me this is excessive. And yet . . .

In the morning he brings me tea in bed exactly the way I like it, with milk and honey and a tiny glass of orange juice with the *New York Post*. Before he goes to sleep he squeezes my hand and says, "God bless." His rule is that every night he insists on giving me a kiss good night whether it crinks my neck or not. Sometimes I just put out my hand for him to kiss. (I know, I know.)

When Marsh is at his most confident, he shows his wonderful goony side, where he'll do a little buck and wing around the bedroom or zing out a great one-liner. He's a guy's guy, and he is my guy and I am very grateful.

Sometimes he'll call me in the middle of the day just to say he misses me. Sometimes it's a half hour after he gets to the office.

❊ 23 ❊

You want to know one of *the* most stressful experiences? Teaching your child to drive. The level of stress is literally unbearable. For both parties. Chloe was behind the wheel and we were driving in East Hampton. She had her learner's permit; I was braced in the passenger seat.

"Okay, put your blinker on," I said. "Turn right." Forgetting momentarily that at almost sixteen Chloe still could not tell right from left. "Turn toward my side," I corrected myself. She did. "Stay to the side, you're a little too close to the middle."

We rounded a curve and coming toward us was a young mother pushing a double stroller with two toddlers. We were heading straight for them. I gasped. "Be careful! Give her plenty of room!" Oh God. Chloe passed the mother without incident and pulled over. "You drive. I can't do this with you."

I turned the main driving lessons over to my husband. Marsh has taught two kids to drive. He and Chloe drove from the city to East Hampton together with Chloe behind the wheel. There is no amount of money you could pay me to do this. A police car pulled up behind them while they were doing seventy in the HOV lane and signaled Chloe to pull across four lanes of traffic to the side of the expressway. Somehow she did this. When they came to a stop, the policeman asked for Chloe's license. She produced her permit and Marsh showed his license. The cop couldn't believe Chloe was old enough to drive; she could barely see over the dashboard.

Connie took Chloe for an early driving lesson. This was in Los Angeles, when we lived off a heavily trafficked street called Coldwater Canyon. Even adults needed nerves of steel. Chloe managed to slowly merge onto Coldwater and proceeded downhill when she saw someone waiting to exit from his driveway. She slammed on the brakes and came to a full stop. *"No!"* Connie yelled, bracing for a pileup. "Don't stop! Keep going!"

"I was just being considerate!" Chloe protested.

"Great, but not here!" Connie told her.

Another time I was riding shotgun while Chloe was behind the wheel and Kris was in the backseat. "You're almost ready to take your driver's test," I told her. "But there's a part similar to when someone gets a pilot's license—it's pretty tricky. It's for night driving, so you have to be able to navigate using only the instruments. You won't be able to see what's around you, just what's on the dashboard. You'll have to wear a hood."

Chloe practically jerked the car to the curb.

"Wow, that sounds really hard." She wasn't sure she was up to that part of the driver's test.

Kris and I started laughing.

She passed the test without our help.

I think it is only fair to say that to this day, Chloe is still not a good driver. When she mentions that she's rented a car to drive out of the city, I look aghast and ask, *"By yourself?!"* Often, on these little work trips, she gets lost and calls her boyfriend in his office. "I'm in Newark and I just passed a Howard Johnson's! Where am I?"

This sense of direction comes straight from me.

❧ 24 ☙

When I finished *Murphy Brown*, I was fifty-one years old. I'd taken a couple of years off to do other things. I was old for movies—I was old, period—when I was offered a role as a conniving beauty pageant director in *Miss Congeniality* with Sandra Bullock. I hadn't acted in three years. The role was tart and funny and my part of the shoot would be only ten days.

So a couple of weeks after Marsh and I got married, I headed to Austin. The last time I was on a set, I'd been executive producer of *Murphy Brown* and could tell everybody what to do. If a guest star wasn't up to the show's brisk pacing, I'd sidle up to the director and mutter, "Goose him up a bit—he's holding too long." Here I didn't know how to behave. Or be. I was playing the part of a former beauty queen show runner past her prime, sitting in the makeup trailer past *my* prime surrounded by these gorgeous dewy young things playing pageant contestants. They'd be chattering away, giggling, thrilled to have a job, while I'd be in the far corner hunched over a magnifying mirror, putting on eyeliner and feeling like an old shrew.

Sandy Bullock was great, everything you think she is and more. It was her first time producing. Michael Caine, who I'd worked with a hundred years before—1968, in *The Magus*—was lovely. But I was nervous. I missed the comfort of Murphy. Here I was, playing this harpy with no redeeming features; it was far less fun.

I tentatively proposed a few ideas to the director. One scene had my character taking her old pageant crown out of a drawer. I thought as she lifted her tiara, she could start to imagine the faint applause from thirty years ago when she was coronated and acknowledge it with a royal wave; they incorporated the idea.

Miss Congeniality was a big hit for Sandy. After its release, when I dropped Chloe off at car pool, the kids would point at me and scream in mock terror.

The imperious shrike. That was my niche. Two years later, I did *Sweet Home Alabama* with

Reese Witherspoon, who played a sweet country girl turned sharp city girl. I played an elitist New York City mayor dead set on breaking up the marriage of her promising son to this small-town wannabe. Patrick Dempsey played the son—charming, self-effacing—just before his huge breakout in *Grey's Anatomy*. Reese had dropped out of Stanford to pursue acting; her production company was called Type A. She is hyper-professional—focused, talented, smart.

From there it was on to *View from the Top*, which starred Gwyneth Paltrow. I played Sally Weston, the "most famous ex-flight attendant in the world," who grooms Gwyneth for a glamorous life working first class in the skies. Small part, big hair, but at least it was a tiny break from shrewishness.

The parts were small, but it was fun to work with smart, strong, interesting women in charge of their careers. I played a wedding planner in *Bride Wars* with Anne Hathaway and Kate Hudson; it was Kate's first time producing. But demand for me never returned to the degree it had been with *Murphy*. Because I had become a cliché: a middle-aged actress marginalized in her career. Jobs dry up. Visibility is gone, and you cease to matter to anyone out there.

And I'm still getting used to having to spell my name to the pretty young thing at the reception desk taking my request for a restaurant reservation.

We were all gathered at Eleanora and Michael Kennedy's house on the beach in Wainscott in the Hamptons for their daughter Anna's eighteenth birthday and high school graduation party. Carol Ryan, one of my closest friends, was there with her husband, my literary agent Ed Victor, and their son Ryan, to whom I am one of many godparents. Chloe was there along with several of her friends who had likewise graduated. It was the week before they were to leave for college: Brown, Duke, Yale, Harvard . . . they had all excelled, made their parents proud. Yet the kids were worried; the parents were in shock.

"I was really nervous," Anna Kennedy said; she was a year ahead of Chloe and knew the drill. "I'd never been away from my parents for more than three weeks."

Lauren, another of Chloe's friends, said, "I'm really nervous too. I've never lived away from home before."

Ed and Carol were dreading Ryan's going off to college. Ed looked at Carol: "She's really struggling with it. When he goes, it's going to be very rough on her. It's going to be 'All hands on deck.' " He turned to his son. "Ryan, who's going to wake you up with a hug and a kiss and bring you tea every morning in college?"

Ryan shrugged. "My gay roommate?"

These were the early Boomers' kids—and many were only children. All had been meticulously, utterly loved. But for certain women, the experience of raising a child had been more. For them, for the women who had almost missed being mothers, it became the reason for living, the Meaning of Life revealed. Diverted by a feminist zeitgeist, they abandoned their careers in a bid not to squander an instant with the child they almost never had.

Feelings lay close to the surface. Carol wept at a sentimental commercial, barely in control. The disbelief that this glorious, vibrant voyage of childhood was over. What was next? Phone calls less and less frequent. Holidays?

My throat was in a constant state of constriction. Often, it was hard to swallow. Emotion was bunching up behind my eyes and in my throat. It ached, there, hoping for relief.

You'd think I'd have a handle on it by now, considering I'd been worried about it since she was born.

She's leaving home. Bye-bye.

We were fighting a quiet, rising panic; many of us were losing.

I'd even had a head start—by a year or two. I'd

get overly emotional as we discussed college tours and years abroad. I'd burst into tears at odd songs on the radio, once even while listening to a funny Christmas carol. Chloe would look at me: "What has *happened* to you?"

Frankly, I couldn't imagine how I would get through her departure. Thank God I had a husband who saw this coming. Thank God I didn't have to go through this alone.

And thank God for my friends. Mothers in their fifties—running to beefy now, the traditional thickening through the middle—we clumped together in our middle-age camouflage: black pants, long sleeves, more makeup than in years past, compensating with wit, attention, intelligence, experience. Bringing to bear not the extra fifteen, twenty pounds we all seemed to be packing but our confidence in who we were. The sizable weight and force of our personalities.

Ann Bancroft told me of her newly empty nest: "It was the worst year of my life."

Joanna Gleason found herself sobbing on her knees in the driveway: "I didn't recognize myself."

Carol declared, "I'm not going to turn this into a personal tragedy."

Some of the parents had gotten puppies in preparation for the empty nests. Others had gotten jobs and planned trips. The kids were helping us get through it. "You'll be okay. You've got such great friends," Ryan told Carol reassuringly.

•••

Chloe had applied for early admission to Brown, where her half-brother, half-sister, and stepsister had gone, making her a triple legacy. We'd gotten snowed in during our campus visit, and she fell in love with the school. The day she was accepted, I was prepared. I put a Brown University sweatshirt on our dog Jerry, and he greeted her when she got home.

On moving-in day, Marsh loaded the car and the three of us drove to Providence. We pulled up at the rear entrance of Chloe's dorm, where we spotted Brown's president, Ruth Simmons, getting out of a car nearby. Chloe was instantly ecstatic to be there. Compared to her wrenching move from LA to New York, this move was easy for her. She loved her roommate immediately.

We had done the ritual Bed Bath & Beyond shopping in Manhattan. We scoured the store with the brilliant checklist and clipboard: sheets, pillows, desk stuff, bathroom caddy. Chloe was very specific about what she wanted. A favorite purchase was a little vacuum cleaner called a Shark. She later told me she had run around to friends' dorm rooms and vacuumed them for pay.

The moment I worried most about was when we left her and all her stuff at the dorm. I remembered the first time Chloe had gone away. She decided she wanted to go to camp. She hated playing tennis, but she said she wanted to go to a tennis camp "by myself." "You don't want to go with any of your friends?" "Nope." We decided she would go to a tennis camp in Carmel, California. She was eleven or twelve. I was practically catatonic. We got to the camp; everyone was lovely. The grounds were very nice, but I was in a state of dread. The two of us were in a corner, both crying; we were pathetic. "You know, honey, you've got to go and try this. If this doesn't work, I'll be back to get you in a New York minute."

After the first days, she snuck in a forbidden phone call. She was depressed and sad and missing me. Then she started getting along with the other girls. But then another call: "You know, Mom, I'd like to come home." I was there the next day. She ran at me so hard that she knocked us both to the ground. We got in the car. "Didn't work for me," she told her friends back home. "I missed my mom too much."

When Chloe was sixteen, she did a six-week summer stay outside Paris. We flew to the city and the two of us stayed at a hotel overlooking the Eiffel Tower. The night before she planned to leave, I sat hunched over on the tiny balcony with the Eiffel Tower in the distance under a full moon while I wailed and heaved with sobs. Chloe lay sleeping in the next room. She was my only child, my one and only, my only one.

The next day I took her to the airport: she was flying out to meet her adoptive French family.

She had her Burberry trench coat cinched around her tiny waist, tears in her eyes. I gave her the present I'd brought: a porcelain locket with an eye painted on it, which she'd admired in Barney's. I put it around her neck. My heart was breaking.

Now, not two years later, she was happily putting up all her posters in her new dorm room. We were both dry-eyed. Marshall was like radiant heat—very much there. We drove home largely in silence.

Back in New York, I mooned. I'd go into Chloe's room all the time and read on her bed, her plastic Japanese cherry blossoms hanging overhead.

Thank God for Jerry. I now had a dog I referred to, talked to, as "my boy." My husband called him "our son." We packed his weekend bag and argued over what toys to take. Me: "Not his bat, Marsh, he doesn't play with his bat," as Marsh packed the rubber-winged bat in the bag. "Sometimes he does," he said stubbornly.

I visited Chloe at Brown two or three times a year. Marina would bake Chloe's favorite Linzer tarts for me to take up to campus and I'd hop on the train. The first year, I stayed in a little club on campus and she'd sleep over. She lived off campus for her sophomore year, and I'd sleep with her there on her mattress on the floor, which was lightly sprinkled with kibble. Her roommate,

Allie, had bought a Pomeranian puppy named Tyrone, who was a messy eater; the trip to the bathroom could be crunchy. We called her group of friends "the Pod," and I loved taking them all out to dinner. They were always happy to be taken to one of Providence's better restaurants.

Chloe would call me on her cell phone, every day, sometimes twice a day, but for thirty seconds or a minute at most, panting as she zipped rapidly from class to class. Ever the multitasker, she'd get all her calls made to me, my brother, my mother, and Connie. I had become an Obligation Call.

She picked a double major: comparative literature and literary arts. I'd get a sense of the scope of Chloe's intellect when we were with a group of people and I'd hear her speak about film, painting, architecture. Hearing the breadth of her knowledge brought me up short. Obviously, she grew up as a child of film, but her instincts about movies were so astute. Once for my birthday, she gave me a day at the Metropolitan Museum where she took me into various galleries and explained the finer points of the art. It was thrilling to see her education come to roost, with her own brainpower driving it.

When Chloe was born, I thought, "This is fantastic—I'm not thinking about myself any-more!" When she left for college, I thought, "Hmmm. I can think about me a little bit now because I can't do anything about her. It's out of my hands." I felt a tiny sense of relief that I couldn't worry to the degree I had. It's liberating for both the child and parent. Free from fear of her getting home safely on weekends, when, as instructed, she woke me when she got home. Free from anxiety about the college application campaign. Free from blanket worrying day to day.

But there was no escaping Empty Nest Syndrome. During her sophomore year, Chloe came home to have her wisdom teeth removed. I took her to the dentist, and during the surgery, I went for a walk and found a pet shop around the corner. When it comes to dogs, I am highly pro-rescue and anti-buying. However, there I saw the cutest little puppy, a fluffy black-and-white designer hybrid rug rat. I could tell she was a leader. She had spark and sass and energy: real presence. I immediately transferred onto this dog; I had to have her. I took this puppy back in my arms to the dentist's office to pick up Chloe, who was staggering from anesthesia, gums stuffed with cotton.

"I'm just going to try her for the weekend," I told her, and that was what I was going to tell Marshall. Of course, I'd already named the puppy: Phyllis.

Marsh said firmly, "No, we can't have another dog." We already had Jerry, a huge white golden-doodle.

Jerry came into our lives when Chloe and I

moved in with Marsh. We'd left Lois behind in California, and Chloe and I really missed having a dog. Finally Marsh told me, "You can get a dog as long as it isn't little." Marina also had an allergy issue, so the dog had to be hypoallergenic. We kept seeing this fantastic white dog in the park. I'd keep stopping the owner, over and over. "What kind of dog is it?"

"The same as it was last week."

The owner, who has since become a friend, had gotten his goldendoodle, named Clemenza, from a breeder outside Toronto, where I was doing a tiny part in *The In-Laws* with Michael Douglas, so I drove two hours outside Toronto to meet the severe Mennonite breeder straight out of *Little House on the Prairie*. She seemed to have hundreds of kids running around barefoot in bonnets and pinafores. On the street people were driving to market in horse-drawn carriages. She took me to the breeding barn.

"I want a tall, lanky dog with a big nose and a sense of humor," I told her.

And that is exactly what we got.

I brought Jerry back home and he bonded with Marshall immediately. Marsh was Jerry's alpha male; he has such paternalism in his DNA that he can't not be fatherly. Having a puppy in the city is complicated: they can't go out onto the pavement for several months because of a highly contagious virus called parvo, which can be fatal. You have to arrange play dates. Thank God, we had a terrace. Marshall would sit out in the dark on the terrace at five every morning and read the papers, waiting for Jerry to do his business. Of course I was sound asleep. We both put in the time training him. Marshall is extremely neat and organized, never much of a dog person. His night table was always pristine: nothing more than a phone and an alarm clock. In no time they were joined by a huge chew stick and a sodden tennis ball, and eighty-five pounds of Jerry was sleeping on the bed.

Walking a dog changes your experience of the city. You meet other people with dogs, primarily, which is lovely. When I took Jerry for early-morning walks, we'd often see attractive, middle-aged guys walking female dogs to which they were very attentive, but no girlfriends. Their only long-term female commitments seemed to be with their animals.

Marsh loved Jerry, but one dog was enough. Phyllis was permitted to stay one night. "It's not fair to her to keep her longer if you're going to return her," he said. As we drove her down to the pet store the next morning, I burst into tears; I was heartbroken. In some weird transference I'd reached the age where women get a little dog. It was predictable: The kids grow up, leave home, and you get the little dog.

Marsh looked at me, said, "I never saw you cry before," and made a U-turn back up Park Avenue.

Phyllis would be an early birthday present, we decided, and we brought her home. I later learned that while he and I were gone, Chloe had turned to Marina and said "Do you want to make a bet that she comes back with her?"

To be honest, my dog judgment proved faulty and Phyl failed to live up to expectations. Her distinguishing trait is loyalty: she never leaves my side. But she's an anxious dog and can't be trusted around children. Also, she's dumber than dirt and, unlike Jerry, has no sense of humor. But she's mine.

Marsh and I rarely walk the dogs in the city. I pay a dog walker, and it's a fortune. When I see commercials for car leases on TV, I think, for what I pay for dog walkers, I could get three mid-sized models.

And the nest still feels empty.

❧ 26 ❧

Marsh knew it was trouble when he woke up because I was laughing so hard beside him that it shook the bed. I was reading a script for *Boston Legal* and it was heaven. I'd been a "full-time wife" for four years. Barely working. He knew enough about my work to know that if I signed on to the show, it was going to start a whole new chapter in our lives.

David E. Kelley is one of the most talented, successful writer-producers in the history of television. He'd created and written shows like *Ally McBeal*, *L.A. Law*, *Picket Fences*, and *Chicago Hope*. At one point he was writing almost every single episode of two of his hit shows, *Ally McBeal* and *The Practice*, simultaneously. He was legendary. No one could figure out how he did it.

He was now working on a new show that had gotten great critical response but garnered only a fledgling audience. It was a spin-off of yet another of his shows, *Boston Public*, and it was called *Boston Legal*. It was set at a high-powered law firm in Boston and starred James Spader and William Shatner. And soon it would star me.

David had written the part of Shirley Schmidt, the only named female senior partner in the firm Crane, Poole & Schmidt, with me in mind. The script was remarkably sharp and funny, fearless and subversive. Each show would explore a hot-button topic in the news, so it was covertly educational. Plus the timing was perfect—Chloe was away at college and I could pop in and out of LA and play this fantastic character created by David. Shirley did not suffer fools, she was highly intelligent, tops in her field, had a caustic wit, and was a workaholic. She was not unlike Murphy and she would be pure pleasure to play. It would be a job, but not an all-consuming one. I couldn't wait.

Of course, the timing wasn't perfect for Marshall—I'd be away half the month—but he saw how excited I was about the script, so he gave me his blessing. I signed on, and they arranged the shooting around my schedule. It takes eight days to shoot an hour-long show; they scheduled it so I'd do the last two or three days of the first show and the first two or three days of the second show so I wouldn't have to travel as much. David originally planned to write me into only one or two episodes as a foil to the other male leads, but the character proved so popular that two turned into ninety-one over almost five years. I loved it in large part because of the uniqueness of the writing; James Spader and William Shatner were wonderful to work with.

James Spader is one of our finest actors. He is truly eccentric, initially a tiny bit prickly, hyper-focused and hyperintelligent. He carves each character he plays by hand—gaining or losing weight, shaving or growing his hair, and making singular wardrobe choices. For the character of Alan Shore on *Boston Legal*, he wanted him to wear Lobb handmade shoes. James found a way of not smacking his gums exactly, but sort of champing on a bit that was very Alan Shore. He has an almost photographic memory, so he learns his lines at one viewing. David Kelley routinely wrote him five- or six-page monologues in court closings, and he would give them flawlessly, only to be sandbagged by a nervous actor who couldn't remember his few words at the end. James never lost his temper with actors and was always generous to work with. The only thing you had to do was be prepared because he not only knew every word of his lines, he knew every word of yours. Plus the punctuation. "Didn't you have a semicolon there?" he asked when someone barreled through a long sentence. "I think you left out your 'for.' " It came from respect for the writing and respect for the craft.

James's dressing room was at the farthest corner of the complex. It took days to reach. He had set up a sculpture studio there for his gorgeous, dear girlfriend, Leslie Stefanson. That was the only way to ensure seeing her during the relentlessly long workweek. (The studio was in Manhattan Beach, which meant lengthy travel times for everyone.) Leslie would often show up with their dog, Mr. Meagles.

James, whom I love, is fiercely quirky. He had, evidently, a traditional series of actions that he went through before going to the sound stage when we were ready to shoot. A string of rituals. If he was interrupted in the sequence and it was unfinished, he would start over from the top. The assistant directors had to consider this when he was called. He would then use his handkerchief to open the heavy fire door to the set as a preventative to catching the myriad germs from hundreds coming in and out. The crew understood he needed his time, and they waited patiently, without speaking, for him to enter the sound stage. He was given every consideration because they had such respect for his work. He never failed them. Every performance was a little masterwork.

Bill Shatner's biggest success had been playing the captain on *Star Trek*, so one didn't have any idea he would be so deft at comedy. But he was versatile and had also played Shakespeare in Canada, where he was born and raised. He had range, he had authority, and now, he had eccentric Denny Crane—one of David's loopiest creations. (The character used to introduce himself by saying, "Denny Crane, cuckoo for Cocoa Puffs.") I watched him as he worked; he threw nothing away. Every line, every look, was specific and important. He took stage with a vengeance. It was truly impressive. You had to stay alert in scenes with him or they were gone and you were roadkill.

Bill had been a huge heartthrob for women, beautifully handsome in his youth, with a strong physique, and he always seemed to take himself a tad too seriously. But now, in his later years, he had put on some weight; it freed him from his romantic leading man roles, and he got enormous laughs as Denny. Stupidly, one day, I asked if he'd ever considered playing W. C. Fields because I thought he would be perfect. He looked shocked. "Well, *no!*" Because he had been a god.

Shatner's dressing room was next to mine. Every morning, I would watch as his dresser, a tall, redheaded woman, prepared his room for him. She turned on his radio at a low volume to his preferred jazz station, turned on the lights, and plumped the pillows. She did this with great care. One morning after Bill came in, I asked him if he knew her name. He looked at me for a few seconds, then said, "Not Cynthia."

Bill was in his early seventies at the time, but he had more energy than anyone on the set, by far. After putting in a long day's work, he would head across town to the Music Center to catch a play. He skied. He bred and showed Tennessee Walker horses competitively. He also bred Doberman pinschers. He rode motorcycles, sometimes to work, which was forty minutes to an hour from his house. Just when he had become the punch line for late-night talk shows, he would reinvent himself once again. He became a spokesman for several products on television, for which he made a fortune because he took his fee in stock options. He somehow always landed on his Canadian feet; I don't know how he did it.

Bill wrote books. He made albums. They were all successes. He won Grammys. He was never still. He had a beautiful, intelligent wife whom he had met on the horse show circuit where she had been a judge. They were married around the same time Marshall and I were. He was happy, he was productive, he was engaged, even exuberant. I respected him for his sheer vitality. It was pure joie de vivre.

Once Marshall came to the set in his Mini Cooper. Bill saw it and asked if he could drive it. Marsh got out, Bill took the driver's seat, and Marsh got in the passenger seat. It was a manual transmission and Bill left a trail of rubber as he gunned it through the parking lot doing seventy. Marsh was ashen when they returned.

David Kelley and his wife, Michelle Pfeiffer, had moved to northern California to raise their kids in a more balanced environment. David would have what he called "tone meetings" with Bill D'Elia and Mike Listo, his producers, by teleconference. They would go over each scene and discuss what was important, what it was meant to achieve, how much humor there should be, what kind of mood it should have. David rarely flew down to the set, and when he did—he was the Invisible Man. He was almost pathologically shy; he never came over and said hello. I would look up and suddenly see him lurking in the shadows, quietly observing. When we saw each other, he was always friendly, polite, and respectful, but he would seldom seek people out.

For an actor, the heart of a show is the hair and makeup trailer. That is where we arrived—in my case, at six o'clock—most mornings and that is where we took off our makeup at the end of a long day. In my experience, it was the best hair and makeup room I'd ever worked in. You felt it the second you walked in because the key makeup head was Jori Jenae Murray, and she was the most welcoming, beguiling woman you will ever meet: warm, relaxed, with a sense of fun. It was a pleasure every time. At the end of the day, she would take off your makeup with heated towels and then put Crème de la Mer on your face.

The key hair guy, Kelly Kline, was the other reason for the perfect ambiance. When we were doing our first hair and makeup test, I said, "I can tell you're really good, but now can we do something a little hipper?" So Kelly came up with a Schmidt bob, a chic shaggy look I loved.

Boston Legal was a joy to be part of: the highest caliber of scripts and crew, the unique quirks of the characters. Shatner's Denny Crane was Mr. Malaprop, routinely mispronouncing words like "You're on a slippery slurp." (It was only in the fourth season we found out Denny was suffering from Alzheimer's.) During a Halloween show, Spader and Shatner dressed up as flamingoes. They did another scene where they performed a tango together very seriously. They not infrequently dressed up as women. Bill drew the line at wearing excessively feminine clothing, but Spader loved it.

I loved playing against Bill and James. Shirley Schmidt had a history with Denny Crane. "You left me, Shirley," Crane told her. "Women don't leave Denny Crane. And for a secretary!" To which Shirley replied, "It was the Secretary of Defense."

My first scene with James was when Shirley barges into the men's room at Crane, Poole & Schmidt to inspect the fixtures—a female assistant was suing the firm under Title 9, claiming the men's room was better equipped. Shirley interrupts Alan midstream as he's standing at the urinal:

Alan Shore: *extending his hand to shake hers.* Alan Shore. It's a pleasure.

Shirley Schmidt: Surely, you intend to wash that first.

Alan Shore: I keep an extremely clean penis. *Walks over to the sink.*

Shirley Schmidt: I know all about you.

Alan Shore: And I, you. There's much written in stall number 2. I pictured you younger. Much.

Shirley Schmidt: A smart attorney recognizes who he can or cannot rattle.

Alan Shore: He also knows a good rattle when he sees one.

Shirley Schmidt: Since I'm your boss, I can't return your sexual banter, but I will say for the record that if I were looking for a rattle, he would be taller, he would be better-looking, he would be more evolved than a junior in high school.

Alan Shore: I prefer the juniors in high school.

Shirley Schmidt: He would be something other than a self-loathing narcissist with a dwarf fetish, and, yes, judging from what I got a glimpse of in the mirror when I first entered the room, he would be bigger. Much.

Once Marsh came to the set to visit while we were shooting a scene in the all-glass conference room. Suddenly, in the middle of the scene, I looked up and saw Marsh nonchalantly walking down the hall in the background of the shot, checking his BlackBerry. The director called "Cut!"

Of course, the work was much less than on *Murphy Brown* since I wasn't the lead. An hour-long TV show's schedule is almost inhuman. Half-hour shows wrap in March, with three months off. Hour-long shows wrap at the end of April, with only two months off before starting back up in July. Unlike a half-hour schedule, there is no week off a month, and the hours are almost twice as long. James was exhausted because he was in almost every scene. The quality of his work was rewarded with four Emmy nominations—and three wins—as Outstanding Lead Actor in a

Drama Series. Bill, who'd won an Emmy for Outstanding Guest Actor in a Drama Series for playing Denny Crane in *The Practice*, got five Supporting Actor Emmy nominations with one win for playing that same character in *Boston Legal*. I was nominated twice for Outstanding Supporting Actress.

Doing *Boston Legal* was hardest on Marsh because it felt like we were back to bicoastal dating. He likes marriage the old-fashioned way. In person. Marsh, who is obsessed with schedules and punctuality, could never compute a schedule that was not fixed. That days went into the early morning of the next day. That shooting schedules changed routinely. He simply could not understand it. He got cranky sometimes. He'd sit me down and say in a soft voice, "This is what I need from you." He'd be very clear, very specific. "When you're going to be away for half the month and we talk on the phone, I don't want it to be on the car phone to or from the lobby of a theater. I want it to be a proper phone call when I have your attention." Note taken. He took projects in LA, like redoing Sony Studios, just to keep himself busy and nearby. He helped me learn my lines.

There wasn't much swag on the *Boston Legal* set, but there was so much cool food. I hadn't done a series for a long time. I didn't know how much progress had been made with regard to food vendors. In the mornings were the omelet-and-pancake guys. Midmorning the taquito guys. Lunch the taco-enchilada guy set up in the sunshine outside the sound stage. Afternoons the Coffee Bean & Tea Leaf truck. Dinner was the sushi guy, and on late nights, the ice-cream guy, a custom handmade-ice-cream truck serving Salted Caramel, the favorite by a mile, and root beer floats. This was years before the gourmet food trucks went mainstream. There were vegan options, of course; it was California. The long craft table was always covered with huge jars of bubble gum, candies, dried fruits, and nuts, and you do gain weight, especially on an hour-long show, because the hours are endless and you eat for energy.

One afternoon I was in my dressing room when I felt a wave of nausea. I called the place where I had ordered lunch. "Do you use MSG in your food?" "Absolutely not," was the reply. Suddenly I couldn't walk across the room without lurching into a wall. I threw up but the symptoms remained. I was convinced it was food poisoning. I asked Alicia, our PA, to please call a car. Marsh was in New York, so I had Kris meet me at the house. He had to help me down the stairs to my bedroom, where I lay awake all night, unable to move. Marsh called my internist in New York. "She's probably had a small stroke," he told my husband.

"She should get to the hospital." With difficulty, I managed to call Rick Gold, my internist in LA. "Get to the emergency room now!" But my synapses were misfiring; I forgot immediately. Instead, I lay awake until six the next morning.

Marsh called Kris; he called Connie and they arrived at the house. After throwing up on the doorstep as a good-bye present, I was taken to the ER at Cedars-Sinai. We laughed as I checked in, but I felt otherworldly, incapable of thinking clearly, nauseated, with no equilibrium. I couldn't walk on my own. An adorable young doctor came in to take my vital signs, check my reflexes, and ask me a bunch of questions to see how lucid I was. "Pull my finger," he said. It was not a fart joke; he was testing my strength. I yanked so hard he fell right onto my bed. He was mortified. "Okay, this never happened," he muttered.

I called Marsh from the hospital. "I'm fine—no problem."

"I'm coming."

"Don't be ridiculous, I'm fine."

A few hours later, Marsh walked into the ER; he'd flown out. He'd told me he was going to a movie in New York with his kids but jumped on a plane instead.

The diagnosis was a TIA—transient ischemic attack, a kind of dress rehearsal for a full-blown stroke. My blood pressure was spiking. I was in the ICU for three days, three more on the cardiac

435

floor. Kris and Connie would visit; we'd start laughing and the nurse would come in to say they were trying to stabilize my blood pressure, not send it skyrocketing. The situation wasn't funny anymore. After my release, I went home and sat in an armchair for hours, muted, not fully present.

Chloe was in Paris for her fall semester junior year abroad when it happened.

She was thriving there. She wormed her way into a tapas restaurant on the Left Bank—simply started helping to serve and clear plates. And that's how she mastered French, the language she'd felt so pressured to learn all her life.

I didn't want her to interrupt her stay in France, so I downplayed the TIA. After all, Chloe had done a stint as an EMT while at Brown, wearing steel-toed boots with her uniform. I worried that she'd rush home if she found out I was sick. Kris accidentally mentioned that I was out of the ICU. "ICU!" Chloe shrieked. "When was Mama in the ICU?"

Chloe turned twenty-one while I was in the ICU. I wasn't cleared yet to fly to see her. It was a big thing not to be with her to celebrate. Louis's youngest brother, Vincent, gave a dinner for her in Paris.

Three weeks after my TIA, I came back onto the set of *Boston Legal*. They took it easy on me the first few shows back. Typically, I'd have a three-page monologue—a lot to learn. The writers cut back on my lines, but it was still a struggle. My first scene was with James. I was moving in gravy, just not reacting as fast as I normally would. I always had to focus more with him anyway because he was so quick. Now I was in a fog. Next up was a big courtroom scene where I'd deliver a long closing argument. I rose from my chair on the set and launched in, but didn't realize I was speaking gibberish.

I don't know if they ever got a clean take; they must have cobbled it together later. The next day our director of photography told me it had happened. I'd had no idea.

I made the mistake of going out to a large, dressy show-biz dinner too soon after the TIA. They seated me next to Joel Klein, a brilliant, dynamic man, then New York City chancellor of education. The poor guy was struggling to make conversation, frantically trying to engage me, but I was just enclosed in some kind of bubble, unreachable behind a membrane. I couldn't help him out, and I didn't know how to tell him. Finally he told me, "I just find you closed off. You're very difficult to talk to."

Marsh and I met in Paris in December to spend Christmas with Chloe. We had a lovely decorated tree in the room at the Ritz. Chloe met me at the airport holding a limo sign: BUNNY. It was like coming home to be with my daughter again. I'd gotten her a present I was so proud of—a rose gold bangle I'd had engraved with all her nicknames: The Mighty One. Dumpling. Muffin Top. Bird. Poochnik. Peach Pit. Bunny. Clovis. French Fry. Honey Bee. Chloe Françoise. Then signed, Mama, Paris, and the date. She never takes it off. Marsh got her a skinny Cartier watch in rose gold.

I was on so much medication and I'd only just been cleared to fly. Marsh was uncharacteristically resentful and severe. He wanted time with me; I wanted time with Chloe. It was hard for both of us. I wept unabashedly in front of him, having no reserves to hold myself together.

Marsh left Paris early so Chloe and I could have two days together in Paris. That was what I needed, the most important part of my recuperation. We could sleep in the bed together, watch movies, and order room service.

Chloe hadn't been given all the details about the reasons for my being in the ICU at Cedars. We had told her it was a spike in blood pressure, which was partly true. In Paris I explained that I'd had a few small strokes, TIAs. I saw the air go out of her for a second. She closed her eyes. Then I explained that I had been put through countless tests—CT scans, MRIs—and that my internist in LA, Rick Gold, was in touch with my internist in New York, David Wolf. I had been put on medication. It was under control.

Social situations were uncomfortable for a while after the TIAs. In *The Dubliners*, James Joyce wrote, "Mr. Duffy lived a short distance from his body." Mr. Duffy was me. I was still commuting.

❧ 27 ❧

My mother died in 2006, nine years ago as of this writing. She had been bedridden for four long years—long for everyone, but especially for my brother, who was there for all of it. She simply kept losing pieces of herself. She gave up trying to walk. Medically, there was no reason why she couldn't, but the impulses sent by her brain failed to arrive or the wiring was so corroded by age they couldn't transmit. Hysterical paralysis is the technical term for it. I think she just gave up.

For four years, we thought every day was going to be her last, but she held on. Thanks to Ubol, her devoted Thai housekeeper, Mom stayed at home for the full four years. Of course, when I say "full" that is a figure of speech. They were anything but. She woke around one or two in the afternoon and Ubol brought her breakfast. Then the bedpan. Then she brushed her teeth and gave her a sponge bath. That was pretty much the only activity she had until she brushed her teeth a second time and washed her face before she went to sleep. Which was late. She would stay up till two in the morning watching old movies and reliving her youth with my father in Hollywood. She knew everyone in the movies she watched— my parents were extremely well connected. My father was famous. She was a beauty. Life was good.

But life at home in her last years was not. It quickly had the power to make anyone who stayed there contract "caregiver's syndrome" plus a severe case of cabin fever. Just being in the house was oppressive, since she liked the shutters and curtains closed and kept it dark. There was no noise of any kind. No life. The place resembled a morgue years before she died.

Kris took Mom to all her doctor's appointments, a nightmare task. Laura, the nurse, helped, but really, four people were needed, at a minimum. She had to be loaded into her wheelchair, pushed out the front door, and then unloaded from the wheelchair into the car, then back into her wheel-chair at the doctor's office. The appointment took another hour or so. By the time you finished the logistics of getting her back and forth it was a miracle if it was still light out. It was exhausting for everyone involved. Then the doctors would say, well, she needs brain surgery or she needs to have her right breast removed or she needs to have her left hip replaced, all of which happened, and we would all rally. She had difficulty breathing because she was a former smoker and had emphysema. Cedars-Sinai Hospital became our family resort, the only place Mom would go to escape her room.

I was working on *Boston Legal* then and was in LA for half the month. I spent every night after work lying in bed with Mom, eating dinner on trays and watching old movies. I'd come straight from the studio and take my eyelashes off while sitting next to her and arrange them on her tray in a smiley shape. She would give me a look: We spoke little, but it was oddly comforting, lying together, holding hands.

She suffered from delirium in the last couple of years, floating in and out of lucidity. She could be a pistol. She was on an antidepressant, which helped a good deal but sometimes not enough. Whenever I stayed there, I would count the minutes until Ubol or my brother or Laura the nurse returned. I stayed there three nights once and it seemed like three years; I became almost as delusional as she was. It was very intense.

Mom could be particularly abusive to Kris, berating him, insulting him, an endless critical tirade. "You're not bright! You dress like a slob. How can you come over here wearing those shorts!" He was such a loving son who paid so much attention to her, but he had to put up with a lot. Mom seemed to have had a minor stroke close to the end, which may have contributed to her anger. She had hallucinations, calling Kris "Jenks," her southern uncle.

Kris kept us laughing, if not Mom. My brother, trying anything to survive the years of constant care, would torture her. It was all in fun, but it was torture all the same.

"I almost committed suicide," she told him in a moment of frustration.

"What would you do—fall out of bed?"

He would climb onto the roof and stomp over the area directly above her room and then minutes later walk in casually. Mom would have the sheets pulled up to her chin, her eyes wide with terror. "Did you hear that!!??" she would whisper.

"That was an Al-Qaeda chieftain, Mom," Kris told her. "They're in training to take over the studio system." Other times he'd claim it was bin Laden. She was petrified.

Another time, Kris jumped from the roof over her room into the pool.

"Kris, did you hear that splash? What was that?" Mom asked when he walked in a minute later.

"That's the squirrel you hate, Mom, the one who's always leaving pine needles by the pool."

Once, after a day when she'd been particularly abusive to him, Kris went into the kitchen, crushed up a Valium and slipped it into her yogurt. She ate it and quickly fell asleep. I think you would call that a draw.

Laura routinely mispronounced the names of the medications. One day Kris was escaping the house after my mother had been unusually harsh. Laura followed him to the back door and asked, "So shall I give her some more Irving?"

Kris stopped. "Sorry, what?"

"You know"—okay, really it was "Ju know"—Laura is Hispanic—"some more Irving. For her to be more calma."

Kris looked at her. "Do you mean Ativan?"

"Jes. Irving."

"Please," he said. As he got into his car, Ubol appeared in the window overlooking the driveway, holding the kitten we had gotten her to help her stay sane—the kitten who turned out to hate people and lived under the bed. Ubol was holding the hostile kitten's paw and waving it up and down, saying "Bye-bye!" My brother shook his head, got himself home, and dosed himself with Irving.

The last time Mom attended a social event was the eightieth birthday party we had for her at my house. When Kris, Chloe, and I planned the party, we knew it might kill her; she was very frail. But we thought if we didn't, she might kill us. And we weren't ready to go.

My mom's favorite color was lavender. She had a custom-painted lavender Thunderbird when I was a kid and then a custom-painted lavender

Mercedes 190SL when I was in my late twenties. Once I happened to walk past it with a friend in Beverly Hills. "Who could possibly own a car like that?" my friend said, rolling her eyes. I shook my head and kept walking. At the party, I had exquisite lavender-accented bouquets on the tables by Suzanne LeMay and the chairs were swagged with lavender feather boas. The house looked festive and fabulous. So did Mom. Her hair had been done; she wore a lavender caftan. My daughter flew in from college and did Mom's eye makeup with a flourish, pronouncing the job "Eyes by Chloe." She looked great. Kris and Marshall wore lavender ties. Chloe and I wore lavender dresses.

We had about fifty of her oldest friends. The guests arrived on the dot; there was gridlock in the driveway. They were very dear. And very old. My house, unfortunately, had a few stairs to navigate and so we had waiters—I called them "catchers"—stationed at the front door and the driveway to help escort the elderly arrivals. Once they made it safely down the stairs, I presented the lavender boas to the women. They all gamely looped them around their necks. Many of the men wore lavender ties. Many of the women wore lavender gowns.

Mom sat in the family room for the first half hour, and people came in to greet her there. She was in Overwhelm. The music was 1940s and soft. We served caviar and blinis, her favorite foods.

When dinner was over, I passed out lavender songbooks for a sing-along. Nancy Reagan, an old family friend, was a great sport, getting up to sing at the piano with Ricardo Montalban. Dina Merrill and my mother had been friends for almost sixty years. Dina looked younger than me, but she was there with her husband, Ted Hartley, and they were singing up a storm.

And then, as one living organism, the guests departed. The staff assembled by the stairs and escorted them one by one to their very nice cars. There were bad hips and knees to be tended to and heart conditions and they were very good sports about all of it. They were grateful to be anywhere in any form. They were all gone by nine. I could have had two other events that night. Chloe sidled up to me and said softly, "I'm very proud of you."

Mom was still on overload but was moved and thankful. Kris, who wore white tie, got her home. Ubol got her undressed and into bed. And that, except for doctors' appointments, was the last time she left the house.

It was a "diuretic day," one where she took Lasix, and Mom, who at that time was still getting out of bed, had an accident because she couldn't get to the bathroom in time. She took these episodes in stride, humiliating as they were. She was embarrassed but dignified about it. "I washed out my panties."

I prodded her to get up and go to the bathroom. With her walker, she moved like a turtle. "Come on, Mom, let's go now just in case. Just try."

"I don't *have* to."

"Well, you might once you get there."

She stood, hands clutching the handles of her walker, laughing softly, aware of the irony of the toddler-like situation she was now in.

"I love you very much," she said simply, patting me on the shoulder.

"I love you too, Mom."

This exchange would be unremarkable for most. But for us it was historic. Fifty-seven years in the making. To be able to tell each other, simply and sincerely that, after all the turmoil, we loved each other.

For my brother and me at moments in these last few declining years, we finally had the mother we always wanted. As she was diminished physically, she had gained in stature. Emotionally transformed. A woman whose primary character defect was seeing the glass half empty now saw it, at last, as half full.

By the time Mom died, it was really a formality. When my mother went to Cedars for the last time, I had just been there two weeks earlier after the second TIA. I was a little unsteady still. My brother called and said Mom was having trouble breathing and they had called an ambulance. Marshall drove me to Mom's house and I talked my way into the ambulance and rode to Cedars with her. She was lucid enough to be frightened, which was natural. She was also initially frosty because I hadn't visited for two weeks.

"I'm so sorry, Mom, but I was in the hospital. That's why I couldn't come see you."

Her eyes widened as she tried to understand. I held her hand. She seemed grateful. We checked her into Cedars and she was taken to the same ICU I had just been in a couple of weeks earlier. We said hello to the same bunch of ER docs and nurses that I'd met recently. "You guys were so nice, I brought my mom!"

Mom lapsed into a coma in the ICU and never regained consciousness. Marshall had to fly back to New York. Kris, Connie, and I were with her when she took her final breath. It was a peaceful death; she was comatose and never in any pain.

I never cried for my mother. Not for my father either. Not ever. I don't know why. I don't want to know why. Kris and I picked out a plot for her ashes at Forest Lawn mortuary, in a little glade with lovely fake rocks and real pine trees. The perfect eternal resting place in LA.

I miss my mom. Kris went to visit her at Forest Lawn at Christmas the first year after she died and told me that families were picnicking by grave sites and had set up Christmas trees. He found it odd and oddly moving.

I went out to Forest Lawn to visit her. I hadn't brought anything. What was wrong with me? I went and stood by the fake rocks, awkwardly, and told her the things she gave me that I am grateful for. Thoughtfulness was one. Consideration of others. Taking time to craft a gift that is personal rather than simply buying something meaningless. Writing thank-you notes. The dreaded notes. But she drilled it into me. And I wrote good ones. And I bought presents that were thoughtful and humorous. Yarmulkes for dogs, for example. Toys that struck my fancy. Snow White alarm clocks. Watches with Mao playing Ping-Pong on the face and the hands were his arms holding tiny paddles.

I thanked her for things that had been surfacing in my memory since she died.

I thanked her for insisting on instilling a sense of values when I was growing up that probably saved my already overprivileged life.

I thanked her for meeting me at the airport in a bus filled with friends when I came back from my sophomore year in Switzerland for spring break.

I thanked her for insisting I move out of my first romantic apartment when I was nineteen and was robbed within two weeks of moving in. She went out by herself and found an apartment that was equally romantic, in a townhouse with a doorman, and then took me to Macy's, which was run by a family friend, Jack Straus, who arranged to get all the furniture delivered on a holiday weekend. Al Pacino sublet the apartment from me years later. He hated it.

I thanked her again for giving Louis and me the splendid wedding dinner after we had married.

She never nicked me about having a child even though I got married at thirty-four and waited five years to do it. I thanked her again for the baby shower with pink Champagne to which she invited all her friends, who hadn't been to a baby shower in years.

Ours was, as they say, a complicated relationship. Stormy. Competitive. Often angry. But being a mother myself has continued to make me more understanding and appreciative.

It surprises me how often I think of my mother and miss her; how I now notice little things she taught me. The loss has grown with time.

Recently I thanked my mother for leaving a sizable foundation for my brother, myself, and Chloe to run together and decide which organizations and charities we wanted to give a substantial amount of money to at the end of each year. Evidently, she spent a long time on this and felt it would be important for the three of us to administer. She was right. Every year, as we winnow our lists of prospective recipients, we tell each other how blessed we are to be able to make these joint donations.

And how grateful we are to her for it.

❧ 28 ❧

There is a sacred ritual in our house and that is the care and feeding of Marshall's shirts. Marsh has a weirdly evolved aesthetic and he is fastidious about his clothing. Especially about his shirts. They are hung in his closet an inch and a half apart, and someone comes in, once a week, to iron them; his name is Mario. It was not easy to find someone to equal Marsh's standard of shirt maintenance, and there was some turbulence in the household until Marina came up with Mario, who is lovely. More important, he has a way with an iron.

I haven't spent an inordinate amount of time thinking about it, but I wonder where this sense of Haute Grooming came from in a kid born in Brighton Beach. He is, in many ways, very princely. He dresses extremely well and often checks with me for color coordination, but he doesn't need to. He is trim; he's been the same weight since college. He keeps clothing for years and years. He likes to shop every so often, and likes me to come with him for that. He has beautiful taste and he dresses in part to please the woman in his life. He doesn't have closets full of things but what he has is of excellent quality. His sweatpants and polo shirts are pristine. When they even begin to appear worn, he gives them to Marina to dispose of; this often means that some end up with me.

This distresses him. We'll set out for dinner and he'll do a double take: "Is that my sweater?" "Yes. And your socks." I disturb the force field around his clothes and speed the aging process of his sweaters. He feels slightly violated, which makes me smile. In 1995, I was inducted into the International Best-Dressed List Hall of Fame. As hard as I try, they can't take that away from me.

Marsh has started coming home around four in the afternoon. That's okay because by this time I've had a day on my own. But at first I was shocked: it was still light out. He started constantly talking about pulling back from work, disengaging. I could see it was traumatic for him. "You know, Marsh, you'll start to get old if you're not working at the office. You're the old fire horse. When you hear the bell, you start pawing the ground." It's just so ingrained in his DNA to be working, problem solving, wheeling and dealing.

There was a little self-interest in my saying that there too. I don't think he caught on. Soon he reverted to his old schedule on his own.

I'm not easy to live with. I'm very messy. After we were married, Marsh came home one evening and said, "You know, living with you is a unique experience."

I nodded serenely.

"Every surface is covered with papers and books and stuff. There's not a surface in the apartment that's clear anymore." He'd have me be a much neater person and I've learned to confine my debris. But I'm winning: Marsh is getting messier. In every way. He's much more his relaxed, loose, fun self.

The biggest sacrifice in being married to Marshall is there's no alone time. He rarely travels on business or even has business dinners. He's there for everything; you can't dissuade him. Marshall doesn't even like to watch TV by himself. He likes to be together all the time.

If you're traveling, he wants to know the itinerary down to the last minute. If you're home in the city, he wants to know the exact schedule every day, even on the weekends. "When are you leaving?" "When are you coming back?" He thinks he's gotten better at letting go of my schedules, of me.

He'll work till he drops. He won't know what to do with himself at home. I will. I'll be playing Scrabble.

✥{ 29 }✥

When Chloe was nine, I made a terrible mistake. I read her parts of *The Diary of Anne Frank*. It was way too early. I read her enough that the damage was done. She started reading books about the Holocaust obsessively, twelve or thirteen of them; I had to forbid her from reading any more.

By the age of twelve, Chloe started going to bar and bat mitzvahs. Most of her friends and class-mates were Jewish, so they happened every weekend. Children would speak about who they were and what they would become, their dreams and ambitions. Parents would speak about how vital their children were to their lives, offer fulsome expressions of love and devotion to their kids. It's a great thing for a child, even if you're not Jewish, to have a ceremony where young people declare themselves, to have a child think about the role of religion in their life, about the person they aspire to be.

"Mom, I want to be Jewish," Chloe told me soon after I started dating Marshall. I told her, "Honey, I'm doing the best I can."

I'm always wrestling with the Jewish aspect of what Marsh has brought into my life. For him, it's about community. In New York, which has the second largest Jewish community after Israel, it's tribal. In LA, people aren't as observant. Of course, most of our friends are Jewish. It fascinates me.

I grew up in Beverly Hills surrounded by show-biz kids, many of whose families were Jewish. Yiddish was my second language. My father was Swedish Lutheran, my mother, Southern Methodist; I was Episcopalian. All Saints' Episcopal Church in Beverly Hills was where we all went to Sunday School. It was run by Father Kermit Castellanos and he was beloved. I took Chloe there a few times as she seemed interested in religion. Once she was playing with blocks and I saw she'd made an altar.

Marsh had grown up in a Jewish neighborhood in Brighton Beach. We were walking to dinner on our first date when I asked him, "Are you religious? Do you believe in God?"

"I don't buy into the program," he said. "I go to temple on high holidays, but I'm not a believer."

Like Marsh, I don't buy into the program either, but I celebrate Christmas and Easter with a vengeance.

When Chloe and I moved back to New York to live with Marshall, he soon learned that for the month of December, there were going to be carols played throughout the day; he can't wait for December to end. He knows the drill: Stockings for all of us, including Jerry and Phyllis, which are

454

filled on Christmas Eve and hung on the mantel with care. Sometimes Chloe and I make it to midnight mass. Before we go to sleep, we put out a glass of milk and a plate of cookies for Santa, carrots for the reindeer. The very polite letters she used to write to Santa stopped when she was nine, as did the replies she would find in the morning thanking her for the snack and complimenting her for being such a caring child. But the late-night Santa supper soldiers on.

We give funny presents for Christmas, nothing expensive. Chloe's priority is stocking stuffers. She loves the teeny gifts. She's an ace gift giver. One year Chloe got Marsh a keychain of men's briefs—farting tighty whities; the next, a basketball that looked like a huge matzoh ball. Another year Chloe gave me a wind-up Kung Fu hamster, which was a fave. Marsh knows how to deal with it; the month will be over before you know it. Besides, all the good Christmas carols were written by Jews.

30

Let me just come right out and say it: I am fat. In the past fifteen years, since I've married Marshall, I have put on thirty pounds. This is due to several factors: I am older, I am on multiple medications that slow my metabolism to a crawl, and I live to eat. None of the "eat to live" stuff for me. I am a champion eater. No carb is safe—no fat either.

A magazine writer once accused me of "warming to the subject of my flaws." I pretend I'm not fat most of the time because I have never been a person obsessed with mirrors. But every now and then, I see myself on film or in a photograph and my overworked heart sinks. How did this happen to me? Ironically, my shock of self-discovery rarely leads me to diet. In fact, I have a certain contempt for women who have a will of steel, those women who never entertain the idea of dessert. I feel a skewed sense of moral superiority to the women who are intensely self-disciplined. At a recent dinner party I shared bread and olive oil followed by chocolate ice cream with my hus-band. A woman near me looked at me, appalled, and I thought, "I don't care."

I look at the tiny upside: my face definitely looks younger. French women knew choices had to be made to accommodate age. They said that when you got older, you had to trade your ass for your face. Fat holds your face up; my skin is stretched to the max. Wrinkles don't stand a chance. But my body? Well, I am almost off the rack when I go shopping.

I always was an eater. Actually, I was a compulsive eater. I think it was because I'd metabolized the idea of "eat before being eaten"—get the first lick in myself. At the girls' school I attended, we'd have speed-eating contests. I could eat twelve peanut butter and jelly sandwich halves in under ten minutes. I had a nice figure; I was slim.

I don't do the compulsive eating the way I used to, but I used to do it a lot. Mostly in my late twenties, probably because of the specter of hitting thirty. Now, on a normal day, I'll have a chocolate sorbet, a little snack, nothing horrible.

In my twenties, when I overate, I tended to take it way past the gratification stage onto the cusp of suicide, headed for total narcotization. In this state, I feel my brainwaves are steady. I'm probably in a deep insulin shock.

I'm not exactly sure what I'm narcotizing myself against. I'm well aware of all my good fortune. I was always perceived as someone who had it all. That was crippling to me; it took away my right to complain if the perfect-looking life wasn't perfect. It probably took me about thirty years to get over it.

Now and then I'll get a frisson of feeling what it would be like to be twenty pounds thinner. I'd be ecstatic, but I don't think it'll ever happen.

Dieting is outside my purview. I think I could count on my fingers the number of days I've been on a diet. I've never managed to last more than a few weeks. I'll start one at my husband's urging, and Marina makes me my meals and hides any cookies and buries my husband's ice cream behind the cutlets in the freezer. Anything tempting is either thrown out or hidden. From me. I literally cannot resist. And see no reason why I should. Until I come face-to-face with myself and my bulk. Then I snap. I crave cookies, Parmesan cheese, all the things that dilate my pupils. It would never occur to me to deprive myself of anything ever.

This puts me in direct opposition to many of my women friends, who are rail thin but at a cost. They maintain their weight by routinely vomiting after major meals consisting of a slice of steak or filet of fish. I am incapable of this.

It was Chloe who came to the rescue. Like me, she is an eater. Unlike me, she stays trim by running crosstown from her apartment to the Upper East Side for a boxing class and then running a three-mile loop back to her apartment before showering and going to work.

Chloe was at the Lamb's Club with a fashion publicist, who ordered a typical fashion break-fast: an egg white omelet with spinach, nothing else. The waiter turned to Chloe.

"I'd like the oatmeal, please."

"With water or milk?"

"With milk. And I'd like a large plate of well-done bacon."

The fashion publicist just gaped.

Three summers ago, she announced that she had signed me up for ten sessions of spinning class, and that I was going and she was going with me to make sure I didn't weasel out of it. Surely she was joking. Spinning? Me? But the next morning, she made sure I was up for the 8:30 a.m. class she'd booked us into. There was no sloughing off.

Spinning is not for the faint of heart. The class was in a room with fifty or sixty bikes, and each one was claimed by an intense, fierce, unsmiling woman. Here and there a guy. The female instructor was chiseled out of granite. The music was really loud. Suddenly the class began; Chloe and I hadn't even figured out how to attach our cycling shoes to the clasps on the pedals. We had no clue how to raise or lower our seats. A friend saw us and came forward to help. And, fifty minutes later, soaking with sweat, at the end of the class, we couldn't get off our bikes. Our shoes were locked onto the pedals. While everyone else in the class was vaulting off and wiping down, we were stranded. Finally, I slipped my feet out of my cleated shoes, leaving them on the pedals. Chloe managed to fall off her bike but wasn't hurt. Strangely enough, later in the day, I felt great. Invigorated. I wondered, had I come back to life? Was this a whiff of the old days? When I was healthy. When I was young.

I decided to keep spinning. Six months later, I

felt better. Stronger. Definitely more alive. Ideally, I'm supposed to be spinning three times a week. And when I'm not spinning, I'm supposed to do the treadmill. In reality, I don't. The treadmill is a bridge too far. Or I'll make the most ridiculous excuses: "I don't have enough time to go spinning, and then get my hair blown out for the radio interview," because we need our hair perfect for radio.

I would like to change whatever's inside me that blocks my higher motives. I would like to be good about exercising. I would like to be good about moderate eating. The weight, most of it, remains.

Let me just say a word about my husband and my gaining weight. The man is a saint. Marsh is a man who appreciates beautiful women. Yet he has been impeccable. When I diet, he is utterly supportive. Okay, last night when he discreetly moved the bowl of Parmesan cheese out of my reach, I was less than thrilled. He also pulled the plate of brownies to the other side of the table and slid them behind the vase of flowers. Out of sight. He'll move my hand away from the peanut M&M's. He's very good about it. He'll ask the waiter quietly to take away the bread, at which point I get prickly.

Marsh pays attention: to what I eat, to my health generally. He has lost one wife; he doesn't want to lose another. "It's not about looks," he says. "It's about your health. We have to stay in the game."

• • •

As someone who is older and overweight, I no longer get the compliments I once received routinely. As I move about in the world, I see how important my looks have been to people. I had no idea how much they mattered. I had always had very little vanity; on the set, I never looked in the mirror. But now that people rarely compliment me on my looks, I miss them.

My parents saved me from vanity with their conscious decision not to focus on my looks. My father armed me: when I was ten or eleven, he would warn me about the pitfalls of being beautiful. "You know, Candy, it's the beautiful women who commit suicide. It's the beautiful women who struggle in life. It's a trap and you must develop all of your talents and your interests and not rely on your looks." The message was: If you rely on your looks, you're an unfulfilled, incomplete person. And maybe a dead one. He encouraged me to focus on my writing, photography, painting, and traveling, because he knew—he dated Ava Gardner.

The difference in men's reactions to me changed in my midforties; I could feel it practically overnight. It was like flipping a switch. After childbearing age, you stop being a focus of sexual interest. It's primitive and the wiring is very basic; the species is designed to propagate.

My hair used to be pretty good. It was fine, but

I had a lot of it. Straight, but with a little wave. The perfect amount. And it was long for most of my life, sometimes to the middle of my back. In fact, when all else failed, I could always count on my hair. That was my primary fallback position. I dried it bending upside down to give it volume and I was out the door. That was my smallest bit of vanity, because if my hair isn't fluffy on this pea-sized head, I look like a golf ball on an enormous buoy. In May of 2000, *People* declared me, at the ripe age of fifty-four, among its "Most Beautiful People." Go figure.

In my sixties, I seem to have gotten somebody else's hair. I think Golda Meir's; it bears no resemblance to my own. First, it's thinner. By a lot. But mostly, it's the curl thing. Seriously. How did this poodle thing happen? Because it's really not working for me. Half the year, I look like an idiot, like my hair had a psychotic break. That would be the summer half. Winter, I'm just balding.

By the way, I am not alone in my elderly hair dilemma. Recently I noticed several of my friends are wearing wigs.

This year I did a few days on a movie written, directed, produced, and starred in by Warren Beatty. We have known each other for fifty years. During breaks when they were doing lighting, he and I sat in a corner of the set and talked about the old days, about being beautiful. There was no one more gorgeous than he. It gives you total access, Warren said, and I agree. What you do with it is up to you. It's an all-access backstage pass.

Of course, there are certain fixes I could make that I choose not to. I could get a face lift. I could get a brow lift. Friends of mine started to get face lifts at around forty. They were beautiful women who looked great before. By now they've had two or three face lifts. Some look absolutely the same to me. Some I can see the scars by their ears. Some wear special hairpieces to cover them.

I did the pilot of *Murphy Brown* au naturel. My eyes were so hooded that when the show was picked up, I got them done. I didn't anguish over it; I went to LA's most trusted cosmetic surgeon, Frank Kamer. It was very discreet. Two years later, I developed these vertical muscular bands beneath my jaw line. The lighting on TV shows is harsh and aging; those neck muscles were catching the light. I went back to Dr. Kamer, who shaved the muscles and sewed them together. Two weeks later, I flew to Cannes to be with Louis. That's been it so far.

I've also tried the shots. I went to a New York doctor who is one of the best. She is whip smart. She has humor. She is chic and always perfectly put together. She has heels by Manolo and the patience of a saint, and somehow, she always manages to fit me in. She knows I'm a pussy.

(Call me what you will; I undoubtedly have gotten there before you.) She spends time chatting with me to calm me down and then, keeping the syringe out of my eye line, she injects me with . . . well, I am not entirely *sure* what it is. Restylane for one. Botox for another.

I made my first appointment before a job. At that first session, she injected me above each eyebrow, which paralyzed the muscles, which somehow resulted in my eyelids looking less hooded. She injected between my eyebrows, which prevented me from getting frown lines, which I never really had. Then she injected the Botox into the two baggy bands under my neck, which tightened them somewhat so I looked less like Eddie Fisher. I think this was good. And I could just manage the pain.

Next came the Restylane, a synthetic filler. Fillers are where women have long ago lost their discretion and end up looking like mummies. Or in many cases, mummy fish, their lips being the focal point of the shots. The lips were where I drew the line; I knew I couldn't take it.

She injected the Restylane above each cheek for starters; this was to lift your face microscopically. By the end, I had slid down so far in my chair that she could no longer reach me. I was also moaning like a wounded warthog. To which she said only, "You know, Jewish women are willing to endure a lot more pain for beauty than Gentiles."

After putting it off a year, I booked another appointment. Before I went, it occurred to me, I can medicate this! Why am I putting myself through this? I'll just take a Valium and two Tylenol. Simple. Then I won't feel a thing. But what I didn't feel was any effects from the pain medication. So I had barely started groaning when I fainted. In the second before I slumped to the floor, I saw the doctor look alarmed and ask the nurse to get a glass of orange juice to raise my blood sugar. I know this remedy because in the 1970s, when it was common for people to pass out at social functions from smoking too much dope or hash or worse, you would grab them under the arms and drag them outside where they would cause less suspicion than in the middle of a hip and trendy restaurant. Then you would put ice on the back of their neck and give them a few sips of orange juice until they regained consciousness. And then you would somehow get them home—usually not my problem.

With half my face injected, I was hustled out of the treatment room and into her office. If you're not special, like me, you're left to rot in the waiting room for days on end. Once the color had returned to my half-lifted face, they were relieved to have me pay and take the elevator down to the car, which is how the special people arrive and depart. I was warned not to incline my head lest the Botox spill into my brain or slosh into the cerebral cortex and paralyze not only my eyebrows but my spine, and that is, I don't have to tell you, ladies, a very different kettle of fish. Once when I was leaving her office, I dropped my sunglasses in the elevator and couldn't look down to pick them up. I had to carefully lower myself and grope blindly. The other passengers paid no notice.

I stopped going for a couple of years and slowly acquired the jowls of a basset. My mouth has grown so thin it cannot be found by the naked eye. My eyes are so hooded by this point that I'm a hazard behind the wheel. After looking in the mirror, I picked up the phone and managed to get an appointment immediately because she is a mensch, and the moaning began anew. I have to make an effort. For my husband. For my old self. I know that I'm one of the lucky ones. In the meantime, I will wear more makeup. And keep spinning.

❧ 31 ❧

For a time I took Prozac. Okay, it was a long time. Several years. A very low dose, but still, enough that I never felt any pain. I had lost the ability. For years, I could not cry. This was risky in so many ways. For one thing, I was, am, an actor and being unable to cry, which is a definite indicator of distress or inexpressible joy, is a professional drawback. And nothing I could do, including trying to squeeze drops of moisture out of my eyes by squinching them, was working. When I was given new scripts to read, the first thing I would look for was if I had emotional scenes. Because I couldn't play them.

The main reason I started taking Prozac was because I was unable to sleep. I would start yawning, turn off the light, then lie there till 4:00 a.m, when I would fall into a dazed short snooze for three or four hours. This began during *Murphy Brown*'s final seasons; I was raising a young child and I was running on empty. Oh, and my husband had died.

When I started seeing Marshall, then fell in love with Marshall, and finally married Marshall, he would find me in various places in the apartment where I had gone to read while waiting till the predictable 4:00 a.m. sleep slot. He suggested I see a man who had been extremely helpful to him when he was dealing with his late wife's illness. So I did, and he was.

This man, a highly qualified psychoanalyst, was exactly what I had been wishing for: a Village Wise Man. He is knowledgeable in all things, psychological, and professional. And his advice is unfailing. This is based on a profound intelligence, a broad education, and a lifetime of observation and experience.

He has, in fact, become the Village Wise Man for New York City. I kid you not. The people I have glimpsed slinking out of his waiting room would stagger you. Titans of Industry. Wizards of Finance. Captains of Popular Culture. Literary Giants. He simply knows how everything works. Life. Children. Marriage. Divorce. Death. Leveraged buyouts. Theater. Film. Plotlines. He is fluent in all fields of endeavor. It is truly amazing. He is charming and nonjudgmental, and he pays strict attention. He has a memory like a steel trap. He is all-knowing and all-seeing. He is the guru of the Big Apple.

The Wise Man is also highly informed medically and able to interpret the complex conditions his exalted patients trot in with. When I first went to the Wise Man, I said, "I need a personality transplant." He put me on Prozac. Later I returned and said that perhaps the Prozac was contributing to my weight gain, which as I mentioned was huge, and he agreed to take me off it.

So for the past few years I have been off Prozac and lost almost no weight but I have regained my ability to cry. This is mostly good. But I am back to inappropriate spurts of emotion at inappro- priate times; I well up often at the least provocation. But, at least I well up. When I told a girlfriend that in going off Prozac, I recovered my ability to cry and was now a chronic weeper, she said dismissively, "Eh. Crying's overrated." I am told this is a condition called emotional lability, usually caused by a stroke. In my case, that manifests as weeping at commercials that feature dogs. And, of course, I am back to being cranky. The surfaces that Prozac smoothed are, once again, scratchy and abrasive. I am short-tempered and Chloe calls me on it. I am impatient and judgmental. I am not nearly as nice to be around, that is true.

I miss the other Kinder, Gentler Self, but I have recovered my ability to cry, and then some. You can't have everything.

⌘ 32 ⌘

Vogue had asked mothers and daughters to a karaoke night for its "Fashion's Night Out"—a Valentino event. My daughter asked me to attend. She knows that I hate those kinds of things, but the magazine told her it would be very important if I came.

Of course it wasn't. I was there for twenty minutes. It was packed with people. Tracy Morgan hosted the karaoke. Natalie Cole sang Nat King Cole. Tracy asked Chloe and me to come up to the mic. Chloe volunteered a few Aretha songs. I just stood behind Chloe and Tracy and clapped. Chloe, who is fearless in those situations, sang— no, she shrieked. That seemed to do it. I left.

The *New York Post*'s coverage of the event

referred to "*Vogue*'s Chloe Malle." Later in the column they mentioned "her mother, Candice Bergen." Chloe was in boldface at age twenty-five. Her boyfriend, Graham, hooked my BlackBerry up to a Google alert for Chloe Malle, and it beeps almost every day. The kid is busy. At twenty-eight, she has over seven thousand Twitter followers. She is a force.

As a mother, I am a backup singer in every way. There's never been a shred of competitiveness. I've always been thrilled whenever Chloe was front and center.

Chloe always had her own ambitions from the get-go. She had two parents who were accomplished public figures and she knew she had contributions to make. She has always made this clear.

After graduation, Chloe came back to live with us for a minute before leaving for a year in Ethiopia, where she volunteered with Dr. Rick Hodes. He is an American doctor who treats severely handicapped kids and had sixteen living with him; they mostly suffer from spinal tuberculosis.

Chloe had wanted to volunteer in Sudan, but our friend Marilyn Hewitt stepped in to steer her away from such a risk-prone place and introduced her to "Dr. Rick." They even visited Ethiopia together six months before. Before she left, she called the Ethiopian consulate and took lessons in Amharic; by the time she left Ethiopia, she had a basic understanding of the language. *Chigger yellum* means "no problem," a phrase she deployed often, even though there was usually a problem.

She lived in Addis Ababa in a little cottage near Rick's house, and her roommate was a premed student named Monica, who was an Orthodox Jew. This advanced Chloe a little closer to her goal of being Jewish. I was sanguine about her absence. I knew it was relatively safe, and if she got sick, she was working for a doctor, who could take care of her. Plus, there was nothing I could do about it.

Marsh and I went to Addis Ababa to visit Clovis at Thanksgiving. It was my second time in Ethiopia; I had been there many years before when I was doing an article on the country for *Travel & Leisure*. I got a five-minute interview with the emperor, Haile Selassie, in his dilapidated Menelik Palace. There were two lions chained to each pillar of the entrance as symbols of his very long title: His Imperial Majesty Haile Selassie I, Conquering Lion of the Tribe of Judah, King of Kings of Ethiopia, Elect of God, a long title for a short guy. These were the oldest, saddest, most decrepit lions I ever saw; they had just given up. Ethiopia in those days was very raw and primitive. Today it is only somewhat less so. There was one nice hotel, the Hilton, in Addis Ababa. All the ex-pats would flock there on weekends to use the pool and have tea. At night we could hear the hyenas howling as they moved into the outskirts of the city.

Now there are two nice hotels, but Ethiopia is still primitive by comparison with developed countries. Chloe met us at the airport and took us straight to meet Doctor Rick at his house. He is a small, trim, attractive man who wears a colorful, knitted skullcap as a yarmulke. He is an Orthodox Jew who is friendly and focused, and he has spent the last twenty-five years healing people in Addis Ababa. He came originally to help in the relocation of Ethiopia's Jews, the Falashas, to Israel and stayed because he saw a huge need for medical assistance.

Chloe helped Rick as he worked out of Mother Teresa's Home for the Dying on the outskirts of Addis Ababa. This is not an easy place to be. It was built originally to handle five hundred people—five hundred dying people, to be precise. It now houses up to eight hundred, depending on the day. The patients are everywhere—on beds, on the ground, on the concrete floor. You have to step over them as you enter and leave. They are cared for and fed for a short term only. Chloe would sit in on consultations, administer pulmonary function tests for TB patients, and distribute medication. Then Dr. Rick would examine them to determine if treatment was possible.

Chloe's had to deal with a lot of things ahead of her time: Louis's early death and the premature death of Ingrid, her beloved nanny. She's very brave about things and fairly knowledgeable medically, not a shrinking violet. She'd thought about med school, which surprised me, because her talents lay in acting and writing, the right side of the brain. The year in Ethiopia, however, burned her out on medicine.

When she got back to New York, she moved right into my old duplex on Central Park South, which I bought when I was thirty, the apartment where Louis and I lived when she was born.

When she started looking for a job, she did it without any help from me. Through a friend, she got an interview at *The Observer* and was given an entry-level job writing about real estate. Marshall, a real estate developer, is friends with the publisher, but he didn't even know that Chloe was going in for the interview. Once she got the job, she started calling Marshall all the time, peppering him with questions: "Do you know this Realtor, that apartment building?" She appeared on MSNBC a month after she started because the top editor was away. She's a tiny thing, five-feet-three, with a high voice, and she looks twelve, but Chloe held her own. *The Observer* moved her to the livelier arts and features beat, where she interviewed architects and painters. Much more fun. Marsh did help her there by getting her an interview with his pal, Frank Gehry. Then she started doing pieces for the Fashion & Style section of the *New York Times* after her *Observer* editor moved there and asked Chloe to write for them. Her first piece was a full page on designer Roberta Freymann, who began her career selling fashions from Vietnam and Thailand out of a miniature souk in her Upper East Side apartment.

Then she was asked to interview Taylor Swift for a cover piece in *InStyle*. Chloe had the random idea to take her riding; she knew that Taylor had ridden as a kid. "Where can I take her?" she asked me. I called Diane English, who has a horse named Chet at the stable at the Los Angeles Equestrian Center. On the day of the interview, I went ahead to make sure the horses were saddled and ready. The stable hand told me, "I'm not going to saddle horses until the rest of the party comes." "You don't understand," I said, bluffing. "I'm going to lose my job if they're not ready." So he did it. I tipped him $100. Mounted on our pathetic-looking, mud-encrusted horses, we met Diane English astride Chet, her handsome paint. Diane and I rode ahead as a security posse while my jug-headed mustang went nuts in mud a foot deep. Taylor and Chloe rode blithely behind us, chattering happily. Chloe got her interview and cover story, and Taylor was adorable.

Word got out that Chloe was talented and charming and well connected. The style editor at

Vogue was leaving and Chloe was recommended by a colleague for the job. In her rapid rise as a journalist, Chloe was interviewed at *Vogue* by ten editors, culminating with Anna Wintour (twice). This for an editorial position overseeing ten pages of the magazine called *Flash*, a mélange of what's happening socially and in pop culture. For Chloe, it was a dream job. A grown-up collage like the ones she'd been doing in her journals since she was nine.

At age twenty-five Chloe became one of the youngest editors at *Vogue*.

Before she started, one day at home she cracked off a massive fart, and I said, "Honey, you are not going be able to fart like that at *Vogue*, you know!" And she whirled around and said, *"Watch me!"*

Now people compliment me constantly on Chloe's pieces in *Vogue*. She writes very well; she is a master of detail. She is piercingly honest and perceptive, and she has a keen sense of irony. Under the auspices of the magazine, she's invited to almost every event in the city. Soon after she started, she flew to Florence to cover a rally of vintage racing cars around the Tuscan country-side, a Ladies Classic Cars Tour. She was the copilot in a 1930s Bugatti with Yasmin Le Bon. When the women first met her, they asked suspiciously, "Are you old enough to have your driver's license?"

She has met almost everyone of note in the city. Valentino and Giancarlo Giammetti invited her to a Valentine's Day supper at their apartment. She appears next to social lions and movers and shakers in the tiny pictures in *The New York Times*. She also edited the magazine's special-interest issue, *Vogue Best Dressed*, the best-selling special issue they'd ever had, as well as *Vogue Weddings*, a lavish coffee table book; and a special issue and a book on the Metropolitan Museum of Art's Costume Institute exhibition and the annual gala hosted by *Vogue*.

Chloe is still the first to volunteer for social outreach projects. When she was in high school, one of my favorite outings was to accompany her as she handed out Christmas meals to the underprivileged or mentally handicapped. Or bought gifts for twenty adolescents at Old Navy for holiday presents. She volunteered every weekend in high school with an organization called Achilles, which provides escorts to disabled athletes. She is now on their board. She's run or walked the New York City Marathon for many years with runners who are blind or have lost a leg. One year she escorted a regular Achilles member named Bill who had such crippling cerebral palsy that he had to push himself back-ward in his wheelchair the entire twenty-six miles. He was given the earlier start time of 7:00 a.m., which is allocated to runners with disabilities, and finished about 7:30 p.m.

A few times on Marathon Day, Marshall and I have driven her at 3:00 a.m. to the gathering place on Fifth Avenue in midtown in pitch dark so the runners with disabilities could be transported to Staten Island for the early start. Buses are lined up as far as the eye can see. Runners in modified wheelchairs came from all over the world: Japan, the Middle East, Australia, South Africa, all gathering in the predawn darkness to compete in a twenty-six-mile race.

I'm thrilled for her and deeply proud of the woman she has become. She's participating in the greatest city in the world at a level most people would never dream of. She has great close pals, The Pod. She's got a lovely guy, Graham. They come to us for dinner, or we go to a favorite restaurant, say, Marea, or a play. She is a young woman in full. What more could I ask?

⊰ **33** ⊱

Now that Chloe was launched, I had the chance to launch myself again; I just wasn't sure how.

Maybe part of it was being the daughter of a ventriloquist; I was waiting for someone to pull my strings, bring me to life. Maybe it came from those mornings sitting with Charlie and my dad at the breakfast table. He'd sit me on one knee, Charlie McCarthy on the other. A gentle squeeze on the back of my neck was my cue to open and shut my mouth so he could ventriloquize me. Charlie and I would chatter together silently, while behind us Dad would supply the snappy repartee for both of us. Charlie had his own bedroom next to mine—and his was bigger. Those were unique circumstances to grow up in. Sometimes I have to give myself credit for being a functional human being.

Before *Boston Legal*, I'd played Judge Amanda Anderlee on the short-lived *Law & Order: Trial by Jury*. It would be such a long time between my lines that I'd sit up there at my bench reading the paper while the other actors played their scene. I'd drift off, then catch them looking up at me expectantly. What was that line: "Denied"? "Overruled"? It was usually one or the other. Once I froze over a speech studded with dense legalese, some in Latin. I could have been speaking Esperanto. It was the first time my brain had been short-circuited by dialogue I was unable to understand. Sam Waterston came up to me between takes and asked, "Is there anything we can do to help you?" I was abjectly ashamed and relieved to finally get through it and go home. After *Boston Legal*, I did a small recurring role as Arlene, Cuddy's mother on *House*.

Then came an offer to do a Broadway play.
The play was *The Best Man* by Gore Vidal.

It's a sparring match between two presidential candidates. Bill Russell is the high-minded intellectual—think Adlai Stevenson with a tiny adultery problem. Joe Cantwell is the ruthless, opportunistic "man of the people," willing to do anything to win. The two duke it out at the nominating convention to gain the crucial endorsement of former president Artie Hockstader. The revival was timely because it overlapped the presidential campaign of 2012.

I was invited to play Alice Russell, Bill's long-suffering wife. Angela Lansbury had already been cast as Sue-Ellen Gamadge, the party's southern female chair. James Earl Jones was playing Artie Hockstader. Angela and James are theater royalty; between them, they've won a tower of Tonys. They are legends. I have known and loved Angela forever; her granddaughter and Chloe were friends in lower school. Eric McCormack would play Joe Cantwell. John Larroquette would play Bill Russell. He is a skilled comedic actor who's won five Emmys and a Tony. He is six-feet-five with white hair, a rubber face, and a commanding stage presence. We'd worked together on *Boston Legal*, so I know he is deeply weird, eccentric, kind, and extremely intelligent. We are pals, and he makes me laugh.

I hadn't been on Broadway since 1985, when I took over for Sigourney Weaver in David Rabe's *Hurlyburly*, a scalding look at self-destructive, drug-addled, low-level Hollywood players. It was directed by Mike Nichols. In general, that early play had been a positive experience, but I was not present. Every night I had to take my shirt off, which was traumatizing for me, even though I was facing away from the audience. The matinees were all older women who would bring their lunches and walkers and talk about you as they pointed from the audience: "She looks like a whore!" I hadn't had my *Murphy Brown* training yet, so I didn't have much instinct and comfort in front of an audience. I just survived by being on autopilot as much as I could. But I was struck by the closeness of the theater community and the tremendous support they showed each other. It was like a tiny village. Hair-dressers would come from theaters two blocks away bearing notes and messages from people on other shows wishing you a great opening.

Nevertheless, when *The Best Man* offer came, I turned down the role of Alice Russell. The part was written for a woman in her forties with two young sons. Hello? I was sixty-five! Also, it was a pretty buttoned-up role, hard to play for comedy.

And I was reluctant to give up domestic bliss, watching the nightly news in bed while Marsh threw the ball for the dogs. He had a routine. Jerry's ball was thrown into the bathroom where he had to jump into the tub to get it. Phyllis's ball caromed off the closet door and shot down the hall. It never got old.

The second I turned the play down, I regretted it. After all, I wasn't getting many offers. The part was small, manageable. I would be surrounded by people I liked and respected, and doing something unfamiliar and frightening, which I believe is always good for one's soul. Counterphobia is a good guiding principle. "You idiot!" I thought. "This has been handed to you. It's a good piece of writing, a wonderful cast, the size of part you can handle that won't be too much for you."

After steaming all weekend, I finally told Marsh that I was furious with myself for turning down the play. He could already tell something was eating at me because of how many orders I was handing out to him on the drive back into the city. "Blinker's on." "You're really close to that car, Marsh." "Turn your blinker off." "Open Jerry's window." "Close Jerry's window." "Does the air conditioning have to be set on arctic?"

I told him what I was feeling. This isn't something I'm used to doing, being half-Swedish, but I'm making an effort at communication. Marsh said if I did the play, he would have periods where he would be cranky, but that shouldn't stop me from doing it. He urged me to ask a close friend to read it for me since he couldn't be the judge; he said I was too conscious of imposing on my friends. I felt better already, just getting it off my chest. I thanked him for being so attentive.

The next day I got a call that if I was still interested, the part was mine. I jumped at it.

The part was still twenty years too young for me. It was still humorless. But it would galvanize me—I hoped. Get me off my ass and energize me. Marsh assured me he would be okay. So, no more hiding out in the TV room. I would try theater again after twenty-five years.

Marsh was beyond supportive; he always throws himself into whatever his wife is a part of. I boxed myself into doing the play because it would force me to focus, but that didn't happen for quite a while. From the very beginning he was on me to get my lines learned, which took ages. Instead of working on the play, I played Scrabble on my iPad. "Don't you think we should do lines?" Marsh would ask. "I'll do it after dinner." After dinner: "Candy, you should work on your lines." Prompting me with, "You sure look purty, Ms. Alice."

I would lie in bed, thinking, "What have I done?" It wasn't just that I was going to make a fool of myself; I was going to bring twenty cast members down with me. A couple of close friends were clearly discomfited; what had I done, throwing myself on a grenade like this? Connie was very anxious. Kris was afraid that it would impact my health, that too much stress might bring on another stroke.

We started four weeks of rehearsals in a large hall on West 42nd Street. They blocked the sets out in the space with tape and fly walls and coat racks. I was not a quick study. There was a mockup of the bed in the hotel room that was a key part of the set. If I didn't have any lines in a scene, I'd read there, oblivious that the other actors would be waiting for me to get off the bed so they could rehearse in the bedroom. "Can't you just do it and pretend I'm not here?" I asked sweetly.

Matthew Farrell, the stage manager, was weeping with laughter. He'd have to take his glasses off and wipe his eyes because I was always running around clueless, hopelessly lost, confused about what tape was marking off what room. "What's going to happen when we get to the theater?" he asked. The same thing happened. Now they knew they had to watch me more than anyone at any age onstage. People were concerned about Angela and James Earl Jones, but they were perfect. I was the one they had to herd. I'm sure the cast thought, "How did she win anything, let alone five Emmys, when she can't even find herself onstage at the right place at the right time?"

I loved watching how the other actors researched and built their characters piece by piece. Everyone did their homework. Eric based his smarmy character on John Edwards and guys from the religious right. I didn't base Alice Russell on anyone specific, but I knew where she came from. My character had supported abortion rights in the 1940s; she was way ahead of her time. I decided she'd be a smoker because several long-suffering wives I had known smoked while watching their wayward husbands. Also, it was correct for the period, the early sixties. Steve, the prop man, got me herbal cigarettes and put gel in the ashtray so the cigarettes extinguished quickly.

It was a particular delight watching Jefferson Mays assemble the character of Sheldon Marcus, a mealy-mouthed fellow who knows something shady about Joe Cantwell's past and isn't eager to share it. He showed up on the first day of rehearsal ready to unveil that character, starting with a Baltimore dialect. He decided that Sheldon would have socks that were pooling around his ankles "because they're too tired; they just couldn't stay up." He wore a sleazy, stained suit with stuff jammed into the pockets and appeared onstage with a sad brown bag holding his lunch. Jefferson wanted that bag to look greasy, so before his entrance he stood backstage dabbing olive oil from a small bowl to give it grease spots. He'd wipe the excess oil from his fingers onto his hair to make it look matted with sweat and put blush on his cheeks and spray them with mist so he'd look flushed. He'd have coffee right before the show to heighten the fever pitch at which he'd deliver his lines. It was remarkable what he did with that character, who got pounced on every night when Joe Cantwell roughed him up. Every time he left the stage after the scuffle, he'd exit weeping. Every matinee, every evening performance. I don't know how he did it. I'd see him on the stairwell offstage, collecting himself.

A handsome man who graduated from Yale, he dresses fastidiously and stylishly. Jefferson is also the most fey, wonderful character, showing up on opening night in top hat and tails. Once when someone brought in a dachshund angling for adoption, he immediately lapsed into flawless German: "*Ach, meine liebchen!*" Jefferson won one Tony for Best Performance for a Leading Actor for his role in *I Am My Own Wife* and was nominated for another Tony for playing eight different characters—men and women—in *A Gentleman's Guide to Love and Murder*.

Kerry Butler, a musical theater star with a voice like an angel, was a whirlwind, planting pots of flowers on the fire escape, learning ukulele from Michael McKean. She was the cheerleader of the group, organizing egg hunts on Easter in the theater between shows for the children of performers in the company. We all helped her hide the eggs; audience members are probably still finding them. She would get everyone together for drinks after the shows; I couldn't go because I had to be home by curfew. Eric McCormack, his instincts honed by his star turn on *Will and Grace*, was a consummate professional. He was absolutely wonderful in the part: sharp and shifty and driven, glad-handing, backstabbing, charming and chilling by turns.

It was the first time I'd met the legendary James Earl Jones. He's an actor's actor who loves his craft, loves the words he speaks each night, exploring them constantly, trying new flourishes on his performance, thinking up new physical business, trying slightly different blocking. He would call rehearsals before curtain with the other actors in a particular scene so they wouldn't be surprised and he could see if his ideas worked.

At eighty-one, James was physically frail. He had a respiratory problem and sipped some oxygen before every performance; he said it sharpened his mind and helped his memory. Producer Jeffrey Richards had built a dressing room specifically for him in the wings just offstage so he would have no stairs to contend with. He shepherds his reserves carefully, but when he enters a scene, he's a force of nature: alive, firing on all cylinders, a twinkle in his eyes. He practically explodes onto the set, creating a larger-than-life entrance for his character, a former president. He's more alive, more connected to the other actors and the scene than almost anyone I can remember. Even after months playing it, he made every line and every moment fresh. I brought someone back to his dressing room to meet him after the play, and they complimented him on his fantastic power. "I was thinking of the energy bursts of Muhammad Ali," he said.

At eighty-six, Angela had the stamina of a horse and she loved to work. She is the undisputed Queen of Broadway. She's won five Tonys and audiences go nuts the second she sets foot onstage. She's taller than I remembered—five-feet-eight and change, with long, shapely legs. She holds herself like the dancer she is, erect and innately elegant. She's let her hair, which she cuts herself, go gray, a lovely silver, and she wears it very short, which gives her an even more youthful appearance. She has two artificial hips and has had both knees rebuilt. Backstage before curtain, she does leg lifts that could knock you flat.

The first night of previews revealed the magic of live theater. Upstairs in my cubicle, over the loudspeaker I heard James Earl Jones stop mid-dialogue and suddenly ask, "Is there a doctor in the house?" He had seen, three rows in front of him, a man slump unconscious in his seat. The production paused, the houselights went up, and paramedics arrived to take the man to the emergency room. A few weeks later, in the middle of the tense second act, there was an audible commotion in the house. It was a Friday night, people had been drinking, and a man vomited on the person in front of him. This, as you can imagine, caused quite a stir. The performance was stopped, the houselights went on, the cleaners came, and thirty minutes later, the performance resumed.

The three weeks of previews were just a shambles for me—I didn't know where I was onstage or off it. I was completely disoriented. Onstage they were performing a political drama, but backstage I was performing a farce.

Backstage is lit low by small blue LED bulbs; it can be confusing until you get your bearings. To me, it was baffling. There were multiple doors to enter the set and I didn't know what set they led to. I'd come barging onto the wrong one at the wrong time because I'd been watching the wrong blinking blue cue light. Helpful cast members, Donna Hanover and Angelica Torn, had to keep pulling me back with a whispered, "Not yet!" The sets were revolving turntables. At the end of the final act, John and I had to walk offstage together, stepping off a brightly lit, moving set onto another set moving in the opposite direction in near darkness. We followed tiny squares of glow tape from one moving platform to the other, but you couldn't see clearly where one set ended and the next began. Thank

God for John, who held my arm in a vise grip so I wouldn't fall. I'd broken my pelvis the previous year and didn't want a repeat.

For me it was a new way to work, and my respect for those who have mastered it is endless. Matthew, our stage manager, wrote the most eloquent, uplifting company notes during previews, with careful words to encourage us to bring out the tiniest nuances:

CB: Clarity: "except when he tells those *long stories*"—careful not to fall off voice.

CB: "But you are very nearly a great man, and I suppose I can endure anything because of that." Good—it's important to stay with her pain here. She has endured a lot, but there is a limit.

CB: "Tough? Only for you. You're the one with the problem." Can slam the dresser drawer at the end of "problem," given your current spacing.

Slam a dresser drawer? At first I could barely manage more than just putting one foot in front of the other and saying my lines. I thought perhaps I might check my watch onstage but realized that, no, even that little bit of business was asking too much of myself.

I couldn't have done the play without John Larroquette. He rescued me repeatedly and told me from the very start: "I've got your back, babe." He proved that over and over when I lost myself onstage, entering a scene early or going up on my lines.

"How did it go?" he asked in character one night as I entered during Act II.

I looked at him blankly and said truthfully, "I have no idea." I'd gone totally blank on my character's line.

As always, John was there with the safety net. "Didn't you have to MAKE A SPEECH?" he prompted.

"YES!" I said, with great relief. "I made a speech! It was TERRIBLE." And we picked it up from there. I have no idea whether the audience knew I was flailing.

One day, I found myself in the middle of the third act onstage with John and Michael McKean, who was playing Dick Jensen, Russell's chief of staff. Jensen was urging Russell to go for Cantwell's jugular; he could knock Cantwell off if he made a tough decision. My character saw how torn Bill Russell was, how it agonized him to contemplate destroying this Cantwell candidate.

In the middle of this long exchange between the two other actors, I drifted off in other directions. Was it better to have a slow death, when you can have some closure, or go out fast with a big bang? Also, it was time to do my hair color—but I wear a wig in the play, no one sees my hair, so maybe I could put it off? Would I have time to go out for dinner between the matinee and evening shows? Did I want to order in? And if I ordered in, did I want to order from Bond 45 or the Thai café on the corner? If I ordered Thai, did I want the coconut soup? If I ordered from Bond 45, I could have the pasta with pesto . . .

Suddenly there was silence. The other actors were looking at me expectantly and I lurched into my line: "Leave him alone!" God knows how long they'd been waiting for me to say it.

Sadly, this happened far too often. I was often onstage for long periods without any lines. There was a lot of standing and listening, of reacting. I had to be conscious of paying attention or off I'd go. Should I invite all the doormen to the play? How could I get them all low-cost tickets? If I invited two, did I have to invite all twelve? And I'd look over and there would be John, giving me that "it's your line" gesture with his twirling finger, conveniently hidden by the couch upstage. At the least, you have a responsibility to your fellow actors to hold up your side of the house, but John had to worry about cuing me on my lines while he was holding up the play.

For me, it was equal opportunity. I forgot lines with James and Angela as well. Angela has struggles of her own at age eighty-six. If I wasn't there to promptly give her the line—"How *is* Mr. Gamadge?"—it threw her off just an inch and made everything a little less crisp. The house of cards started to tumble.

Another time during previews, I was backstage, waiting for the onstage cue light. I got distracted fighting back the hair in my face from my wig. When I looked up, the cue light was blinking! Ken, the assistant manager, had to run from stage right to stage left behind the set to call "Candice!" because there was no sign of me. So they put multiple backup systems in place—someone stage right and stage left in case I drifted off. It was a constant battle to focus. I hired a woman to come every Friday to speak French with me and subscribed to *Paris Match* to tune up my brain.

With all those previews, I didn't think opening night would be a big deal, but I was pleased to discover that opening night rituals were observed in a very respectful manner. John tipped me off the day before that you were supposed to give out little tokens to your cast mates. Kerry Butler, who played Mabel, Joe Cantwell's lubricious, ambitious wife, gave out glasses engraved with one of her favorite lines: "Now don't get all het up." Eric McCormack printed up beautiful cards with his favorite quotes as well. Donna Hanover, who played a reporter, gave everyone little food containers engraved with THE BEST MAN and the opening night date. Matthew, our wonderful stage manager, likewise gave us all bottles of branch water—a key prop—inscribed with the name of the play and date. My favorite gift came from James Earl Jones, whose wife, Ceci, had found it: a bracelet made out of campaign buttons from the 1950s; it was a brilliant present and I wore it every night. I scrambled at the last minute to find a cast gift and got most of them a hefty cast-iron door stop of the Wicked Witch of the East's feet wearing the ruby slippers. No one seemed exactly sure what to do with it; Jefferson thought it was the world's heaviest Christmas ornament. I gave Angela and James solar-powered Queen Elizabeth statuettes, which gave jaunty waves on sunny days. Because of old theater traditions, people refrained from giving good-luck wishes to actors on opening night. In my case, they were very sweet about my earlier fractured hip: "I'd wish you to break a leg, but I believe you've already done that."

Chloe came to visit me in my minuscule dressing room after the first preview. She took note of the huge applause that Angela got the second she stepped onstage: "You know, Bunny, this is something for you to keep in mind." She figured that in twenty years, I could be playing Mrs. Gamadge and get some applause and attention of my own.

The producers knew when critics would be in

the audience, but they didn't tell us lest it unsettle us. It might have focused me a little more. The reviews were more than kind; James got a much-deserved Tony nomination for Best Actor, and the play was nominated for Best Revival.

New York magazine did an interview with me. I was hoping it wouldn't be brutal; it was not. Maybe people are a little gentle on you when you're older. I was surprised when people waited for me by the stage door for autographs. "You'll always be Murphy to me!" There were a few ghouls, tiny clusters of the living dead who have no life but autograph seeking, but mostly the fans were lovely.

No one's in the theater for the money or the perks. When we were in rehearsals, the only place nearby with edible food was a Pax deli on 42nd Street. The cast would eat our lunch there on plastic trays every day. There was no enchilada man, no frozen mocha blendeds, no handmade-ice-cream truck—quite a change from the elaborate catering on TV sets.

We had actors in the cast who lived hand to mouth. Broadway pays nothing, but they were grateful to be in the play with this cast, doing two or three tiny parts. They played hotel maids, reporters, delegates, secretaries. They're the lucky ones. Every day I got picked up by a driver from a company that employs a great many triple and quadruple threats—highly trained, multitalented people who can sing like birds, act, dance, and play instruments. They cannot find work—so they drive old, successful actors who sometimes can. It kills me.

My tiny dressing room was next to the toilet on the boys' floor with John, Michael, and Jefferson. The door to the rat gray toilet was always open, so I could see the vacuum cleaner jammed inside. I sort of enjoyed that. It was like being in a dorm. With every male in the cast running up to that bathroom, I got to know them very well. Every now and then I'd hear snatches in the hallway of testosterone-fueled conversation: "Thank God I didn't fuck her . . ." "Ha ha ha ha." *This is another species,* I'd think.

On his way in, John would stop by my dressing room to chat while I did my makeup. When they were working out my contract, I naively asked, "Do you think I could use Angela's makeup person?" "Honey, you're your own makeup person.") John would watch as I tried to put on my false eyelashes; I'd glue my eyes together and have to peel them apart and pull my own eyelashes out.

Michael McKean would pass my dressing room as well, often with a hearty "Candela!" He is a total life-enhancer. He'd walk around with his guitar, playing and singing Johnny Mercer songs. Once between shows, Marshall came to have dinner with me near the theater. As we walked back from Orso, I heard someone yelling "Candice!" I looked up. Michael and Kerry had climbed out their dressing room windows onto the fire escape. With Michael on guitar and Kerry on ukulele, they were serenading all passersby.

Everybody had a dresser. Mine, darling Andrea Gonzalez, helped me pull on my Spanx; I was always gasping afterward. Then she helped me put on my stockings. "I can get it from here," I told her, but she always corrected me: "Candice, this is my job." Among many other things, they keep your personal comfy shoes just offstage. Once I saw Angela padding around in fleece-lined pink Crocs, so I brought in my own Crocs, which Chloe had festooned with Disney stick-on characters. When I was done I stepped offstage and walked up the thirty-five stairs to my room on the third floor—I counted them every time. Other cast members' dressing rooms were one and two floors above us—I don't know how they did it.

I am stunned at how hard all the actors work: eight shows a week, with vocal warm-ups for fifteen minutes before every show. Everyone lines up onstage and vocalizes at full pitch—"The lips, the teeth, the tip of the tongue!" "Whatever the weather, we're in it together!" "Lullagully, gugalully gaga ga!"—while hopping back and forth and swinging our arms up and down to get the circulation going and pump air into the lungs. (Michael McKean told me that an actor he knows warms up by shouting, *"Hey, that's my car!"* at the top of her lungs.) You just stand there vocalizing in front of the ushers stacking programs at the back of the house and bartenders setting up behind the bar. Not being a theater actor, I was unfamiliar with the vocal warm-ups; I'd always just sung "Do-Re-Mi" from *The Sound of Music* in the shower at five in the morning before work. James Earl Jones was always there for the warm-ups with that legendary voice. How actors sing *and* dance onstage is beyond me.

From warm-ups, we'd go upstairs, put on our makeup, and get into our wigs and wardrobe. Then we'd hear Matthew give us a countdown to show time through the speakers. "It's an hour to curtain . . . it's fifteen . . . it's five . . . it's places . . . and it's *Saturday night on Broadway!*"

To work with these actors is especially rewarding and engaging. It's also bittersweet because you get close to people, yet you know it will end in a matter of months.

Every performance, James and Angela gave 150 percent—everyone did. It was the love and respect of the game. When I was offstage, I'd watch the other actors from the wings. They were always experimenting—doing different line readings, giving different responses, changing it up in minute ways. John varied the most because he liked to work that way. He was wonderful in the part, bringing so much detail. I especially loved to watch him when he downed the "scotch" onstage—he's been very public about how he used to be a raging alcoholic, so he's got that behavior down. Michael McKean's acting was invisible; I never caught him working. He was rooted in the moment, powerful, spontaneous.

Backstage, I would often hear Matthew announcing, "Understudy rehearsal!" I always thought, Is that really necessary, to have an understudy for every part? (Often actors would be assigned two or three small roles to understudy.) There were, however, no exceptions; there was always a backup planned. It seemed redundant until it wasn't. Midway through the run, Michael McKean was walking on Broadway on the Upper West Side and heard a car he knew was going way too fast. It jumped the curb and hit Michael, who left a bathtub-sized imprint on the windshield. He sustained a broken leg and lacerations and needed multiple stitches. He was in the hospital for days and had to drop out of the play. He went home to California. His publicist said, "It's the first time he will have ever missed a curtain in his entire life. His understudy has never gone on in forty-plus years."

It was interesting to see how the terror of doing Broadway lessened. Once I got over the scared shitless part, I got more and more comfortable every week. About a month in, I realized that I was feeling at home onstage. That was a major accomplishment for me. It was very gratifying, very engaging work. I liked starting and finishing something every night. I loved the mystery of the audience: every day it's different. At first, not having a second take was terrifying for me. Then I surmounted the big hurdle—I actually looked at my watch onstage without losing my timing.

Marshall saw the difference in my mood, the level of comfort that came with a few weeks of doing it. He was very proud of me. He went to see the play for the third time with another couple. They told me they spent most of their time watching him watching me, because he had such a big grin on his face. He likes the fairy dust of being the husband of that actress in that play.

Faith Ford and Grant Shaud, my old castmates and pals from my *Murphy* days, came to see the show. We dragged John Larroquette to Bar Centrale, next to Orso, one of those unmarked, hole-in-the-wall bars for theater folk. John Lithgow was there, along with the cast from *Death of a Salesman*. It was all very relaxed, a fraternity of theater people, a club without the burden of membership.

I'd sent Marsh an email to tell him I'd be home late. Unfortunately, he didn't get it until the next morning, and he was expecting me home at the usual time. When I got home late, he was not a happy camper.

When you have the luck of marrying a husband who pays attention, there's a downside, which is that you have to return it. It's never tidy with work and a relationship; you have to give up some of each. At this point in my life, I don't think there's any way around that. It's a bit of a sacrifice, because I slipped so easily into the theater world and enjoyed it so much; it's hard to have limitations placed on that.

The producers asked me to do the play for two more weeks; I said no. The last thing I wanted was to be on Times Square in July. I wanted to come home and pay more attention to Marsh.

"We only have thirteen shows left!" Kerry Butler said as we clustered backstage for curtain call one night at the tail end of June. We'd started rehearsals on February 1. One month of previews, then three months of performances. These five months had brought me back to life, back to my tribe: the actors' tribe. Not the show-biz tribe, which I grew up in, but a world where people put the love of their work, their love of the word, before the love of their double-wide Star Wagon. And finally, at age sixty-six, it had given me a newer, deeper respect for acting and actors. The love of the work was so palpable you could feel it.

We'd become a family, with everybody conversant with everybody else's lives. In a couple of months, they'd all be scattering and moving on. I'd been getting unexpectedly emotional for the final few weeks, even though I sometimes caught myself checking my watch offstage: "I have two hours and fifteen minutes . . . one hour and forty-five minutes . . . a half hour . . . before I'm finished and into my car." Then at one point in the second act, an old John Philip Sousa march would strike up to signal a scene change, and backstage a conga line would form, with all of us doing the cha-cha, jump-kicks, boogeying down, reveling in the nether world of the low pale blue lights that connected us.

My last performance in the play was the Sunday matinee. I was emotional at curtain call; Angela had tears in her eyes. Part of that might have been that she wished she were leaving along with me. Part is that we had become friends. Everyone was adorable, writing lovely notes, coming upstairs to give a good-bye hug. I took the cast to a bar nearby for drinks and then slipped off home, where Marsh and Marina had arranged a surprise dinner with Chloe, her boyfriend, Graham, and my brother, Kris, who had flown in from LA for the last performance. Marina had printed up a "program" of the dinner in imitation of the play-bill, welcoming "Our Best Woman" back home. She'd outdone herself with the meal: barbecued ribs, chicken, sausage, corn on the cob, macaroni with four kinds of cheese, berry cobbler with vanilla ice cream.

And I, who had dreaded the play ending and the relationships with everyone in it—and Marsh who had dreaded the experience of me leaving the play and the depression that would follow—well, we were both fine. Glad to be back together. Happy to be home.

By that Wednesday, I'd started to resume my old schedule. Sleep by midnight, up by seven. Okay, seven-ish. Marsh and I had our first Wednesday dinner in months and we had it alone. I mostly listened. It was the first time since March that he had my total attention. He talked about work problems, family concerns, but he was lighter, visibly happier. This is a man who is all about connection, and he had reconnected with me. We chatted walking home. As we walked in the door, Jerry was barking that he was ready for his ball, which Marsh threw the length of the hall. Jerry, now twelve years old and mostly blind, retrieved it by scent and sound. Then we curled up in the TV room and watched an episode of *Foyle's War* on the BBC. At nine o'clock, we put it on pause and got a frozen yogurt, which we ate with tiny espresso spoons. This was our old routine and we are very attached to it. And this is partly why I turned the play down in the first place; I had missed this.

Chloe has always written. I started buying her journals when she was seven. Every night she would scribble down thoughts and observations, dreams and dreads. She writes very well. She is perceptive, observant, intelligent, and wry. Part of the reason she latched on to writing, I think, is that in our family, where her father and I had separate professions in which we were recognized, writing was her own. She had staked her turf in which she could also be recognized and it belonged only to her. Louis wrote and coauthored screenplays but it was not a second skin. What he did, and did brilliantly, was direct. I, of course, was an actor and not a very successful one until I got *Murphy*. Chloe would have been a wonderful director, yet I always felt that she was equally gifted as an actor.

For Chloe, growing up mostly in LA until she was fourteen, acting was always on the top of the menu. The part of her that was attracted to acting, to the very real and challenging and rewarding possibilities of it, was also restrained by not wanting to be predictable. And what could be more predictable for her than wanting to be an actress in LA? And perhaps she felt my resistance to her doing something that could be so bruising and full of disappointment. My resistance to her doing what was predictable.

We first knew she was good when she played a Noo Yawk mother in *Bye Bye, Birdie* in ninth grade. We went to a costume store for her wardrobe and they put her in a housedress over a fat suit, a green snood, knee-high support hose, rhinestone-studded glasses, and a raccoon coat. She moved like an old grandmother, she tawked like one. It was as if she had grown up in Brooklyn. She was hysterical and got huge laughs. This wasn't channeling me; it was channeling Lucy. Connie had introduced her to *I Love Lucy*, and she watched it every day after school. She was such a fanatic that one Halloween she went dressed as Lucy; her best pal, Shane, did her the great favor of being Ethel.

At Brown, a small theater group was thinking of producing *A Doll's House* but they couldn't find anyone who could play Nora. Chloe auditioned and then they could. She was about to start rehearsing when she came down with a horrible case of mono. I flew up to bring her home; she was in the infirmary with her head swollen to twice its normal size. It was shocking to see. The production was canceled when she got sick; I always thought that was a decisive moment. I think she would have been a magnificent Nora, although the effort would have cost her hugely. To keep up with classes, coedit the independent school paper, and learn one of the most challenging roles for women ever written—it would have been asking an insane amount from someone. But I think the fire would have been lit and she might have changed course.

I think Chloe will always feel torn between writing and acting, wondering what if. This is where Louis's guidance would have been invaluable. If I had it to do over, I would have presented her with acting at its best.

She once asked me why I had always discouraged her from doing something that could be so stimulating, so engaging: to tackle a great play and understand an interesting character and speak thrilling words. Why indeed? I had not always seen the nobler side of the profession; in fact, I didn't know it at all. I had only done two plays in college, by Tennessee Williams and Jean Anouilh, but I had gotten more than a whiff of the seamy side and I wanted to protect her from it.

My feelings about acting are still sorting themselves out. I don't even know what real acting is made of. When I see a theater actor attacking a great dramatic role, I wouldn't know how to begin to probe it or put that role together, how to know the stage well enough to use it and control it. That kind of acting is daunting to me.

There's a hierarchy in acting: theater is greater than film is greater than television, although I don't think the hierarchy is as sharply defined as it used to be. I'm not a real actor. To call myself that, I'd have to have graduated from a school like Juilliard and then have performed an anthology of the great plays or done substantial parts in films. I would have to have committed. If I had studied acting when I was younger, if I had assembled the basic tools of the craft, it would have given me the freedom to enjoy the work and spared me the anguish born of insecurity.

I always felt my success in *Murphy Brown* and *Boston Legal* owed almost everything to the quality of the writing, which was exceptional. When I won the first Emmy, I was so unaccustomed to winning anything that it seemed a voting error, a miscount. I knew the work I did on *Murphy* was good, especially after the first few years. And for me, comedy was my comfort zone. There were many moments I was proud of. After the fifth Emmy, I decided not to submit my name for nomination; it just felt greedy. When my publicist, Heidi Schaeffer, called and said, "Candy, you haven't submitted yourself for nomination yet," I said, "Well, I'm not going to." Once the news broke, it became a big deal. That it was even considered newsworthy surprised me; it was a casual decision. I didn't mention it to anyone.

There were lots of times I struggled with scenes, and then, with the cast's help, I would find a way to play it and would have a little rush of satisfaction, a sense of a job well done. But I've also been flummoxed by moments in jobs where I haven't had a clue.

I think it's very healthy that Chloe is recognized on her own turf, that she's valued where she works; actors are usually not, since the competition is so fierce. And yet I feel a little pang in my heart, because I know she would have been able to appreciate the experience in a way that I have not.

⚜ 35 ⚜

I have made a lot of money. Most of this is the incomparable TV Money. Nothing like it.

Until *Murphy* I had made money but not that much, and I needed to work to support myself. When Louis and I were married, we flew coach to France; upgrading to business class was a big deal. We rarely flew first class, which I flew routinely for work.

The first year of *Murphy*, they paid me peanuts, in part because I was far from their first choice for the role; they'd wanted the younger, juicier Heather Locklear. After I won the Golden Globe and the Emmy in the first year, however, my salary went up and kept heading in that direction over ten years. I managed to keep what I made per week a secret. The financial success from the show was a cushion of warm air around me all the time.

I was the highest paid woman (or man) in television by a lot for a few years. But we lived modestly. We had a small house that was large on charm. The first years I drove the Jeep that was provided by the studio, then got myself a BMW, which I bought during my lunch break. I single-handedly bargained with the sales guy and got him down $3,000, along with free floor mats and pinstriping. I was inordinately proud of myself. I kept that car twelve years. I loved it. As I said, we did not flaunt.

My family was always discreet about money. It was not something we spoke about—even to each other. Mom was very responsible with money and rarely spent on herself; she was well trained. Louis's family was even more discreet. First, the French, by nature, are discreet above all else, but especially about money. The display of wealth is considered extremely déclassé. And Louis was from old money. Even after the family sold their control of the business, sugar packets in France still say Béghin-Say. Louis's mother was a Béghin. She was also very discreet.

When I did *The Best Man* on Broadway, Harry K. Smith interviewed me for *30 Rock with Brian Williams*. When it aired, the piece, which was lovely, proclaimed that I "met and married billionaire philanthropist Marshall Rose." I was appalled. Seriously? Marsh is very smart about money, and about finance generally, but a *billionaire?* Please. As a result of this rumor, which was everywhere online, people assume I married Marsh for his money, which I really find infuriating. First, I married him because I was and am in love with him. Second, I have always paid my own freight, always; that is a key principle with me. Marsh is extremely generous and romantic and buys me incredibly thoughtful personal gifts, but that's it. True, once we were married, he automatically oversaw my financial affairs because that is what he does; he takes care of people around him. He has doubled what I had when we met, and I am very grateful, but it was unnecessary; I had plenty.

When I was doing my Broadway run, the other cast members enjoyed going out after the play for a drink. Although I did bring John Larroquette home once for an early dinner Marina made, I made a conscious effort to keep my theater friends separate from my home life. Why? Part of it was not wanting to flaunt what I perceived as the grandeur of the apartment—which I still think of as Marshall's, not ours, after sixteen years here— given our modest theater paychecks. If I still had my old apartment on Central Park South, it would have been perfect. That was a spectacular pad, but boho-chic. Slightly funky. But that was now Chloe's. I'd made the big TV money, but these gifted theater stalwarts, who worked equally hard, had never enjoyed that kind of payday. Plus I didn't want the cast to think of me as the wife of a rich man, someone on loan from life as a staid Upper East Side matron. I am a proud Elder of the Tribe of Show Folk.

Sometimes I see how other women live and what a natural impulse it is for them to seek out a guy who will provide for them financially and take care of their every need. The assumption is that that's their entitlement. I know and am friends with many women who never supported themselves at any point in their lives. Obviously, I'm blessed to be in a profession in which I am insanely overpaid, but I never asked for or received any unearned money. Ever.

Dad paid for my first year of college, but after that, I have always paid for everything. I remember proudly paying the rent on my first apartment at age nineteen from proceeds from my modeling and movies. I'd been told that I'd receive a small portion of my inheritance from Dad in my twenties, but he kept moving the age of entitlement back later and later, like Lucy with Charlie Brown's football, perhaps because he found me financially irresponsible, until finally no more mention was made of it.

My father had a safe in his study. Soon after he died, my mother and I sat down on the floor in front of it. She hadn't a clue what the combination was, but she knew that there were valuables inside. We tried birthdays and addresses and phone numbers. Finally, she transposed "Charlie" into numbers and, of course, it opened. Inside were beautiful pieces of jewelry that Dad had bought and kept secretly as investments and never let her wear. She didn't know they existed; he hadn't wanted to pay taxes on them. A large marquis diamond ring, a beautiful diamond necklace with an aquamarine the size of an egg.

Mom had no clue how much was in the estate. I remember sitting with her and the estate lawyer in her living room as he read the will. One section of it stood out for me:

I, Edgar Bergen, give and bequeath to the Actors Fund of America the sum of Ten Thousand Dollars to be held as a separate fund, to be known forever as "The Charlie McCarthy Fund." It is my sincere wish, and I request, that said fund be managed, invested, and reinvested . . . to give gratuitous and charitable performances of ventriloquism at orphanages, welfare homes, homes for crippled children and other such similar institutes for destitute and handicapped children. . . . Especially, I make this provision for sentimental reasons which to me are vital due to the association with Charlie McCarthy (the dummy), who has been my constant companion and who has taken on the character of a real person and from whom I have never been separated even for a day.

Charlie McCarthy was included in the will. I was not. I'd chased my father's approval all my life and here was proof I'd never get it.

Kris Edgar Bergen was born when I was fifteen, and he grew up in a completely different household. By that time, Dad was barely working, playing country fairs, his star dimming. Dead. "You know, pal," Kris told me, "when you were growing up, Charlie had his own room. When I was growing up, he had a suitcase in the hall."

I knew my father loved me, but with his Swedish reserve, it wasn't his nature to tell me. Even though he was never physically affectionate or demonstrative, we did stuff together. We'd get in his plane. He would prop me up on phonebooks and let me fly it. Or we would go fishing in Yosemite, go for long breakfast rides on horseback in Palm Springs. When I finally overcame my terror to tell Dad that I loved him, it was a triumph of will. That was a force field you didn't cross. It made him too uncomfortable. His reaction? He would just pat my hand and move on.

Still, I was hurt, shocked when I discovered he had left me out of his will. Mom was clearly embarrassed. She offered some sort of apology. Kris, who was sixteen when my father died, was also surprised. I felt like it was my dad's chance to give me the seal of approval and he withheld it. Everything would have been settled. I didn't need the money, obviously; I earned a good living. I was acting. I was writing and photographing articles, usually for *Esquire* magazine, because he encouraged me in that. Part of me thinks his withholding of money was his way of preparing me, giving me a sort of armor. But the rest of me is still baffled.

My mother tried to make it up to me. Although her husband never included her in any financial discussions, we soon started calling her the "stock witch." Suddenly she was in charge, and she tripled, then quadrupled, the estate in twenty years. She had help initially from close family friend Justin Dart and her business manager, but she clearly had a flair for finance. Who knew? By contrast, my only goal when meeting with financial advisers was to stay awake.

Chloe has always been very disciplined about money and restrained about buying more than she needed. When we shopped together and she would see a dress or skirt that made her eyes light up, I'd say, "Try it on. Let's get it." "No, it's too expensive," she'd say, or "Nope, I don't need another skirt." There was no changing her mind. She has always earned a living and she is extremely budget-conscious; she lives within her means. Well, almost. She can't afford the maintenance of the apartment I gave her, but she lives modestly. She eats at moderate restaurants. Hip but reasonable. She appreciates living well and loves traveling first-class with me. But on her own, it's coach.

Not me. I am grateful every day that I can afford everything I need and a lot I don't. I can give away chunks of money to people, children, animals, the environment. I can make a tiny difference.

Since my *Murphy* windfall, I have a much smoother ride; I don't feel the bumps.

❈{ 36 }❈

Marshall and I were riding bikes in East Hampton, cycling by the pond in the village. I had my eye on a nearby swan because I didn't want to tick him off when all of a sudden, Marsh braked hard in front of me. There was the sound of bikes gnashing and the next thing I knew, I was lying in the middle of the street. Once I hit the asphalt, I couldn't move. It was a new frontier of pain; I was delirious with it. I saw stars.

Marshall didn't know what to do. So he called Marina, who always does. "Bring the car, because we had a little thing."

Over my protests, Marina called emergency services. "No, I want to go home," I told her. "I don't want to go to the hospital." Standing up was a bad idea, considering the explosive pain radiating from my hip. I changed my mind about the hospital. Soon the police, the fire department, and an ambulance were on the scene.

They managed to hoist me onto a transfer board and into the ambulance, which in East Hampton is volunteer. The wife was the driver and the husband was the EMT. The wife drove like a bat out of hell. They put the siren on, so it was very exciting. Everyone at Southampton Hospital was terrific; they're so used to stupid summer people crashing into things that they have the drill down. The nurses were nice, the morphine nicer.

The diagnosis was a fractured pelvis, which was completely incapacitating. I was told it would be at least six weeks before I could walk unassisted. I'd never not been able to walk, so I had to learn the world of incapacitation. It was interesting to experience the view from a wheelchair. People don't see you; you're beneath their sight line. They walk by and they don't even look at you. The first two weeks were the worst. It's not easy to wheel yourself around in a wheelchair; in fact, it's exhausting. You need someone strong to push you. The chair itself is incredibly confining and constricting. Just navigating a block was a challenge. Of course, I was worried that Marshall would hit a bump and send me flying out to break the other side of my pelvis. He'd take me for long walks in the park. Such a weird dynamic in our relationship—older husband pushing his younger wife around. It gave me a new vantage point on life.

Eventually I graduated to a walker. I learned to love it, with its pockets for my books and glasses and money and Chap Stick. I learned what it's like to be terrified of crossing the street on a walker because you're afraid the light will change before you make it to the other side. I'd ask people on the corner to walk across the street with me; I'd get across just as the red light was blinking. And when I went to an event, people made room.

Chloe's boyfriend, Graham, got me a special lifting chair, like an upholstered catapult, to move me from sitting to standing. This saved my life. It still took twenty minutes to get up and go to the bathroom.

The first time Marshall wheeled me into the orthopedist's building, everyone in there was in a wheelchair or had a walker or cane. I burst out laughing. One woman my age had just had an accident jet skiing. Another guy, a state trooper, had a stainless steel rod through his calf bone. You could see him in that zone of painful concentration. He was *really* screwed.

Ironically, I lost weight during this time because I wasn't able to go into the kitchen to forage; it was simply too far for me limping on my walker. Much to my amazement, when I got on the scale after so much time away from the gym, I discovered that I had dropped nine pounds on the Broken Bone Diet.

Bringing me all my meals and taking care of me sent Marina into a nervous breakdown. In six weeks, to the day, I threw away my walker. That was when I discovered, much to my astonishment, that I'd lost nine pounds because I couldn't amble down to the kitchen. When you're confined to quarters, it cuts down on your snacking options.

The accident was a preview of myself in a decade or two.

"We're just a couple of geezers," Marsh said.

"I'm *not* a geezer," I said, flaring up just a little.

We're all getting older. When I fall now, I break. I have fractured an arm and a pelvis. There's only one possible ending. We have come to an age where another's death is like our own. It brings it too close. When Nora Ephron died, it was all anyone talked about for weeks.

"Nora had always intimidated me," I said. I was chatting with three or four people after she died. "We were all afraid of her," someone said. Afraid of being judged, feeling stupid or inadequate. Nora did not suffer fools lightly. I know I'm intelligent, but it's very finite: it doesn't expand when fed.

If you have the gift of that level of intellect and wit, you can choose to modulate it by being excessively generous to bystanders or people you're in conversation with. Mike Nichols made that choice, so people were not frozen by his firepower. Nora did that more in the last few years of her life. She softened in the years after she was diagnosed with leukemia; her persona relaxed. The edges became smoother. And I had gotten older. When I mentioned something about it to her in the most apprehensive way, she waved her hand and said dismissively, "Oh, I was another person then." She knew who she was.

We met in the late 1960s; she was first married to Dan Greenberg. She worked at *Esquire* then. I knew her when she was married to Carl Bernstein. One time, my friend Rusty Unger took me to their house in Sagaponack for lunch. Nora was playing with her youngest son but staring daggers at Carl across the porch the whole time. If looks could kill, the man was toast. A couple of years later, she wrote *Heartburn*, the single most perfect revenge on a cheating husband.

So I had known Nora for more than forty years but I didn't know her well. We led overlapping lives in New York City. For the last ten or twelve years, Marshall and I would occasionally have dinner with Nora and her husband, author Nick Pileggi, either at our apartment, at our house in LA, or more often, at their apartment or their houses in East Hampton and LA. We were on a boat together once, in the Caribbean, for a week.

She was an authority on, it seemed, everything. In St. Barths, she came back to the boat with six-packs of some juice no one had ever heard of and then drank all afternoon. She decided the menus on the boat, she did the seating at every meal, she chose the games after dinner and the movies we would watch. She knew everything, and the best of everything.

When I fractured my pelvis, she and Nick sent a bouquet of perfect roses. Once, I saw her at the hairdresser and watched how respectfully she spoke to the shampoo girl, acknowledging her with kindness. Trust me, this is not usual in the city. We had the same hair colorist, and a stylist there named Chris came up with a cut and style for Nora that almost changed her life. She had it the last few years and it, too, was perfect. Nora had her hair done regularly twice a week. It made her feel better, she said. And she always looked great.

What knocked people silly is that no one knew Nora was sick. No one. All anyone knew was that she had a blood disease—she was never specific about which one. But she always seemed healthy, always looked fantastic. She even had her hair done at the end in the hospital. (She'd famously written, "Sometimes I think that not having to worry about your hair anymore is the secret upside of death.") Some of her closest friends had lunch with her two weeks before she went into the hospital and they discussed future projects. She did not tell a soul. Except Nick and her boys, her sisters, and two friends. And then she was gone. I only got word the day before her death that she had been hospitalized and it was close to the end. I was at the hairdresser's and the owner there took me aside. "You're the only person I can tell about this," she said. "I just heard Nora is dying." She had heard from Nora's hairdresser, who was at the hospital.

The last time I had seen Nora was a month before. She had come with Louise Grunwald and Sandy Gallin to see *The Best Man*. We met for dinner after. Nora had loved the play and was very complimentary. We had dinner at the Lambs Club and she looked and seemed in great form. She took the check after dinner and we all protested. There were cries of *"Nora!"* She smiled and shrugged her shoulders. In hindsight, it seemed as if she were saying, "What difference does it make?"

Around the same time, Nora had a dinner at her apartment for about fifteen of us, all people who knew and liked each other. It was the first week of May. I brought her some lilies of the valley in a hand-painted glass. She thanked me for them, examining them closely. "I love lilies of the valley!" Nora, of course, made the dinner, and as she beckoned us into the dining room, she said, "It's a Thanksgiving dinner." And it was. It was a perfect Thanksgiving dinner with all the trimmings, and it was delicious, as Nora's dinners always were. I think it was the last dinner party she gave; Thanksgiving had been her favorite meal. After dinner, we were having coffee in the living room, and several of us commented on how exquisite the plantings were on her small terrace. "Yes," she said, "and this tiny terrace costs me as much to garden as five acres."

We all played these last moments with Nora over and over, giving the tiniest gesture immense weight. It was impossible not to wonder how she got through it. How could she bear it and never acknowledge it? How could she know that she was going to die shortly and face leaving it all? Leaving her boys and Nick, her terrace, her beloved garden in East Hampton, her charming house in Beverly Hills. Her perfect life and her stellar career. She was always busy, writing books, plays, and screenplays, making movies. Discovering the best new restaurants, the best coconut cake. In *I Hate My Neck* she wrote about "Things I Will Miss," among them, "the twinkling skyline of Manhattan as you cross the Triborough Bridge." Imagine the insane bravery of a woman who loved life and lived it with such gusto, knowing that she was about to leave it and saying nothing. Each miraculous moment. How could she bear it?

Nora orchestrated her own memorial down to the last detail. She'd stolen the idea from Henry

Grunwald, the former editor of *Time*, who'd had a funeral with an orchestra in a magnificent venue. She'd been close to Louise, his widow, who told her that Henry had written out the plans and kept them on his computer in a file marked "Exit." Nora put a file by the same name on her own computer.

The memorial at Alice Tully Hall at Lincoln Center was a marvel. Nora specified the choice and order of speakers: Martin Short, Tom Hanks, and Rita Wilson, her wonderful sister Delia, Rosie O'Donnell, Mike Nichols, Richard Cohen (the *Washington Post* columnist whom Nora used as a model for Harry in *When Harry Met Sally*), Meryl Streep, and Nora's sons, Max and Jacob Bernstein. The music: Cole Porter, "It's a Wonderful Life." The flowers, done by David Monn as arranged by Louise Grunwald, were exuberant, voluptuous, enormous bouquets of hydrangeas, tall, full clutches of berries and leaves, like her East Hampton garden. Of course, the list of eight hundred guests who were the social, political, and artistic elite. Everyone from Steven Spielberg, Meg Ryan, Diane Sawyer, Paul Simon, Sally Field, and Steve Martin to Barbara Walters, Arianna Huffington, Martha Stewart, Diane von Furstenberg, Barry Diller, Tina Brown, Mayor Michael Bloomberg, and Police Commissioner Ray Kelly. And she determined the length of the service: forty-seven minutes.

Meryl perfectly summed up how gobsmacked we all felt by Nora's sudden passing: "She really did catch us napping. She pulled a fast one on us. And it's really stupid to be mad at somebody who died, but somehow I have managed it." Her sister Delia sighed that the world was "practically opinionless" without Nora's sure-footed declarations.

Every note was pitch-perfect. We each received one of Nora's famous recipes with our programs, which featured a beautiful photo of Nora. And as we filed out, there were waiters serving her favorite pink Champagne.

In the space of three months I lost three people who were once very close to me. My dear friend John Calley, at eighty-one. Bert Schneider, an old boyfriend, at seventy-eight. Sue Mengers, my agent and friend of thirty years, at seventy-nine. And now Nora, at only seventy-one. When it happens, it brings you up short; those people have been part of the texture of your life for so long and then they're gone. I'm trying to sort through it. It feels as if the fabric of my life has begun to fray, to become threadbare, to fall away.

Life seems to go at a steady, even stately, pace and then, suddenly, toward the end, it stutters, lurches, and it's over in a New York minute. There seems to be no time to wrap it up nicely, tuck in the corners, fan out the bows.

Even at a young age, I started thinking about how to dispense with my body after I was dead. I remember lying in my dinky bed in my dorm room in Switzerland on a late winter afternoon, pondering it all. I'm only half-Swedish, but I fully identify with the depressive side of that culture. I'd read something about Herod's wife being pickled in honey; that sounded like a good alternative. I never liked the idea of being buried because of my claustrophobia. I thought the Maasai have a good method; they just lay you out in the savannah as a buffet.

Among my generation, there is a sense of panic creeping into the eyes. Squelched successfully in some cases, less in others. It's the Death Thing and the reality of it is gathering focus. We are, after all, the hip generation, but we have now become the "hip replacement generation," and family friends' conversations about their hip surgeries, which once made us snicker, have now become our own. We grew up in the 1960s, did drugs, knew good music, saw the Beatles launched on *The Ed Sullivan Show*, protested The War. Baby Boomers, I believe we're called. We refused to grow up. To grow old. But that isn't working so well anymore. Because we *are* growing old—the ones who aren't already dead. My older friends, people in their seventies, some in their early eighties, are simply freaking out. They are still mentally astute, alert, informed as ever. They can remember passages of books and plays as if they just set down the pages. But they are more and more often in hospitals. They know they're in the vulnerable age group. They see The End in sight and they do not like it one bit. How do you do that gracefully? With acceptance? Without religion? How does one come to terms with it?

6

Au Revoir L'Enfant

❦ 37 ❦

Chloe and I met at Orso before going to see *The Glass Menagerie* with Cherry Jones and Zachary Quinto. As usual since working at *Vogue*, she looked incredibly chic. Atypically, she was all in black. She swooped in like a cute raven and settled into her seat. Borrowed Louis Vuitton lace-cut leather and chiffon dress, black tights, black dropped boots with high heels in which she walks almost effortlessly. The teetering is gone. Her hair, which is long and usually worn up in a bun or chignon, tonight is worn down, stick-straight, and parted in the middle. It looks like wings till she settles into her seat. "It's called 'The Ali,'" she giggles since she has known Ali MacGraw literally from the day she was born. "They also had a 'Farrah.'" She looked insanely gorgeous and glamorous.

Chloe takes after the French side of her family, but also a little of mine. She looks like neither of us, really. She is original. Her hair is auburn, which comes from my eccentric maternal grand-mother, Lilly May. She has small, fine features and blue eyes and what they used to call "porcelain skin." She is beautiful, which matters very little to her. She has no vanity. She's in her late twenties but still looks twelve—she's five-feet-three, which adds to her ever-youthful demeanor—unless she's made up, which is rare. Then she looks smashing and adult and chic and behaves very much like a grown-up. She has the confidence of a beautiful woman and an adored only child. From a very young age, she would step forward and introduce herself to people, announcing, "I'm Chloe," extending her hand for a firm handshake. She is petite but her personality is vast.

During the play Chloe had put her hand lightly on my knee. It felt like a feather. We do not have the intense intimacy, the giddy banter we once had. I remember friends telling me years ago that that was what happened with their relationships with their daughters. They become friends. There is a distance. There are boundaries. That will never happen to us, I thought. Our relationship is unique. Our bond will go the distance. But it has happened; I have to cave on this. Chloe and I are no different.

A few weeks later I met her at my old place on Central Park South, which is now hers. We had organized a meal with eleven French friends; I'd arranged for the catering, since these were family friends of Louis's and mine. The evening was delightful: a lovely buffet supper, which reminded me of the casual buffets Louis and I would have with friends sprawled around the living room, only this time, I was with Marshall and we were the guests, not the hosts. Chloe had music by Cole Porter, Ella Fitzgerald—the same kind I used to play. There was intelligent conversation about film, pollution, and politics in China. Our guests all spoke flawless English, although Chloe and I threw in a bit of French. We do the attitude perfectly.

The apartment looked absolutely beautiful, with its twenty-five-foot ceiling candlelit. When Chloe was a teenager and I couldn't bear to sell the apartment, my plan was that when she was twenty-five, she'd move into it, which she did. On her twenty-seventh birthday, I signed the apartment over to her. It is now officially hers and she lives there with her boyfriend, Graham. I didn't realize how much I'd miss it.

Soon after moving in, Chloe had decided to redecorate the apartment and make it her own. Nothing had been done in the thirty-five years since I bought it in 1976. I paid for it, in the hopes of having some say in the renovation. We looked at pictures of kitchens; we looked at paint chips and swatches. I respectfully asked to be included in the site meetings. For me, the apartment was sacred. I loved exactly how it looked and wouldn't have done anything, just freshened it up.

But there was no denying that after renovation, the place looked gorgeous. Chloe has her own taste and a good eye. With the help of decorator Susan Forristal, she had added a long, dark red tufted banquette below the window overlooking Central Park. Our apartment is across the park from hers, and if I look out from our bedroom, I can see the twenty-five-foot mullioned windows if the lights are on. But I don't look; I am not a stalker. Wraparound bookcases and a proper mantel designed by architect John Murray in the vernacular of the turn of the century were newly installed, but looked as if they had always been there.

When I took the Tiffany lamp to the apartment on Fifth Avenue, Chloe was sad to see it go. The only remaining trace of me was several boxes of letters, clippings, and other memorabilia, plus much of our furniture from LA and some art. A few weeks later, Chloe called to ask me to get my boxes out of "her" apartment. They were in the way, I was informed. I felt outraged. I was being evicted from my own apartment? Why, I hadn't even been invited to dinner yet! Chloe remembers this differently. She told me, "I asked you if you could please go through your many boxes at the apartment because you said you would for six months and I offered you the alternative options of putting them in storage or bringing them to Fifth Avenue or East Hampton and you bit my head off!"

Weeks earlier, Louis's nephew, perfume maker Frederic Malle, had been invited to Chloe's place for dinner. I was not included. She told me that he complimented her on the place. "Chloe, did you do all of this yourself?" "Well, Candice helped a lot."

The dinner with our French friends was the first time I'd been to the apartment for dinner. At some point in the evening, I walked into the back of the apartment, the once-cozy nest where I'd burrowed in with baby Chloe. There were my boxes, huddled in a corner. I was so moved to see them there, thrilled they hadn't been incinerated. In time, I will move them. But not yet.

I still feel like I'm dressing up "Marsh's apartment." Moving the Tiffany lamp helped a lot. I've gotten some pillows made, bought some quirky things. Ellie Cullman redecorated the study, the dining room, my office, and the master bedroom. John Stefanidis redid the living room years ago and it is beautiful, but I want to make it younger, less adult. I'm more willing to stake my rights about what I want. Whenever Marsh starts to cock his eyebrow, I tell him, "Hey, you wanted me to feel at home." He buttons his lip. It's a stuffy building, but it's a nice building, with lovely doormen. The older I get, the more I like nice.

I'm loosening Marsh up. And he's had a civilizing influence on me, all to the good. I pay more attention to him than I used to. I know now what I can do to give him a little of the attention that he likes. I know not to make a phone call to him from a car, to give the conversation its time, make it quietly, really listen. When he comes home, I don't just glance up from my Scrabble or Boggle; I actually get off the couch and ask him if he'd like a cup of tea. I'm a better partner. I know to ask him about things before I do them if they involve the two of us. I'm more inclusive.

It's not always easy. Marshall wanted to leave Chloe's dinner party early. I was resentful of him taking me away from "my" apartment. It felt weird leaving because I'd felt like I was home. It was confusing. I felt torn.

The caterer would be cleaning up after the dinner. It would not be Louis and me washing the dishes, hashing over the party. That marital ritual would be reserved for Chloe and Graham.

Like all the other daughters, Chloe is a miracle. Motivated, compassionate, hard-working. She takes nothing for granted. I am so very proud of who she has become. But I miss those years from her childhood. They had fairy dust.

❧ 38 ❧

Last Thanksgiving, we were all in East Hampton, where we had a holiday meal for twelve friends and family. Marina makes a dynamite turkey and trimmings and she did not disappoint. A few days earlier, Chloe and I had been on the sofa alone in the sitting room, playing our usual Boggle. After a few games, she asked if I would help Graham choose a ring. This was the most specific reference to marriage she had made in a long time. I told her I would be thrilled to help, but he has to *ask* me first. The next day, he did.

The following Monday, I set out to reconnoiter rings. On my way, I passed an inflated six-foot reindeer tethered outside of the EAT Boutique on Madison Avenue. After scouting for rings, I was going to have lunch with a friend who hates Christmas, and this seemed like the perfect gift. Because it wouldn't fit in any taxi and I didn't have a truck, I wrestled it down Madison, stopping at one of the chicest jewelry boutiques in the city, Stephen Russell. I parked the deer in the space between the pair of security doors and asked to see a small, elegant, understated ring with a pale pink diamond set between two white diamonds that caught my eye. It seemed like a good starting point. It wasn't. It was $345,000. I thanked them and moved on.

Farther down Madison, I went into Fred Leighton Boutique, a legendary antique jeweler who specializes in one-of-a-kind pieces. Unique, very fine, rare jewelry. They also lend pieces to celebrities for awards shows and events and are very accommodating. I got wedged between their pair of security doors with the deer and pushed him into the store ahead of me. Rebecca Selva, who has been an executive and PR director for years, was there and I told her I was looking for an engagement ring, preferably vintage, for a petite person who happened to be my daughter.

Out came the trays. Everything they had was ravishing. We found a few possibilities that I thought would work. One was an Art Deco sapphire and diamond ring, very fine, elegant.

It would look beautiful on Chloe; we put it aside along with two others. The next day, Graham met me there and we looked at the rings together. He went immediately to the sapphire, with a beautiful contemporary ring, which I also loved, as a second choice. Since it was a major decision, we called in consultants. Marshall came in and said no question, the sapphire. My stepdaughter, Wendi, went for the contemporary one. Graham brought his sister to weigh in. She and Chloe have become very close over the last sixteen years, and Chloe regards her as a sister. Rebecca has the patience of a saint and the cunning of a jewelry merchant. It was not her first rodeo; she has done this many times before. Graham decided on the sapphire, sure of his choice.

Chloe and Graham would be together with us in LA over New Year's: D-Day. They went to San Ysidro Ranch in Santa Barbara for two days, where he proposed. She accepted. Frankly, I am abbreviating this because I had given him specific instructions for how to present the ring, which I had suggested be placed under the silver cloche that covered the dessert that they would order from room service, where she would discover it. That's how I would have done it.

Instead, Graham went his own way and proposed on a hike. He'd planned to ask Chloe at one of the scenic view sites, but they were all filled with people, so he had to make do. He had the ring in a Kleenex in his pocket, which he pulled out for the proposal. She experienced a moment of terror; then all was fine.

"A *Kleenex?!*" I kept asking when they briefed me afterward. "Graham, didn't you have a little suede pouch to put the ring in?!" The important thing is, the deed was done. They then decided they—well, let me be precise, *Chloe* decided she would like to be married a year and a half later, during the summer, at Le Coual. This is where Louis and I were married and the place she loves most in the world. Of course, Le Coual is insanely inconvenient to get to—a half-day's travel from Paris, in *la France profonde*—and there are no real hotels nearby, but she was firm and the flurry of emails commenced. Hotels. Party planners. Florists.

But first, Chloe and Graham decided they would like to have an engagement party in the spring in New York. I thought that was an excellent idea. Graham came up with the site in

Williamsburg, Brooklyn: the Williamsburgh Savings Bank, originally built in 1875 and now magnificently renovated and renamed Weylin B. Seymour's. The new owners, an Argentinian family, had spared no expense and just completed a $27 million renovation. The two-year project was finished weeks before. We visited it in February. It was staggeringly beautiful, a masterpiece of rehabili-tation, down to the tiniest details, reproduced faithfully to match the original period. There was an entry hall with a 75-foot dome that opened into a vast space crowned with a 110-foot, hand-painted, lit dome. There was a massive bank vault on one wall and one of the city's first cage elevators on another. The bathrooms featured old-fashioned hand-pull chains. The lighting fixtures were exquisite Tiffany reproductions. It was a jewel.

On one of our frequent visits to the bank in the following weeks, I dared suggest to Chloe that she make the party the wedding ceremony. Everyone she cared about would be there. It would be so simple. Tidy. Her face became a mask of horror. "DON'T!! You're stressing me! I want to enjoy the process. Now I'm stressed." Her hands had balled into fists, her breathing heavy. I backed off immediately. We would proceed as planned.

Preparations went on for almost four months. Chloe, who has her finger on the pulse, knew of an artist named Happy Menocal who hand-paints whimsical invitations, so we all went to discuss what she wanted: Chloe, Graham, Wendi, Marsh, and I. Chloe also knew Bronson van Wyck, a stellar party planner, and she and I met in his office a few times to refine the details. Bronson said he wanted the first hall to be filled with a thousand candles with a path running through it.

"That would be beautiful, but won't we need a fire marshal?" I asked.

"I have a fire marshal," he said, "And EMTs." It was a new frontier in party planning.

In a few emails to Bronson, I said I wanted to have some sort of surprise for Chloe at the party. A Big Reveal; a Ta-Dum moment. What about a band? I asked. And that is what we decided. Chloe had wanted a band, but she thought it would cost too much money; she'd insisted we hire a DJ. In secret, however, I hired a band, Veronica Martell, which became a whole hoo-hah, because the band was eleven pieces, and we needed a stage and a curtain to drop for the Ta-Dum moment. Planning the engagement party was all-engulfing and it was really fun. It was fun because it was joyous to plan something that celebrated the happiness of someone I loved so much.

And that happiness is something real. After five years together, Chloe and Graham still make each other laugh, still enjoy starting the day together. They are a young, vibrant couple, and it is lovely being in their glow. She lights up when she sees him. And why not? Graham is a dashing-looking, deeply decent guy. He gives Chloe an anchor, a base. He evens out her highs and lows. Ever since they've been a couple, I haven't worried about her getting overtired or cranky. Chloe calls him her "handler" and, in no small part, he is. When she gets exhausted and hyper and wants to keep going, he suggests relaxing and going to bed early. Chloe says that, for her, a perfect evening is going for a run in the park together, stopping at the huge Whole Foods near them, going home and cooking dinner and watching endless episodes of *Masterpiece Mystery*. That is her idea of heaven.

We both put an inordinate amount of time into preparing for the evening. For me, it was the equivalent of getting ready for an awards show. Chloe arranged for me to borrow a spectacular pair of fire opal earrings and a cuff from Irene Neuwirth. I actually owned my dress, which was an iridescent orchid taffeta trench coat from Akris. I decided to not wear pants. For me, it was the same as other people going topless. So I asked Chloe to find me a spray tanner, which she did. This was the third time I'd be doing this spray tan thing and it has never gone well. A lovely woman came to the house, hosed me down, and when I woke up the next morning, I was the color of mahogany. I called Chloe at work. "I look like a mulatto!!!" I heard her stifle a laugh, then she said firmly, "First of all, you *cannot* use that term. It is extremely politically incorrect. Use 'mixed race.' And second, it will tone down. Or you can rub it off with baby oil or lemon."

She was right, as usual, and soon I looked like I'd spent a short weekend in Miami. I picked up Chloe's borrowed jewelry from our now close friend Rebecca at Fred Leighton. Rebecca was happy because when the editors at *Vogue* saw Chloe's engagement ring, they decided to do a piece on "nontraditional wedding rings" becoming the new fad. Chloe wrote it, describing her ring as "a petite blue flash of elegance. People don't automatically know that I'm engaged—and I actually like the hesitancy and uncertainty. The simple fact of being engaged at twenty-eight is, frankly, far more conventional than I had hoped to be. Thank God the ring isn't." It was two pages and featured a huge close-up of her actual ring and its Fred Leighton provenance.

For the engagement party, Chloe borrowed a beautiful pair of pink diamond starbursts insured for $50,000. She also borrowed a halter neck white ankle-length dress sprinkled with pink flowers from Valentino. I went with her to try it on. She was reluctant to ask them to alter it. I was not. I politely asked if they could raise this and shorten that and they very kindly did. It was a magical dress and she looked perfect in it.

Chloe wanted everyone important to her to be at the party and, for the most part, they were. Kris flew in from LA, Connie as well. Her brother Cuote came from Paris with his stellar wife, Ashley. Her godmother, Tessa Kennedy, flew in from London and her godfather, Mike Nichols, came from 84th Street. Her sister Justine had stayed with her in New York the month before, so she remained in Paris. The Pod from Brown was present in force. Three close girlfriends and a guy friend from Addis Ababa showed up. The guy, Hussein, is an Ethiopian friend who plays soccer with Graham and had introduced them. I suggested that Chloe host a dinner at her apartment for all the people who had flown in. She did and it was lovely.

The next day I asked Graham to make sure Chloe had a nap so she would enjoy her party. She had breakfast with my brother and Connie and laid low for the rest of the day.

We all arrived at the venue early for a pre-check and when we came up the marble staircase of the entrance, the bronze doors opened to the enormous domed room lit entirely by a thousand candles. They covered the floor like a river of light with a path winding through it.

It was staggeringly beautiful. No one had seen anything like it and it became the site for photo ops throughout the evening. Then we proceeded into the even bigger domed room and tears came to my eyes. It had been transformed into an English Great Hall, replete with dark blue velvet chesterfield sofas, Persian rugs, tables of varying heights, and a ten-foot bar topped by a stuffed peacock. There was a huge swagged teal blue curtain dividing the two halls, and at the other end of the room was a stage faced in teal with a hand-painted drop curtain. This was for the "reveal" of the band. There were silver bowls of spring flowers on all the tables and an exquisite four-foot arrangement at the end of the bar. What was an empty, cavernous, but ravishing space had been transformed into a series of intimate, cozy nooks that would comfortably seat two hundred for dinner.

Chloe and I stood together and greeted people as they arrived. Many of them we had never met, as they were friends and family of Graham's. Marshall, however, had thrown himself into the fray and was busily introducing himself and welcoming people with élan. Chloe turned to me. "Marsh is really at his peak in this setting," she said. I nodded. Together with the caterer, Scott Skey of Bite, we had chosen four personalized drinks for cocktails: the Earl Greyhound, which was grapefruit juice with Earl Grey–infused vodka; a Rita Hayworth, which had tequila; a Savannah Smash, which was bourbon-based; and The Airmail, which was gin. Dinner was extraordinary, served family style. Chloe and I had chosen to have all the platters and serving dishes on the table, which people would pass themselves. This seemed less formal and more relaxed. Desserts were bite-sized and delicious. Strawberry shortcake, which I had requested, was a large strawberry stuffed with sour cream, shortbread, and brown sugar. There were mini profiteroles, tiny lemon tarts. Yum.

Tables were cleared and removed instantaneously. I took the mic to welcome people and on a prearranged code word, the curtain fell back for the Big Reveal of the Veronica Martell band and the dance floor. I was watching Chloe, who looked baffled and said she was wondering why the DJ needed so many people. I knew she was in Overwhelm. She looked stricken, barely able to react. Something similar had happened when she was little. Before her seventh birthday, she told me she would love a surprise party. So I'd asked all her friends to a kids' hair salon, and when Chloe and I walked in later, they all jumped out and shouted *"Surprise!"* And Chloe had fainted.

The band was sensational. It was also really loud. The party itself, I found frankly overwhelming. I didn't know most of the guests, and parties are not my strong suit. What I loved was the planning process, discovering the singular space of the bank, seeing it magically transformed, meeting with Bronson and Chloe a few times to make decisions about the look and the feel of it. What I loved was celebrating my daughter's engagement and planning every step of it with her. Marsh and I slithered out around eleven thirty. We felt far too old for the crowd.

Two days later, Chloe, Graham, and I started talking about the wedding next summer. As usual, Chloe knew exactly what she wanted. She wanted it very small: only immediate family and closest friends in the garden at Le Coual. And she wanted it like a village fete: strings of colored lights swagged in the trees. In the garden, huge bouquets of sunflowers in mustard-colored clay pots. Picnic tables and a large buffet with regional cuisine. There would be a DJ and dancing in the barn after dinner. She wanted the actual ceremony held at dusk in the *cours* in front of the house facing the fields, and when I asked who she wanted to officiate, she and Graham looked at us and said, "Well, we would love it if Marsh could do it."

That night, in East Hampton, Chloe and I decided to take Graham and Marsh to the movie theater to see *Maleficent*. When we told Marsh we were going to see *Maleficent*, he asked, "Who are the Levinsons?"

When Chloe was five or six, the two of us would have dinner on trays in bed and watch Disney movies: *Lady and the Tramp*, *Peter Pan*, *Dumbo*, but the favorite was *Sleeping Beauty*. Princess Aurora is out cold and the spell cast on her by Maleficent can be broken only by the kiss of true love. That is given by an extremely plucky prince who, undeterred by walls of thorns and raging dragons, arrives at her bedside and kisses her softly. Aurora awakes, he gently scoops her into his arms, and they, we confidently assume, will have a long and happy marriage. They have earned it. The famous Tchaikovsky standard, "The Sleeping Beauty Waltz," gracefully swells over the end credits and tiny Chloe, tears in her eyes, would softly sing along with it. Then we would get up and take our trays to the kitchen.

In *Maleficent*, which we found to be a totally satisfying film, wonderfully made, with excellent performances, especially by Angelina Jolie, the ending has been tweaked in a surprising twist, which Chloe and I loved. Marsh said it was better than he expected. A new version of "The Sleeping Beauty Waltz," sung by pop star Lana Del Rey, filled the theater. Sitting next to me, Chloe sang quietly:

I know you, I walked with you once upon a
*   dream*
I know you, that look in your eyes is so
*   familiar a gleam*
And I know that it's true that visions are
*   seldom all they seem*
But if I know you, I know what you'll do
You'll love me at once, the way you did once
*   upon a dream.*

I, of course, was crying.

❧ Acknowledgments ❧

When I asked editor Betsy Rapoport to help me with this book, it was supposed to be for the period of a year, which was my deadline. I told her I needed an "extractor," as the book would include material I wasn't comfortable sharing and I needed someone to assist me in that. Four years later, Betsy sat in our study, her head in her hands, her shoulders shaking convulsively. "Betsy," I asked, "are you laughing or crying?" "I don't know," she said. "I just want this to be over." I told her she would miss me, and soon I stopped procrastinating and it was finished. If this even resembles a book, it is thanks to Betsy, who has shaped and sequenced it into something certainly book-like. She did this with hundreds of para-graphs, which grew into pages sent to her by me from my iPad, with thanks to the Pages app.

If Betsy doesn't miss *me,* I miss *her.* Besides being excellent at her job, she is intelligent, witty, engaged, and good-hearted. She was great company to keep as I drew the process out beyond her limits and, finally, my own.

Over the endless course of this process, Marina Borges, chef extraordinaire, provided sustenance in the form of exquisite lunches.

Marcia Hemley, my college roommate and lifelong friend, encouraged this book and suggested many of the topics. Ed Victor, a friend for a shockingly long time and later my literary agent, has been trying to get me to cough up another book for thirty years. I hope his perseverance is rewarded.

Priscilla Painton, my editor at Simon & Schuster, saw deadlines come and go, yet somehow never gave up on seeing a final manuscript. She was also pure pleasure to work with and set me straight on droit du seigneur.

BB McLeod, a close friend for many years, with a dry sense of humor and the patience of a saint, has been a mainstay in my life and I am forever indebted.

Heidi Schaeffer, dear friend and fellow dog lover, used her consummate professional skill set to muster a readership. She did this as she does everything, with energy, humor, and a great spirit.

Connie Freiberg, my pal since eighth grade who has since become part of our family, provided many of the photographs in this book and gave us a record of Chloe's childhood, which we will always cherish. I'm also extremely grateful to my brother, Kris, who's been a constant source of joy for me since his birth, and then for Chloe since hers.

The writing of a book, while often stressful for

the author, is also stressful for her family. It is not unlike the lobbing of a tiny grenade into one's home, then waiting for the inevitable explosion. My husband, while ducking shrapnel, has been loving and discreet beyond measure, and my daughter infallibly encouraging and supportive. I am extremely grateful to them for that and so much else.

◄⊰ **Photo Credits** ⊱►

❧ About the Author ❧

Candice Bergen's film credits include *The Sand Pebbles*, *Carnal Knowledge*, *Starting Over*, and *Miss Congeniality*. On television, she made headlines as the tough-talking broadcast journalist and star of *Murphy Brown*, for which she won five Emmys and two Golden Globes. She later starred with James Spader and William Shatner in the critically acclaimed series *Boston Legal*. A gifted writer, Bergen has penned numerous articles, a play, and a previous best-selling memoir, *Knock Wood*.

Center Point Large Print
600 Brooks Road / PO Box 1
Thorndike, ME 04986-0001 USA

(207) 568-3717

US & Canada:
1 800 929-9108
www.centerpointlargeprint.com